Philosophy of the Medium

Also Available from Bloomsbury

Julia Kristeva: Live Theory, John Lechte
The Human, John Lechte
Peirce's Philosophy of Communication, Mats Bergman

Philosophy of the Medium

The Age of McLuhan in Question

John Lechte

BLOOMSBURY ACADEMIC
LONDON • NEW YORK • OXFORD • NEW DELHI • SYDNEY

BLOOMSBURY ACADEMIC
Bloomsbury Publishing Plc, 50 Bedford Square, London, WC1B 3DP, UK
Bloomsbury Publishing Inc, 1385 Broadway, New York, NY 10018, USA
Bloomsbury Publishing Ireland, 29 Earlsfort Terrace, Dublin 2, D02 AY28, Ireland

BLOOMSBURY, BLOOMSBURY ACADEMIC and the Diana logo
are trademarks of Bloomsbury Publishing Plc

First published in Great Britain 2024
This paperback edition published in 2025

Cover design: Ben Anslow
Cover images: Marshall McLuhan and Buckminster Fuller (© Dick Darrell /
Toronto Star / Getty Images); Retro old television (© PitukTV / Shutterstock)

A catalogue record for this book is available from the British Library.

A catalog record for this book is available from the Library of Congress.

ISBN: HB: 978-1-3502-9918-4
PB: 978-1-3502-9922-1
ePDF: 978-1-3502-9919-1
eBook: 978-1-3502-9920-7

Typeset by Newgen KnowledgeWorks Pvt. Ltd., Chennai, India

For product safety related questions contact productsafety@bloomsbury.com.

To find out more about our authors and books visit www.bloomsbury.com
and sign up for our newsletters.

In memory of Harry Redner, 1937–1921 and Bernard Stiegler, 1952–2020

Contents

Note on the Text

Except where otherwise indicated, all translations from French texts are my own.

Introduction

The time is ripe for a philosophy of media.

– John Durham Peters (2015: 1)

This study indeed takes its cue from the epigraph from John Durham Peters with the modification that it is the medium, in the first instance, that is the object of study rather than the pluralized version, with which we are all familiar. And it is the age that Marshall McLuhan first rendered visible that is to be brought into question in what follows. McLuhan's message that the 'medium is the message' corresponds to the notion of medium specificity – sister, as it were, to the social construction of reality era – and it is this that the following discussion seeks to challenge.

But, according to Graham Harman, McLuhan's work 'remains underutilised' (2016a: 99). McLuhan, he continues, 'is one of the neglected major thinkers of the 20th Century' (100).

Underutilized and neglected as a thinker McLuhan may well be, but the influence of medium specificity ('the medium is the message') that he brought into being in the 1960s remains pervasive in many quarters.[1] This is so, despite the criticisms of McLuhan's work, not least the perennial one of technological determinism. Indeed, even if the greater part of McLuhan's writing can be consigned to another era, the notion of media specificity as an explanation of the nature of the medium lives on. As Herta Wolf, a contemporary proponent of the principle, says: 'I am convinced that the special impact of photographic

---

1 As the thinker who could be dubbed the French Marshall McLuhan, Jean Baudrillard writes 'beware … , you are yourself constantly selected and tested by the medium itself' (1993: 64). And, with regard to opinion polls, in light of McLuhan (64): 'It is in fact the medium … that rules the process of signification' (65). Indeed, Baudrillard's concept of the simulacrum, it could be argued, is the medium in full view.

images, their power, can only be explained with reference to their media-specificity' (2007: 68) (cf. also: Doane 2007; Hepp 2012; Maras and Sutton 2000; Uricchio 2014).

To clarify and deepen an understanding of the notion of medium specificity, a chapter will be devoted to an analysis of McLuhan's *Gutenberg Galaxy: The Making of Typographic Man* (1967), first published in 1962, and to *Understanding Media: The Extensions of Man* (2008), first published in 1964.

While proponents of medium specificity abound – the proliferation of *media* departments implies this[2] – it is also true that at various points in the last forty years medium specificity – if not McLuhan's work as such – has been the subject of critique (e.g. see Carroll 1985). However, for the most part, critics of medium specificity concern themselves with enumerating the correct or incorrect characteristics of media rather than reflecting on the nature of the medium and on how it works.

Indeed, in terms of the subtlety of argument concerning the medium *qua* medium, Sybille Krämer's *Medium, Messenger, Transmission: An Approach to Media Philosophy* (2015) is without peer. As if reflecting Krämer's argument, that of the following study will be that a medium's essence is 'manifest' in its 'disappearance' (2015: 30–1).

When compared to Krämer's work, however, the approach here will take the principle of the 'disappearance of the medium' into new territory, specifically that of technics, as set out by Bernard Stiegler and that of Object-Oriented Ontology (OOO) as delineated by the philosopher Graham Harman. Moreover, in play and as addressed, amongst other things, in the Conclusion is the prospect that the problematization of presence as proffered by Jacques Derrida in a reading of Husserl on indication and expression is ultimately about the notion of medium. The medium, in this regard, is essentially that which – *qua* medium – is not present.

I also conclude by pointing out that it might be possible to interpret Kant's 'noumenon' in terms of the medium, and I show that phenomena such as the mirror and *trompe-l'oeil* art might constitute possible challenges to the notion of the essential transparency of the medium.

---

2 On the Chicago School of Literary Criticism and media specificity in contemporary media studies, see Jagoda (2018).

*

To reiterate: by focusing on the medium as such, this investigation questions the influence of the principle that the 'medium is the message' and the idea that the best we can hope for is a knowledge of the world that is medium specific, where this specificity, rather than medium content, becomes the exclusive object of interest. As Harman explains: 'McLuhan's most famous phrase, "the medium is the message", also expresses his central idea: that the content of any medium is largely irrelevant compared with the structure of that medium itself' (Harman 2016a: 103). As a result, the following aspects need to be addressed:

1. The extent to which 'medium specificity' is the dominant approach, in the themes considered in this study, needs to be appraised.
2. Medium specificity (that, e.g. in photography one experiences a uniquely photographic view of reality), which entails that no image or text is transparent, needs to be subjected to critique.
3. The prevailing view that it is philosophically naïve to accept transparency as an explanatory term when it comes to the medium needs to be questioned. It will be seen that, in key instances (e.g. with McLuhan's theory of medium) a macro approach to the medium is often foisted onto its micro articulation.

The origin/etymology of 'medium' and associated terms: middle, milieu (context), *medias* (*medias res*), median, means, implies, as will be shown in Chapter 1, that a medium cannot be apprehended as an object. This, however, tends to remain occluded in current usage of the term, 'medium'. As the noted German media theorist Friedrich Kittler points out: 'ever since Thomas's great idol Aristotle, that particular matter which all but evades our senses yet facilitates sensual perception in the first place is called *to metaxi* ("the middle", Latin *medium*). Aristotle, in other words, shaped the concept of media' (Kittler 2006: 54). Despite this acknowledgement, the medium, for Kittler, disappears, once digitalization becomes prolific. Or, rather, since the advent of the digital, there is only one medium, and it determines the nature of the 'message'.

For her part, Krämer, responding to Kittler's take on the medium, proposes that: 'We can cook meals, drive cars, calculate with zero, etc., without needing to understand which chemical, electromechanical, and numerical-theoretical relations inform these processes. We can use technology without needing to understand how, and especially why, it works. In practice, Kittler also refuses to make this distinction' (Krämer 2006: 104).[3]

Another – also German – media theorist clearly vaunts the importance of a material approach to cultural techniques and, by implication, to the medium:

> Hence doors, as well, are a fundamental cultural technique, given that the operations of opening and closing them process and render visible the distinction between inside and outside. A door, then, is both material object and symbolic thing, a first- as well as a second-order technique. This, precisely, is the source of its distinctive power. The door is a machine by which humans are subjected to the law of the signifier. (Siegert 2013: 60)

To cite this passage from Bernhard Siegert is thus to be made aware of the very materialist strand of media theorizing that characterizes the work of a number of key German practitioners in the field. Kittler falls into this category, as does the work of media archaeologist, Wolfgang Ernst, and the implications of this will be taken up further in this introduction and in Chapter 4, which will focus on the thinkers who treat the medium primarily as an object, whether virtual or physical.

The approach to be adopted: The disappearing medium

This book is only incidentally concerned with medium as understood in terms of the classic sender–receiver model in communication theory. The following statement by Krämer – one echoing the passage cited earlier with regard to Kittler – evokes the approach I will adopt: 'that while enabling something to emerge media themselves remain invisible' (2015: 31). This is why Krämer says (to reiterate): 'A medium's success depends on its disappearance' (31). These statements introduce an approach to the medium that could hardly be less like McLuhan's. And indeed, the 'German approach' (whether objectivist or not),

---

3 Without directly addressing the medium as such, Derrida makes a similar point when he says with regard to using a computer that he has to 'comply with the law of a machine about which basically I understand nothing' (Derrida 1999: 7). And the philosopher continues by stating that this is what marks 'our dependence with regard to many instruments of modern technology' (7). In effect, the medium disappears.

oriented as it is towards a philosophy of the medium, is an indicator of the orientation of the following study. Aristotle had already noted the necessary transparency of media and Aquinas after him. The medium, then, despite approaches that dispute this, is immaterial and disembodied in their use (see Krämer 2015: 34).

Luhmann and the medium

Although his work will not be addressed in detail, Niklas Luhmann's characterization of media as having a high degree of 'dissolution' (1987: 101) seems to imply the notion of disappearance. Indeed, matter as medium is defined as 'that which is undetermined in itself and thus receptive to form' (101). On the other hand, as the social theorist 'reads' the medium through the prism of materiality, the question becomes, in each case: what kind of materiality is the medium?

In discussing Plato's *Khora* in the Conclusion, we shall return to the medium as undetermined in itself. And in Chapter 7 on the medium and Object-Oriented Ontology (OOO), we will return to Luhmann's theory of art.

The notion of art as understood by Luhmann expands the concept of medium in a way that is in keeping with the position adopted in this investigation as far as medium as materiality becomes equivalent to environment. Thus, air can be a medium; the human body can be a medium; institutions can be a medium. Overall, though, unlike Krämer and this study's approach, the focus on materiality tends to lead Luhmann to reduce a medium to an object rather than understanding it in terms of its disappearance as object. Or: one can never experience a medium *as* medium, but only in terms of what the medium makes possible. Here, Luhmann seems to endorse the idea of the medium's presence over its disappearance: 'No medium gives only a single form, for then it would be absorbed as medium and disappear' (1987: 103).

Medium as immaterial and material object

Luhmann's focus on the medium as materiality leads into another strand of German media theory, one that explicitly promotes the medium as concrete object and thus challenges the idea that media are what disappear. And it is important to address this theoretical and historical orientation. Indeed, despite appearances to the contrary, with the approach inaugurated in the modern era by the 'age of McLuhan', the study of the medium remains dominated by the idea that the material support, historically inflected, *is* the medium. No doubt this implies not only that the medium appears as such, but also that it is essentially found in the historical evolution of technics, culminating with the digital revolution and the dominance of computers. Hence, we recall again media theorist Friedrich Kittler's famous statement that 'the general digitization of channels and information erases the differences among individual media. Sound and image, voice and text are reduced to surface effects, known to consumers as interface' (1999: 1). In the wake of the digital revolution: 'any medium can be translated into any other ... a total media link on a digital base will erase the very concept of medium' (2). Despite what Kittler says, the virtual materiality of the digital image might mean that focus must now be on the image as such and not on the medium as material support. This, at least, is a key aspect of the thesis to be pursued in what follows, where the medium will be understood to be that which does not appear vis-à-vis what does appear, namely: images, meaning, message, information, knowledge, feeling/ sentiment, idea, space, time, personality, memory, music and so on.

For his part, Wolfgang Ernst refers to media as essentially measuring instruments. In this regard, it will later be confirmed in Chapter 4 that Ernst tends to be ambivalent, so that what remains unclear is whether or not measuring by the machine provides a machine view of the world. Technics will thus be defined as media. As such, Bernard Stiegler's work on technics, as outlined in Chapter 6, will have a special significance.

In the interest of finding an answer to this question of the ultimate status of the medium, Ernst's key text, *Chronopoetics*, will be the focus of analysis in Chapter 4. To gain a fuller picture of medium as object, reference will be made in the same chapter to Friedrich Kittler's texts, *Gramophone, Film, Typewriter* (1999), and *Discourse Networks, 1800/1900* (1990).

And emerging in the wake of the putative dissolution of media is Rosalind Krauss's formulation of a 'post-media' reality. This notion will also be treated in more detail in Chapter 4; suffice it to say here that, as a critique of 'post-media', Krauss, inspired by Benjamin, endeavours to rehabilitate obsolescent media – in effect, media as object – the better to gain a deeper understanding of that which in its operation was entirely taken for granted (see Krauss 1999a). Obsolescent media can, Krauss proposes, come to assume a 'redemptive' role by bringing to light the 'necessary plurality of the arts' (305).

*

As should now be clear, each of the following chapters in this study will form part of the development of a philosophy of medium that is at odds with the historical appearance of material supports that are designated 'medium' or 'media'.

However, in order to clear the way for the full elaboration of a philosophy of medium as transparent, it is as well to address now some possible objections to this approach.[4]

One might object, for example, that materiality cannot be ruled out of any definition of medium; for to do so is to eliminate the possibility of the undeniable connotative potential of this materiality. Tzvetan Todorov's reference to a message announcing an insurrection written in blood as an example of connotation would seem to be evidence of the signifying capacity of the materiality of the medium.[5] And Heidegger, in similar fashion, famously points to the difference between handwriting and typewriting in terms of personalization. Compared to the putative individualizing character connoted by handwriting, 'the typewriter makes everyone look the same' (Heidegger 1992: 81). Moreover: 'The typewriter veils the essence of writing' (85).[6] Here, via connotation, as it were, the medium, for Heidegger, becomes the message.

More broadly, one might wonder how the differential history of technics and with it, media specificity, can be denied. Surely, media evoke eras – the era of radio, for example. This issue will be addressed at various points throughout this study, but here it can be said that an acknowledgement of the reality of media specificity at the level of connotation does not entail that the medium as such is the message. If it were correct, as Don Ihde has reiterated (2010: 104), that 'machine' writing was in no way individualizing, as Heidegger claims, then

---

4 As already indicated, the Conclusion will also treat examples of media that might also constitute a challenge to the claim that the medium is essentially transparent.
5 Todorov elaborates: 'The message of the letter later called "the bloody letter" is found to be very well confirmed and illustrated by its material aspect' (1967: 17).
6 We will return to Heidegger and the typewriter in Chapter 4 in relation to Kittler's media theory.

the very relationship between authorship and printed works – and between Heidegger and his printed works specifically – could not be sustained.[7]

Another issue to be addressed in more detail concerns the apparent problematizing of the transparency of the medium and the emergence of medium specificity in the examples of time and the mechanical versus the atomic clock. Indeed, one might ask about what is to be made of Harrison's chronometer as an agent in the accurate calculation of longitude. On one level, the chronometer conforms both to Ernst's archaeological view that media are essentially instruments of measurement and to the notion that every medium connotes something, in this case, with the chronometer, the historical era of Cook's voyages. Could it not be said that the instrument (clock, chronometer) signifies itself to the extent that it gives an *in*accurate reading of time? In other words, we are seemingly faced here with an instrument (medium), or medium-specific view of the world.

But this is to view the clock or chronometer after the event of the presentation of time – after the voyager returns from the voyage and the discrepancies noted. At sea, the chronometer is necessarily a transparent vehicle of time, even though it also 'speaks' in its own name (is inaccurate) and thus needs to be corrected. A true reading of the chronometer is thus one that makes the necessary correction with regard to the time that it presents.

Dasein and the clock

'Temporality', says Heidegger, 'is the reason for the clock' (1978: 466). The medium in Heidegger's study, *Being and Time*, can be equated with 'ready-to-hand' in as far as 'ready-to-hand' equipment is taken for granted, not commented upon, is entirely inconspicuous – transparent. Awareness of equipment – as occurs when a tool breaks down – is 'present-at-hand'.[8] As 'present-at-hand', the tool can assume medium specificity. If the clock 'is manufactured for telling

---

7 In this regard, after the publication of *Sein und Zeit*, Heidegger is quoted as saying: '"I have at the very least proven that I can get something into print" (6 October 1927)' (cited in Kisiel 1995: 453). It can be assumed that Heidegger believes that if he is misread, it will not be due to the fact of 'print'.
8 An elaboration of this theme in Heidegger will be taken up with regard to Graham Harman's object-oriented philosophy in Chapter 7.

the time', it becomes present-at-hand when it ceases to work. This is when time becomes 'clock-time'. As such, it conforms, in Heidegger's conception, to 'modes of conspicuousness, obtrusiveness, and obstinacy [which] all have the function of bringing to the fore the characteristic of presence-at-hand' (Heidegger 1978: 104). A sign *qua* sign is always in the mode of 'ready-to-hand'. That is, a sign is essentially transparent: 'The sign is *not* authentically 'grasped' ["erfasst"] if we just stare at it and identify it as an indicator-Thing which occurs' (110). Time is temporalizing. The *'measurement of time … is grounded in the temporality* of Dasein' (468). The clock is the measuring of time. The clock as we have seen is 'ready-to-hand', even if time comes to be 'present-at-hand' in a ' "flowing stream" of "nows" ' (474).

For Françoise Dastur, interpreting Heidegger on time:

> Time is not something objective, it is not a being, as we know already: time is not, but 'there is time', i.e., a process of temporalization so that if time were to be the *Es* of *Es gibt Sein*, it would mean that the alleged subject of the giving process would be nothing else than the process of temporalization itself. (2014: 411)

Through emphasizing 'temporalization', this statement confirms that time emerges through the medium that, as such, is 'ready-to-hand', and, as a consequence, is inconspicuous and transparent. But is this Heidegger's ultimate position on the medium? In Chapter 7, we will attempt to provide an answer to this question.

Middle voice as in Heidegger

As is known, Heidegger argues that the 'essence of technology is nothing technological'. Again, in Chapter 7, we will examine the implications of the parallel claim that the essence of the medium is nothing concrete. More broadly, the issue to be clarified is the connection between medium and 'middle'. A consideration of 'middle' in relation to medium will call attention to the way passages in Heidegger's *Being and Time* exemplify the implementation of the middle voice. What, we might wonder, are the implications of this for an understanding of Heidegger's philosophy? Does it have to do with the effort to render the text transparent? More will be said about this in Chapter 1.

The work of Mark Hansen as an introduction to the philosophy of the medium

In the chapters to follow, we will see that the majority of writings on the medium treat it as – in Heidegger's terms – 'present-at-hand' and thus as endlessly available for analysis and interpretation. Indeed, Marshall McLuhan's approach to media precisely follows this thread. 'The medium is the message' means that the medium is always 'present-at-hand', that it is captured in the notion of media specificity.

As Mark Hansen's writing on media raises in a sophisticated manner the issue of media specificity, it offers a unique window through which key themes in media philosophy can be introduced. For instance, Hansen claims that because there is 'no time-in-itself'[9] there are only various media temporalizations.[10]

As with Ernst, the issue is not whether time appears via media temporalizations, but whether the latter are media specific rather than the emergence of authentic time. Thus, the question to be addressed and elaborated upon is: are such media judged to be transparent or opaque?

Rather than remain within the province of forms of media temporalization, Hansen adds another twist: it is the notion of the 'unboundedness' of time (2009: 307), time as distinct from any media capture of it, which Hansen also calls 'technical time inscription' (308). But this is to imply that the time of media capture is only the media version of time, not time as unbounded – that is, not time as such.[11]

Hansen addresses the theme of media ontology and thereby adds another dimension to a philosophy of medium. Specifically, Ernst's work is interpreted in part by way of a critique of Timothy Morton's hyperobject version of Object-Oriented Ontology (Hansen 2016). What is significant, according to our theorist, and what we will elaborate upon in Chapter 8, is that, via

---

9 Cf.: 'there simply is no time-in-itself (or time in its basic structure); time only comes to exist through the myriad temporalizations that generate its fundamental heterogeneity' (Hansen 2009: 297).
10 Thus: 'in today's world, human beings temporalize in conjunction with and on the basis of largely-autonomous technical inscriptions of time by computational machines' (2009: 298). This is basically in keeping with Ernst's view of time as what is measured by machines.
11 Hansen invokes the work of experimental film-makers Pierre Huyghn and Lynn Marie Kirby as a way of illustrating his thesis.

'medium-oriented ontology' the reality of phenomena *is* their manifestation; there is no 'deep' reality involved. Initially, however, the 'physicality of the medium' (383) is insisted upon, a point that has significant implications for any understanding of the medium.

The increasingly accepted version of quantum phenomena (as opposed to a quantum object) is that they are the result of the measuring media. How this is so will again be discussed in Chapter 8, where it will be a matter of assessing in what sense the nature of the measuring media is equivalent to quantum phenomena. Similarly, as concerns climate, if there is no climate object as such, as Timothy Morten and OOO maintain, but only climate simulations, what are the implications of this? Hansen's response is that, like quantum phenomena, like time as instantiations of temporalization, 'the data of climate simulation … simply is the phenomena of climate. There is no true climate, no real climate, no climate *qua* hyperobject that stands behind these phenomena' (400). This claim will be one of the foci of discussion in Chapter 8.

*

Again, with regard to Hansen's theory, in McLuhan's case, it is a question of medium *and* the message: 'more of an expansion', says Hansen, 'in the scope of hermeneutic analysis to include the material-technical support for the message' (Hansen 2006: 298). That is, perhaps, both content *and* medium become the message. Here, the concept of medium is given wide scope. Human and medium are inextricably linked. But the question of whether the medium is entirely transparent is still not resolved.

In a paper on affect as medium, Hansen claims, with regard to the works of the artist Ken Feingold, that we can understand 'affectivity as the very medium for communication as such' (Hansen 2003: 222).

Clearly, if affect is the medium, it presumably does not appear as such but only in various modes and dispositions of the body – in this case, the face. Hansen does not make this fully explicit, the result being that he gives the impression that the medium can appear, a position that is the reverse of the one defended regarding time, and perhaps also as regards quanta or climate simulation.

It is no doubt fair to say that with regard to the medium taken in its materiality, Hansen, like Ernst and Kittler (as we shall see in more detail later), share an ambivalence as to whether or not the medium in its performance is transparent. Certainly, all three endeavour to highlight the specific nature of the materiality in question, but do they also maintain that it is this materiality itself that 'speaks'? Such is the issue to be further illuminated in our investigation.

*

The foregoing commentary has aimed to introduce some of the issues that pertain when the medium is conceptualized as object. In the chapters to follow, Chapter 1 aims to establish the meaning and signification of the term, 'medium', the better to understand the notion of 'media specificity', as employed by media theorists. 'Media specificity' relies on only one possible meaning of 'medium'. Of particular interest is the fact that etymologically, medium derives from the Latin *medius* (neuter of medium) meaning 'middle', so the chapter will elaborate on this by considering the sense in which the middle appears as such. Also, to be considered is the Greek term for 'middle', or 'in-between', *metaksy*. It will be shown that if a medium is defined as an object, it becomes an end – that is, it ceases to be a medium. Krämer offers a point of departure here in her discussion of medium as middle, as spatial, as intermediate and neutral (see Krämer 2015: 36).

Painting, photography, sculpture, music – media in a word – as much or more than individual works – or *an* individual work – dominate critical discourse. More often than not a particular work is viewed as an instance of what can be achieved in/by a specific medium.

Medium can also be understood as the Third element in relation to the well-known, tried and tested principle of the excluded middle (either/or 0–1). Is the 'middle' equivalent to the medium? The issue of bi-valence (both/and: 0–2) arises. The excluded middle is part of (or constitutive of) logical formalism. It is not medium specific, at least not while the middle is absolutely excluded. Nevertheless, the form here is the medium in the sense that it is the condition of possibility of propositions.

Medium, can, in addition, be viewed as a means not an end. An object, by contrast, is an end in itself. Moreover, three-dimensional space can be considered as a medium: Clement Greenberg opposes the illusion of three-dimensionality in two-dimensional space (the canvas).

Methodologically, it is important to be aware that an excessively analytical approach that attempts to reveal medium as medium only serves to obscure rather than reveal the nature of medium. This is because analysis presupposes the *presence*, or manifestation, of what is being analysed. Analysis has difficulty dealing with transparency.

The main focus of Chapter 2 is the theme of McLuhan and the history of media. In this regard, it is important to acknowledge the apparent plausibility of McLuhan's historical approach to the evolution of communications media. This entails considering macro and micro approaches to the medium, and noting that there is a genuinely macro approach to the medium (to technics), thus to literacy (the phonetic alphabet, the printing press, cinema, digital recording, etc.), that McLuhan reveals. It might well be that, at this macro level, the medium can be observed to change the human – that at a macro level 'media specificity' can have palpable effects. At the same time, it is necessary to consider the medium at the micro level. While opacity marks the medium at a macro level (i.e. the notion that the 'medium is the message' is palpable), at a micro level, there is transparency – transparency in the sense of Sartre's philosophy of the image, where the image becomes a mode of access to the real.

The problem for philosophy is that the macro approach has come, in a majority of cases, to be its default position. This is the one that allows philosophy to treat medium purely as an object.

The key question to be addressed, then, is: What is the effect of a medium being actively – as opposed to passively – utilized? Here, it can be proposed that an active user of language, because of the need for transparency, problematizes the notion that 'the medium is the message', which also means that such an active user problematizes the notion of medium specificity.

The subject of Chapter 3 is the work of Sybille Krämer. As we have seen, Krämer's central thesis is a determining one for this study. Krämer discusses the medium in relation to the traditional concepts fundamental to communication theory, such as 'messenger', 'transmission' and 'sign' as well as in relation to the syllogism in Plato's philosophy.

As has we have seen, Chapter 4 will include a further elaboration of the medium through a reading of key texts by Ernst and Kittler, along with those of Rosalind Krauss on the notion of 'post-medium'.

Chapter 5 centres on Michel Serres's series of five volumes, called *Hermès* (plus his work on the parasite and on angels as messengers). Only a selection of chapters from the *Hermès* series has been translated into English. Serres's books in the *Hermès* series were published between 1968 and 1980 (Serres 1968; 1972; 1974; 1977; 1980), so embraced all of the 1970s, the period when the theory of the medium as the message was taking root. Serres's approach notably shows the influence of the mathematical theory of communication, initially developed by Claude Shannon (see Shannon [1949] 1998: 29–125). This explains why Serres's underlying approach to communication is animated by the notion of the presence or absence of 'noise in a channel' (cf. the parasite (Serres 1983)) and by the relation between order and disorder. That is, the medium will be what is not present. 'Noise', by contrast, is the presence of the medium over the message. To be investigated, therefore, is the extent to which Serres presents a paradigm of communication that is – or is not – at variance with that of McLuhan. In this respect, the following themes will be considered: (1) Hermes, as messenger, thus as the figure of medium par excellence: the catalyst of communication as travelling between regions, whether these be scientific, poetic/metaphorical or artistic. (2) Noise versus communication (indecipherable writing as noise). Here, the parasite is also the 'noise in a channel'. The possibility is thus introduced that what is of most interest to Serres is the objectification of medium as noise, as joker, as parasite and as harlequin. To be considered, too, are the figures of messengers, such as Hermes, Mercury and angels. This might lead, somewhat ironically, to the invisibility of the medium so as to render the invisible medium visible is to be led astray regarding its true nature. (3) For mathematics, abstraction is the elimination of the irregular, the inexact, the material, the empirical – thus, the elimination of noise as the third party, or element. How matter relates to the abstract is what becomes crucial. (4) The theme of the Third as excluded – as 'nothing' and 'everything' (Serres 1991: 87) – will be considered. Here, we take up Krämer's argument that communication is not dialogue but dissemination (2015: 20–5; 68–74). Consequently, it remains to be seen as to whether 'the Third' – as noise, poetry as the noise of science and mystery (as in Jules Verne) – constitutes a version of the medium. Does Serres ultimately follow McLuhan and privilege media specificity in his conception of communication and noise? The answer will be that he does not. With media specificity, there is no engagement with noise. Noise can be broadly understood as: chance, turbulence, chaos, disorder, *clinamen*, entropy – everything, in short, that challenges the working of the medium as the facilitator of communication.

There is also in Serres the idea that the messenger ultimately dies or at least disappears in relation to the message, which obviously puts him at odds with McLuhan.

Chapter 6 examines the relationship between technics and medium. Thus, while technics must be acknowledged to assume the status of an object, it is not as object (as opaque) that it is technics. Objectivity is not what is essential to it.

Bernard Stiegler's view of science as application will briefly be compared to Serres's notion of science. Then, in the wake of Stiegler's work, how technics define the human will be addressed. Indeed, to be without technics is not to be human. Does this mean the medium (technics as media) is *in* the human and thus should not be thought of as an object outside the human? Or, as Stiegler, following the prehistorian Leroi-Gourhan puts it: with the evolution of language and tools the essence of the human becomes external to it. Or again: technics is equivalent to the human as exteriorization. But what needs to be investigated is whether or not the exteriorization of the human is ontologically and epistemologically neutral. A McLuhan-inspired answer would be that they are not. Does Stiegler – and Leroi-Gourhan, for that matter – follow McLuhan on this? What is the implication of Stiegler's notion of epiphylogenesis as the evolution and maintenance of life 'by means other than life' – that is, by technics as the exteriorization of the human? Is it that technics is a medium and as such 'disappears' into the human?

The study of cinema by Stiegler will be taken as a key indicator of his position regarding the medium and technics. Cinema here corresponds to Krämer's cartography as a medium 'test case' (Krämer 2015: 187–209). His analysis of film (a medium) results in the claim that consciousness is cinematographic. Moreover: cinema is the realization of Husserl's temporal object that incorporates the tri-partite structure of retention (past), attention (present) and protention (future) in the flux of time (cf. Husserl's analysis of melody).

For Stiegler, Husserl's temporal object is deemed to show how consciousness works. This is to be evaluated.

To say that a film is a temporal object is to comprehend it, first of all, *as* an object. As an object, film is not comprehended as medium. It also remains to be shown how consciousness can be equated with a cinematographic format. Is consciousness the object in itself or a medium (of thought, of perception, of knowledge of the world)? In this regard, the following quotation raises the question to be addressed: 'The temporal object, as flux, *coincides* with the stream of consciousness of which it is the object: the spectator's' (Stiegler 2011: 12).

For Stiegler, the phenomenological attitude is to pose consciousness as constituting the world, not the reverse, in which case consciousness, as argued here, is not a medium but an object (see Stiegler 2011: 21).

Another theme to be addressed in this chapter concerns memory as medium. If human memory is one of retentional finitude (selection and forgetting), then surely memory as medium becomes an instance of media specificity. Memory aided by all kinds of supports (tertiary memory) would seem to reinforce the reality of media specificity. However, memory supports are part of the human as exteriorization, and as such, are essential to it. Without memory supports there would be no memory of a past not personally lived. This will be discussed further in the chapter.

Because cinema, as a temporal object, is homologous with consciousness, Stiegler's controversial notion of adoption (of cultural habits, artefacts – of a 'way of life', in effect) becomes plausible. But this entails that the cinema ceases to be apprehended as in terms of the medium as object and is interpreted at the level of its content. The media specificity of film (especially its American version) amounts to its potential to conceal its media specificity. In a 'war of images' America uses, and has used, Stiegler controversially claims, cinema in order to have the world adopt '*the American way of life*' (Stiegler 2011: 116; emphasis in original).

With his privileging of the medium as message and object and his dismissal of media content, McLuhan could never have reached Stiegler's conclusion regarding adoption.

The key theme of Chapter 7 is the medium as it emerges in OOO. The latter has become a significant movement in contemporary philosophy.

Prior to looking at OOO in relation to art, an examination of Harman's reading of Heidegger on 'tool-being' – foreshadowed in the introductory section of this study – is appropriate as it evokes the reality of medium. Thus, in the distinction noted earlier between the 'ready-to-hand' and 'present-to-hand', the tool in the former sense disappears in its use, while the tool in the latter sense appears as an object. It has already been proposed that the tool as 'ready-to-hand' is the tool as medium. The tool only appears to consciousness (as 'present-to-hand') when it breaks down. Harman's point is that 'tool-being' ('ready-to-hand') applies to all entities, not just to the examples of tools that Heidegger explicitly invokes. What needs to be determined, then, is whether the notion of medium as disappearance can encompass Harman's tool-being. Given that Harman explicitly says that 'there is no basis in tool analysis for any fruitful theory of modern technology' (Harman 2002: 4), the challenge is on.

The chapter also offers further insight into the role of the medium in art. In this regard, the question that calls for a response is: does OOO's notion of the role of the medium confirm or refute the notion of media specificity? The art criticism of Clement Greenberg sets the scene here, as Harman takes up Greenberg's position on the medium as the point of departure for his thinking. In painting, the medium for Greenberg is essentially the 'flat canvas'. This is Greenberg's way of confirming the dictum that the 'medium is the message', a point that will be taken up in relation to OOO in what follows.

We will also see that Harman claims that 'literalism' in art occurs when an object is made equivalent to its qualities (see Harman 2019: 26). By contrast, aesthetically, an object, for Harman, cannot be reduced to its qualities. To conceive of the message as the disappearance of the medium is a form of literalism, which is not necessarily Harman's position. In fact, to all appearances, Harman places art content on the side of literalism and the medium on the side of what is unique in art. Ultimately, literalism transcends the difference between content and medium, so that there can be a literalist interpretation of medium as there can be a literalist interpretation of content. Here, much will depend on what counts as 'content' and what as 'medium'.

Ultimately, we will see that what is lacking in both Harman's and Greenberg's accounts of painting is a nuanced notion of content. For instance, while the viewer of a Cézanne painting might become aware of the pigments of which the picture is made, this is paint within the frame of the picture – it is paint *as* content, something very different from the paint outside the frame. This is the point to be developed at length by considering various examples of abstract art. The result of this consideration is that the medium as such – which is the medium in its implementation – cannot be depicted.

The focus of Chapter 8 is crucial because a consideration of the medium in relation to fields like quantum objects opens the possibility not only that the medium is explicit but that it is the medium as measurement that creates the object. An overall picture of what is at issue has been gained from Mark Hansen's discussion of media archaeology in relation to OOO.

By effectively making quantum physics the measure of the world as such, the medium constitutes the world in as far as it is essentially implicated in the creation of appearances – of phenomena. Contra OOO and the positing of a noumenal realm withdrawn into itself and inaccessible to any media, there would be nothing else but the phenomenal world.

The question still remains as to whether the measuring set-up in relation to quantum objects is transparent or opaque. A detailed investigation of the approach of quantum physics is obviously required. Nevertheless, it is difficult to imagine that it is the measuring set-up that is visible over and above what is measured. What is measured/produced is still what appears, not the measuring medium. And when this is extrapolated to the world in its entirety, it can be argued that it is still the world that appears, not the medium.

When, for instance, it comes to a computer simulation of climate, the issue once again is about the computer model 'creating' the reality. If, in certain fields such as meteorology the object is probabilistic, does this mean that we are getting the medium's-eye view of things? An answer to this question is to be developed, but the hypothesis is that, as with the quantum object, the medium 'disappears' into the 'plurality of realities'.

Although the OOO position of there being a deep reality of climate (cf. work of Timothy Morton) beyond the phenomenon of weather might be problematic, there can be no doubt that Morton's concept of the hyperobject does not privilege media specificity, which is what the opposing view can lead to if due care is not taken to avoid this.

*

The aim of the conclusion is to consolidate the fact that a profound consideration of the medium leads into hitherto unsuspected philosophical territory – ontological territory, in a word. This is the basis on which Husserl on communication and Kant on the noumenon – as well as the schema – are to be invoked. The issue of medium will be addressed in relation to interior monologue, or soliloquy, as found in Husserl's thought and as analysed by Jacques Derrida in his now famous text, *La voix et le phénomène* (1976). The aim is to show that, for Derrida, the absence of medium is equivalent of pure – therefore, unqualified – self-presence. But what, precisely, does the notion of the *presence* of the medium mean? Is it the case that medium is never present as such? Is it in the place of *différance*? The significance of this for the notion of 'media specificity' – already addressed in relation to Stiegler's philosophy of technics as epi-phylogenesis – will be examined in the context of Husserl's theory of consciousness and the possibility of an interior monologue or soliloquy.

As concerns Husserl's notion of interior monologue, or soliloquy, the following statement by Husserl is crucial: 'In a monologue words can perform no function of indicating the existence of mental acts, since indication would there be purposeless. For the acts in question are themselves experienced by us at that very moment' (Husserl 1970: 280). We know that Derrida argues in response that: 'With regard to the certainty of interior existence, it does not need, Husserl thinks, to be signified. It is immediately present to itself. It is the living consciousness' (Derrida 1976: 48). The implications of this for the notion of medium will be set out.

Husserl will show how the issue of the medium can emerge in phenomenology. Thus, if expressions 'serve the hearer as signs of the "thoughts" of the speaker, i.e., of his sense-giving inner experiences, as well as of the other inner experiences which are part of his communicative intention' (1970: 277), these same expressions could be deemed to be transparent, as, for Husserl, they enabled – through a 'pure' expression – access to an other's interior being, or inner experiences. Derrida thus concludes that: 'The relation to the other as non-presence is therefore the impurity of the expression' (Derrida 1976: 44).

With 'inner life' there is no indicative because there is no communication (78). There is no second person in inner speech – or if there is, it is fictional.

For Husserl, the voice allows absolute auto-affection, absolute self-proximity without remainder. The voice does not operate as a medium. One hears oneself speak: speaking is an immediate hearing. There is no signifier (medium).

Speaking is immediately present to hearing. Does this mean that speaking and consciousness are identical? This question will be developed.

The Conclusion will also consider arguments against the transparency of the medium, such as might be exemplified by the mirror, *trompe-l'oeil* and camouflage.

As foreshadowed, a further consideration will be the relation of the 'appearing' of the Kantian object in itself. The fruitfulness of the medium as transparent is that the notion of a modal ontology can enable the realm of appearance to be understood as the appearance of the in itself (the noumenon) in its transparency (i.e. in its disappearance). Such is the way that even the *Critique of Pure Reason* can assist in bringing the age of McLuhan into question.

And, finally, Plato's *khora* will be considered because it must remain distinct from its content. In short, the *khora* – at least in one of Plato's characterizations – must not appear as such. In its non-appearing, it would thus evoke the medium.

1

The meaning and signification of 'medium'

This chapter aims to establish the meaning and signification of the term 'medium', the better to understand the notion of 'media specificity', as employed by media theorists. 'Media specificity' relies on only one possible meaning of 'medium'; compared with *via media*: a middle way or compromise between extremes.

Although Raymond Williams recognizes media historically as an 'intermediate agency or substance' (1985: 143) he, nevertheless, considers media largely objectively (as words, newspapers, radio). That is, Williams offers a media-specific definition of media.

Etymologically, medium derives from the Latin *medius* (neuter of medium), meaning 'middle', so it will be worth elaborating on this by examining the sense in which the middle appears as such.

Excluded middle, bi-valence, carnival and the novel

Medium can be also be illuminated by considering it as the third element in relation to the excluded middle (either/or 0–1). Here we can ask: is 'middle' the medium? Is bi-valence (both/and: 0–2) not equally valid? However, the excluded middle is part of (or constitutive of) logical formalism. It is not medium specific, at least not while the middle is absolutely excluded. Nevertheless, the form here is the medium in the sense that it is what enables propositions: the sun rises in the east *or* the sun does not rise in the east. The principle of the excluded middle is the medium of this statement even though it does not appear as such. The latter is true because the law is the condition of possibility of non-contradiction in reality. It would be the medium as non-appearance (or as non-presence to use Derrida's terminology) that will be seen to constitute the essence of medium.

As has already been signposted, the thesis being defended is that the nature of the medium entails that (*pace* McLuhan), in its operation, it never appears as such. Does the notion of bi-valence change this? Carnival as Julia Kristeva presents it (see Kristeva 1982 and 1998) becomes the incarnation of bi-valence, also called ambivalence (both/and). Clearly, univalence connotes the constitution of identity. The latter is always singular, homogenous: One. This does not rule out the possibility that two things could be in every respect identical (a mirror effect). (Kristeva was looking for a principle that would do justice to the drive-based semiotic as the basis of poetic language. The logic of the semiotic would be the carnival logic of 0–2, while the logic underpinning the Symbolic (sphere of rationality, and law of contradiction, etc.) would be 0–1.

The bi-valence of carnival evokes the presence in it of both identity *and* difference. The carnival is a medium that has no outside. It is all inclusive. Or, if there is a position outside, it is of no significance. In the words of Mikhail Bakhtin, pioneer theorist of carnival in the European Middle Ages: 'Carnival is not a spectacle seen by the people: they live it, and everyone participates because its very idea embraces all the people. While the carnival lasts, there is no other life outside it' (Bakhtin 1984: 7). Carnival, therefore, is a medium and, as such, transparent. The principle of either/or of the excluded middle evokes the medium even though the latter does not appear as such.

The carnival principle implies that what is normally excluded comes to be included in the carnival experience. Opposition, the negative, otherness, evil perhaps, noise (as Shannon and Serres, as we shall see, define it), poetry, emotion come to be part of the carnival scene. What we have is an attempt to provide a formal principle that would capture the reality of the overturning of the normal state of affairs: hierarchies of power are overturned for a period of time; normal moral values are not adhered to; sexual licence pertains, and so on. Would this be how the medium appears?

Carnival, then, challenges (the hegemony of) binary logic. Perhaps the carnival principle (0–2) even embodies the difference between Analytical and Continental philosophy.

Dostoyevsky's novels, as initially illuminated by Bakhtin, can be characterized as carnivalesque because they include all voices, all points of view. This is why they can be designated as 'dialogical' (as opposed to Tolstoy's novels, which are monological in the sense that they present a singular view of the world). But if it is accepted that there is no particular subject matter that is excluded from the novel in its modern guise – if, that is, the modern novel is essentially open ended – then the novel, as a medium, is essentially carnivalesque, with *Finnegans Wake* leading the way. Indeed, Joyce's novel demonstrates how the 'letter' can oscillate between a status of the medium as disappearance with its apparent presence – not only in punning, where one letter might replace another (cf. 'The letter! The litter!' (Joyce 1975: 93)), but also in the focus on letters as such – on the medium, on 'HCE', as the sigla for 'Here Comes Everybody', 'Hush! Caution! Echoland!' (1975: 13), 'Humphrey Chimpden Earwicker' in the 'alphybettyformed verbage' (183). There is also the description of the letter on the *Tunc* page of the Book of Kells (122), and the text refers to 'a colophon of no fewer than seven hundred and thirty two strokes tailed by a leaping lasso' (123). The letter, then, is featured in *The Wake*.[1] Perhaps we 'see' the medium. Even McLuhan is alive to Joyce's focus on letters in *The Wake* and points out that: 'everywhere in *Finnegans Wake* Joyce reiterates the theme of the effects of the alphabet' and urges all to "harmonise your abecedeed responses?" ' (Joyce 1975: 140 cited by McLuhan 1967: 152).

However, it is necessary to observe that there is a *story* of letters, and it is also letters that give rise to the narrative of *Finnegans Wake*. The reader is not just involved in a forensic study of the alphabet, but is embroiled in the plot, such as this can be ascertained. Or, again, the reader is captivated by the sounds of letters, sounds that make punning possible. As the text says, it is a matter of 'soundsense' and 'sensesound' (121). In short, to read *Finnegans Wake* – or indeed any novel – is to become immersed in the text; the reader enters an 'irreal' world. In Jean-Paul Sartre's words: 'objective signification

---

1 Even the allusions to the crimes in Phoenix Park, Dublin, involve the letter, 'e' used in the spelling by forger, Richard Piggott, of 'hesitency'. Piggott had forged documents incriminating Charles Stewart Parnell (Irish Nationalist leader) in the murders of Lord Frederick Cavendish and Thomas Henry Burke in Phoenix Park. By misspelling hesitancy in court, Piggott gave himself away as the forger; cf. 'his hes hesitancy Hec' (Joyce 1975: 119).

becomes an irreal world' (2004: 64), where disbelief is suspended and events, characters and materials become 'real'.

To return to the excluded middle, even 0–1, when understood in digital technology as 'on–off', or 'yes–no' in relation to – as Wolfgang Ernst says – the 'rhythm' of algorithms, the issue of time as event-based and differential evokes the 'in between' (= difference) in the relation of 0–1. The medium, then, is to be understood in the context of time as difference – or as '*différance*', which evokes delay. I will elaborate on this later in the text.

In Michel Serres's work (see Chapter 5 of this volume), it is noticeable that the excluded middle becomes a key element in the philosophy of communication. In effect, univalent logic is found to be limiting. We can intuit that what tells against the excluded middle as being ranked as important is its character of non-appearing: as that which does not appear as such.

Hermes, as messenger, is the figure of the medium par excellence: he is the catalyst of communication as travelling between regions, whether these be scientific, poetic/metaphorical, artistic.

Noise is, at first blush, opposed to communication: indecipherable writing counts as noise; the parasite is also the 'noise in a channel'.

Middle

With carnival, then, medium can also mean milieu or environment as water is the medium for fish. This calls for analysis as it implies that for the creatures involved there is nothing outside the medium.

To be in the *middle* of the ocean, or desert, suggests being 'submerged in' to the extent of being unable to comprehend where one is. Compare: '*in medias res*' ('into the middle of things') much used in literature and cinema. Thus:

> There is a pile of clothing on the side of the train tracks. Light-blue cloth – a shirt, perhaps – jumbled up with something dirty white. It's probably rubbish, part of a load fly-tipped into the scrubby little wood up the bank. … The train jolts and scrapes and screeches back into motion, the little pile of clothes disappears from view and we trundle towards London. (Hawkins 2015: 1)

As Peter Fenves explains: 'a pure middle would have to be an immediate middle: not a middle determined by an act of measurement but a middle that immediately announced or otherwise activated its own middleness. Such a middle would be less a "means" than a medium, and this, too, is implied in [Walter] Benjamin's strange term *reine Mittel'* ('pure medium'; Fenves 1998: 48). In a note, Fenves adds: 'The [German] word *Mittel*, which is generally translated without further thought as "means", at first meant "middle" and then came to mean "medium"' (1998: 48–9, n. 3).[2]

Gilles Deleuze's philosophy is often described as being based on the 'middle' (milieu) because it seeks to avoid being dominated by oppositions, but also because thinking is always undertaken in a pre-existing milieu that rarely, if ever, appears as such. This, of course, requires further investigation. We need to know whether the middle is supposed to appear as such in Deleuze's thought. The evidence suggests that, in fact, it is a very elusive notion.

Medium, as frequently noted, meant middle in Latin (also, note that middle in French is 'milieu'). We can think, too, of: median. Consideration will be given to whether it can be represented. Sybille Krämer offers a point of departure here: 'Occupying the middle is precisely what the position of medium represents. This "middle" can be understood in three ways: spatially as an intermediate position, then functionally as mediation and finally formally as neutralization' (2015: 36).[3]

Medium can also be studied in terms of it being a means not an end. An object, by contrast, is an end in itself.

*

Three-dimensional space can be considered as a medium: Clement Greenberg opposes the illusion of three dimensionality in two-dimensional space (the canvas).

For Greenberg, the 'flat canvas' is the medium of painting. But the canvas does not appear (see Harman 2019: 108). This might seem odd as most people would say that paint is (also) the medium of painting. It is a bit like saying that paper is the medium of writing to the exclusion of the substance (ink, etc.) of writing. The flat canvas is simply a conventional surface support. But compare

---

2 On this, Fenves references the Grimm Brothers (1954, 6: 2381–93).
3 Interestingly, Freud, in his struggle to provide a rigorous definition of the ego, initially saw it essentially as an '*intermediary* between the id and the external world' (Freud 2001: 145, emphasis added). Indeed, the definition of the ego in Freud would seem to oscillate between medium and object (= total personality).

the cut canvas in the works of Lucio Fontana.[4] The canvas appears as such. However, at issue, is the idea that, ultimately, only a two-dimensional space is integral to painting, not the illusion of perspective. For Greenberg, abstract art is in harmony with the two-dimensional character of the medium. But then again, a canvas, as a whole, is not, strictly speaking, two dimensional. Only its surface is. Impasto technique (cf. van Gogh) adds a third dimension to a painting. These issues call on us to think more profoundly with regard to the medium.

*

It will become clear that the medium has no identity in any simple sense. In the example of translation, medium becomes difference. Linked to translation is metaphor as medium; compare with Gk *metaphorein*: to transfer. Metaphor becomes the medium of transfer of meaning between two different contexts. Here, recall that McLuhan frequently referred to the notion of metaphor as transport.

Analytic-synthetic distinction, as found in Kant, evokes the medium. How is this so? An excessively analytical approach that attempts to reveal the medium *qua* medium only serves to obscure rather than reveal the nature of medium. In this regard, if a medium is defined, analytically, as an object, it becomes an end – that is, it ceases to be a medium.

Painting, photography, sculpture, music – media in a word – as much or more than individual works – or an individual work – dominate critical discourse. More often than not a particular work is viewed as an instance of what can be achieved in or by a specific medium. As though the medium as such could be revealed in its status as medium. But the medium is never present as such – this is the thesis to be developed.

*

It remains, now, to establish, through an elaboration of the points raised, the meaning and signification of the term, 'medium', the better to understand the notion of 'media specificity', as employed by media theorists. 'Media specificity' relies on only one possible meaning of 'medium'.

---

4 See: https://www.tate.org.uk/art/artworks/fontana-spatial-concept-waiting-t00694 (accessed 19 October 2022).

It is a matter, then, of highlighting the way that medium and its synonyms are deeply embedded in culture and society. This will also include a diverse range of philosophical and linguistic meanings attached to 'medium'. Against the self-evident approaches to this term, I am going to imply that medium and its avatars exist in a diverse range of contexts, the experience or knowledge of which will provide us with a closer approximation of what 'medium' truly stands for. It might be said that the trajectory proposed resorts to an esoteric or to an at times obscure response to the notion of medium. But it can equally be said, I believe, that the impact of the medium occurs via unseen, if not invisible, places in language, technical objects and philosophical thought. As the medium is not what appears but is the condition of possibility of all appearing, it is understandable that tracking it down calls for thinking.

Aristotle

As has been noted, etymologically, medium derives from the Latin *medius* (neuter of medium), meaning 'middle', and I have already elaborated on this. But it is also worth considering the sense in which the middle appears as such. As we have seen, Friedrich Kittler points out that for Aristotle, medium means '*to metaxi* ('the middle', Latin *medium*). Aristotle, in other words, shaped the concept of media' (Kittler 2006: 54). Recall, too, that in 'On the Soul' (*de Anima*) Aristotle says that bodies in air (medium) do not notice the air, just as bodies for whom their life-sustaining medium is water do not notice 'wet surfaces' (Aristotle 1984: 423b 30). Aristotle could be said to be the first philosopher in the history of Western philosophy to raise the question of the medium in relation to perception. In *de Anima* he points out that if taste amounted to the taste of the tongue itself, as can occur when someone is ill, the taste mechanism ceases to function (422b 5). Although Aristotle, when discussing perception, specifies that the medium will have a concrete form, it does not appear in what is perceived. As the philosopher says: 'in the perception of objects of touch we are affected not *by* but *along with* the medium' (423b 15). Moreover, while there must be bodily flesh for touch to be possible, 'flesh is not the organ but the *medium* of touch' (423b 25). Let this mention of Aristotle on the medium as *to metaxi* suffice to indicate perhaps the first instance of the conception of the medium in relation to transparency and materiality. As the example of the tongue in relation to taste also shows, Aristotle is the first to raise the issue of medium specificity, even if this is to remind us of its dysfunctionality. Thus: to taste is not to taste the tongue; to see is not to see the eye; to hear is not to hear the ear; to touch is not just to feel one's own skin (on this, see Merleau-Ponty on the chiasmus of touch: touching touched).

Middle voice

A significant evocation in relation to medium is the middle voice. Supplementary to the Heideggerian notion of 'ready-to-hand' is another element relevant to grasping what is essential to the medium. It can be pointed out that, potentially, the middle voice offers a way into the transparency of the medium in that it is quite distinct from any subject–object appropriation of language and from media specificity. If, for Heidegger, logos can be explained in terms of the middle voice, this is because, 'λόγος [logos] lets something be seen (φαίνεδθαι [phanesthai]), namely, what the discourse is about; and it does so either *for* the one who is doing the talking (the *medium*) or for persons who are talking with one another, as the case may be. Discourse "lets something be seen"' (Heidegger 1978: 56), just as the clock, as 'ready-to-hand', lets time be measured.

For Charles Scott (1988), Heidegger's text exemplifies the appearance of the middle voice and of a way of thinking outside of subjectivity. Thus, in speaking more generally about the middle voice, our author says that: 'I note particularly the intransitive uses of the middle voice since that is one form of the middle voice that is difficult to retrieve in our languages now, but one that plays a significant role in contemporary efforts to think outside of the domain of subjectivity' (1989: 746). Hence, the emphasis in Heidegger on 'letting things appear'. As an instance of Heidegger's writing in the middle voice in *Being and Time*, Scott cites section 7 (the phenomenological method), but more pertinently, the sections on time and 'historicality', namely, 74, 75, 76 and 80 (1989: 746 n. 4).

Hence, the middle voice is the voice that does not appear. For Scott,

it is linked to metaphysics. It is not the medium as such, but one can deduce certain characteristics that relate to the medium. The middle voice enables thinking outside the domain of subjectivity, as Heidegger aimed to do in *Being and Time*. Although Scott also relates self-overcoming in Nietzsche's thought to the middle voice (1989: 753–4[5]), it is the brief reference to Heidegger that is of interest. Scott says that it is through the middle voice that Heidegger can point to the letting be, letting appear – the showing – of beings. Thus: 'The middle voice function is not primarily one of representing or designating. It shows out of itself. The "*what*" that is shown is not central or peripheral. ... What is shown is in self-showing. And since self-showing is not a what or who or an action, the present time as a determinant now does not dominate the concept' (Scott 1988: 162). In other words, it is not 'agency-centered' (162). Effectively, the middle voice gives rise to complete transparency and neutrality, something hardly thought possible for thinking governed by media specificity, where the medium, if not subjectivity itself, would assume a certain agency. No doubt the rise of the dominance of the principle of media specificity – the age of McLuhan – can be equated with the fall into desuetude of the middle voice. In Scott's words Heidegger's *Being and Time* 'will be a "medium" that shows something other than the totality of its contents and other than what it speaks directly about' (163).

For the theorist of general linguistics, Émile Benveniste, the middle voice serves to define 'the subject as *interior* to the process' (1966: 173). As an example, we have: 'he bears gifts'. And one can add: 'the shop closes at 6 pm'; 'this book sells well'; 'the battle begins at dawn'; 'The medium remains concealed'. As, formally, there is no middle voice in English, these examples are only approximations. However, they indicate a mode of voice that is more nebulous than the active or passive voices: Paul hit Peter (active); Peter was hit by Paul (passive).

Benveniste's theory of the middle voice centres on a discussion of the active and the passive voice: 'I say flat earth theory is untrue' (active); 'It is said that flat earth theory is untrue' (passive). How does the middle voice figure in this context? According to Benveniste, the Greeks formulated a third category – the middle voice – as a voice of transition, or mediation – between the active and the passive voice. The passage from active to passive

---

5   Thus, Scott says: 'In *The Genealogy of Morals* the process of self-overcoming is thus a middle voice of Western morality' (754).

needed to be marked in some way. Indo-European also marked the middle voice. For a time, the middle voice displaced the passive voice, so that the opposition was between active and middle voices. Latin has '*media tantum*' (middle only verbs). With active verbs, the subject is external to the process; with middle voice verbs, the subject is interior to the process (1966: 172). Of course, the passive voice also corresponds to the 'third person'. Outside a linguistic analysis (diathesis), the third connotes 'the in between'. Overall, and no doubt speculatively, the middle, passive and third connote 'interiority' – like interior to the milieu.

In an extremely interesting engagement with Benveniste's definition, Philippe Eberhard suggest that:

> The force of the middle voice is that it fosters a *both- and or both-and-more* way of thinking in terms of the subject and the verb instead of the subject vs. the object. In the middle voice, the process the verb expresses happens to the subject who is *also* its subject. It encompasses the subject without reducing him or her to a passive entity. Thus, in the middle voice it becomes possible to conceive of an action without an exclusive single agent opposed to an object. The question the middle voice elicits about the subject is not one of identity but locality, not 'Who or what is the subject' but 'Where are we?' (2006: 127; emphasis added in the first line)

Here, we find an implicit evocation of carnival logic (0–2 – 'both/and'), as well as the implication that the middle voice as the voice of events occurring. It facilitates the event rather than being the event – as can occur with the active voice: 'I can see the water falling on the men in their small boat below' (the event is the narrator seeing). By comparison, the middle/passive voice says: 'the water from the waterfall inundated the boat; the men drowned'. The middle voice thus lends itself to narration (to being a medium), even though structuralists have in the past argued that a narration of events cannot be separated from the event of narration. The work of Gérard Genette (1980) can be consulted in this regard. Or again, the work of Hayden White on historical discourse. A structuralist approach rarely treats the medium as transparent and is instead interested in medium opacity, which is a way of alluding to media specificity.

Eberhard also points out – in light of Gadamer's philosophy – that play (as in to play a game) – is also indicative of the middle voice: 'A game is something we play, not something we do. The players do not master the game. They are involved in a process that happens to them yet not without them' (2006: 127). In other words, a game cannot exist as a pure form; it only becomes a game in being played. A game, then, is what it allows to appear (the content of the game).

In more speculative fashion, we can recall Derrida's reference to the middle voice in his essay, 'La différance'. In this regard, the philosopher proposes that the Latin verb, '*differre*' – which evokes the sense of delay, detour, lateness and reserve – means, in effect, to 'temporalize' and forms the basis of the French verb, différer: to differ, defer, delay. We will see that this view of time in relation to difference has influenced Ernst.

Recall, too, that the trace effaces itself in presenting itself (Derrida 1972: 24). Is it not like the medium?

But *différance* evokes the middle voice because neither the active nor the passive voice can do it justice: Thus, we read that: 'We must consider that in the usage of our language the ending –*ance* remains undecided *between* active and the passive. And we will see why that which lets itself be designated "*différance*" is neither simply active nor passive, announcing or rather recalling something like the middle voice' (1972: 9).

Perhaps, again like the trace, the middle voice is the disappearance of voice in its appearing. What appears is what happens: 'the bookshop closes at 5 pm'.

The active and, to a lesser extent, the passive voice, tend to evoke the appearing of voice as such: '*I* closed the bookshop at 5 pm' (active); 'The bookshop is always locked at 5 pm' (passive).

Overall, we are dealing with what has an effect, or impact, in its non-appearing – like the medium.

Foucault and the middle voice

Vincent Pecora has noted that Foucault embraces the middle voice at the end of the *Archaeology of Knowledge* when 'attempting to characterize the positivities of discursive practices in relation to their enunciating subjectivities' (Pecora 1991: 219). But more than this, if the episteme as articulated by Foucault does not exactly qualify for being characterized as the incarnation of the middle voice (which, I believe it does have a claim to), it does qualify to be considered as the medium. For the *episteme* is not what appears but is the condition of possibility of what does appear:

> By *episteme*, we mean, in fact, the total set of relations that unite, at a given
> period, the discursive practices that give rise to epistemological figures,
> sciences, and possibly formalized systems; the way in which, in each of these
> discursive formations, the transition to epistemologization, scientificity, and
> formalization are situated and operate; the distribution of thresholds, which
> may coincide, be subordinated to one another, or be separated by shifts in
> time; the lateral relations that may exist between epistemological figures or
> sciences in so far as they belong to neighbouring, but distinct, discursive
> practices. (Foucault 1972: 191)

Crucially, Foucault adds that: 'the episteme is not what may be known at a given period … it is what, in the given positivity of discursive practices, *makes possible the existence* of epistemological figures and sciences' (192, emphasis added).

The episteme has all the aura of the medium. This is why discursive formations are not to be explained by the work of a subject or subjects, nor by the notion of a historical era, world view, ideology or zeitgeist. Nor again are discursive formations to be explained as the expression of a group, a class or an individual. Instead, a discursive practice 'is a body of anonymous, historical rules, always determined in the time and space that have defined a given period, and for a given social, economic, geographical, or linguistic area, the condition of operation of the enunciative function' (117).

Certainly, Foucault, following in the wake of structuralist 'anti-humanism' (even though he denies the connection), lends a certain autonomy to events, an autonomy that evokes the middle voice. The controversial aspect of the Foucauldian episteme is that the human apparently has no conscious agency as far as the form of the episteme as medium is concerned, but it is nevertheless the case that it is human actions unconsciously articulated that give form to the episteme. In other words, the latter configuration is not prior to human action even though it gives the pattern of human action, most notably, thinking. Without going into further detail, we simply note here that in his preface to *The Order of Things* (1982), Foucault refers to 'order' as that 'which has no existence except in the grid created by a glance, an examination, a language; and it is only in the blank spaces of this grid that order manifests itself in depth as though already there, waiting in silence for the moment of its expression' (xx). This 'grid' is thus redolent, we could say, of the medium. There is also reference in the same text to the middle: 'Thus, between the already "encoded" eye and reflexive knowledge there is a middle region which liberates order itself' (xxi). Moreover: 'This middle region, then, in so far as it makes manifest the modes of being or order, can be posited as the most fundamental of all: anterior to words, perceptions and gestures, which are then taken to be more or less exact expressions of it' (xxi). Even though – let us admit it – Foucault's language is ambiguous at times, it is the appearing of the episteme via the 'middle region' that again evokes the medium. There is, to be sure, much more that could be said here but it would take us too far afield, suffice it to say that I propose that the critical element in relation to the episteme is that it constitutes a historical event and as such is waiting to be documented in light of the requisite research. This is, after all, what 'discontinuity' between the different epistemes signifies. Hence, the importance of synonyms for 'discontinuity', such as 'threshold', 'rupture', 'break', 'mutation', 'transformation', terms listed in introduction to *The Archaeology of Knowledge* (1974: 5).

Agamben and mediality in a 'model ontology'

For Giorgio Agamben, the medium – or 'mediality' – appears (see Agamben 2005: 62 and 2015: 172), but 'the middle term, the *qua,* the "as" is unthought'. Of course, he is not alone in this. Thus, we can refer to the notion of 'divine violence' (*Göttliche Gewalt*), as discussed in Walter Benjamin's 'Critique of Violence' (1986), which is equated by Agamben with pure means – that is, with pure mediality. With regard to the latter, my thesis is that a large part, if not all, of Agamben's thinking is organized around the notions of 'means', 'mediality', 'medium' and 'middle' – the latter especially in light of Émile Benveniste's linguistic theory. Of particular interest in this regard is Agamben's development of a philosophy of 'modal ontology', where an entity's being would be understood to be inseparable from its 'mode' of being. That is – to put it another way – where an entity is inseparable from its 'form of life' (see Agamben 2015: 147–75). Here, it is intriguing to see that the *middle* voice (cf.

' "to walk oneself" '), 'situated in a zone of indetermination' (2015: 28), is invoked as a way of explicating the notion of modal ontology. Thus, in referring to Spinoza on substance and mode, we read that: 'in order to think the substance/ modes relationship, it is necessary to have at our disposal an ontology of the *middle voice*, in which the agent (God or substance) in effectuating the modes in reality affects and modifies only itself. Modal ontology can be understood only as a *medial ontology*' (163, emphasis added). The medial is given a broad reach, as the whole idea of 'use' is 'a *medial* process of this kind' (163, emphasis added). All of these terms ('means', 'mediality', etc.) raise the question of the appearing of the medium – of the appearing of that, which to be what it is, normally does not appear.

It is thus through the notion of mediality that violence is brought into proximity with the image. Whether or not Benjamin is correctly interpreted here, the notion of violence as pure mediality needs to be rethought when considering violence in Agamben's theory of *homo sacer*. The latter, despite all the commentary on it, remains to be fully illuminated. In particular, what remains to be determined is the extent to which the *homo sacer*, or bare life, is essentially a point of mediation in Agamben's discourse on politics. In short: this figure has no value in itself but provides the basis for an understanding of the political framework of the whole of the modern era. Thus: 'In Western politics, bare life has the peculiar privilege of being that whose exclusion founds the city of men' (1998: 7).

Séance

Let us note in passing that *séance* in French is translated as 'session'. How did *séance* come to take on the meaning it has in English – namely, as a kind of spiritualist or mystical session, where there is a real or attempted communing with the dead via a medium? Derrida might have liked to follow up on the origins of the English *séance*.

It is not necessary to believe in the power of a medium in a séance to understand what is being aimed at: contact with the dead in the sense that the dead person speaks through the medium. In other words, if the medium is in fact speaking the whole exercise is thrown into disarray. The goal of the medium, therefore, is to be absolutely transparent, even if sceptics will not be convinced and propose that it is the so-called medium who speaks throughout, not the deceased.

Can this be connected with Derrida's 'hauntology'? How does the spectre appear to disrupt the present? Two notions of spectre are pertinent here: the ghost revealed by the text – or by whatever medium – and the spectre haunting the text, a spectre that can never be fully revealed. The first approach, as Colin Davis (2005) has shown, is that of Nicolas Abraham's and Maria Torok's psychoanalytical approach; the second is the one taken up by Derrida in *Spectres de Marx* (1993). In the first case it is a matter of finding the secret (the ghost) at the heart of the text; with Derrida it is a matter of showing that what haunts a text or other symbolic formation can never be fully revealed. The spectre becomes the medium.

Again, as concerns the medium in the séance, we read in *Spectres* '[Marx] must describe the table become merchandise as, indeed, a rotating table in a spiritualist séance' (241).

Questions arising in light of Derrida's text are as follows: in what sense can the ghost or spectre *appear*? Does a spectre need a medium in order to appear? Or is the spectre the medium that enables entities to appear? In what sense does Derrida's text enable the appearing of the spectre – the spectre of Marx? But in what sense can the spectre of Marx appear in a text that focuses on the spectre *in* Marx's text (or in Shakespeare's *Hamlet*). In a footnote towards the end of his thesis, Derrida refers to the medium: 'each epoch has its phantoms …, its own experience, its own *medium* and its own hautological media' (243, n.1; emphasis added).

Predictably, we are in the realm of paradox in our attempts to work out how that which cannot appear (the spectral, says Derrida, '*is not*' (14)) as such, appears. A spectre *qua* spectre strongly evokes the medium in the sense that it, too, does not appear but perhaps appears in a certain sense.

What is clear is that the logic of the spectre is that of 'both-and' (0–2), not either-or (0–1). This is clarified when Derrida speaks of there never being a scholar who does not think that there is a clear distinction between 'the real and the non-real, efficacy and non-efficacy, the living and the non-living, being and non-being (*to be or not to be*, according to the conventional reading), the opposition between what is present and what is not, for example in the form of objectivity' (33).

A spectre always raises the question of repetition: 'un spectre est toujours un revenant' (32). The spectre is always an apparition, or, literally, what returns. This is what 'haunting' evokes. In what sense does a medium always return? Implied here is the notion that the medium is not present. Looked at in terms of medium theory, this means that the medium is a pure condition of possibility, not an actual reality. 'What', Derrida asks, 'is the mode of presence of a spectre?' (69). Ditto for the medium.

Derrida also reminds us of the fact that in the Trinity, the medium corresponds to the *Saint-esprit* (Holy ghost). 'The holy ghost assures the mediation, thus the passage to unity' (200).

In *Hamlet*, the ghost says: 'I am thy Father's spirit'. Spirit – like medium – is naming what cannot be named.

Economy of the medium (Mondzain)

The medium (Holy ghost) is what assures the relation of Father to Son in the trinity. In Marie-José Mondzain's explication, 'economy' is implicated with the image, especially in relation to Christ in the Trinity: 'Christ is … par excellence economy in every sense of the term, since he is intrinsically a part of the trinitarian distribution … . He is image, relation and organ' (1996: 51). In Mondzain's commentary on the theology of the image in the debate between the iconoclasts and the iconophiles, if the image is a medium, its 'essence … is not its visibility' (110). A contemporary approach to the image as medium is of course often the opposite of this.

Time and medium: Ernst

If, as Ernst argues, time is fundamental to technical objects in their operation, then time and medium come together. Technical objects as media are time incarnate. Therefore, via technical objects time becomes a medium. This is time as Aristotle's counting movement, or as the rhythm of Greek poetics, or as the pulse of computer algorithms, as we have seen that Ernst has pointed out. Schematically, we have operationality, which leads to time as rhythm/event/differential, which leads to the medium.

Énonciation and the medium

In his linguistic theory of pronouns Émile Benveniste – inspired by the work of Roman Jakobson – made a distinction between *énonciation* (act of stating) and *énoncé* (statement made). In invoking personal pronouns (I/you; we/they), and demonstrative pronouns (this, that, here, there, tomorrow, yesterday), meaning takes place only in the act of language – that is, at an existential level. Once made, a statement can be analysed independently of, or in conjunction with, its *énonciation*. The important thing to note here is that the chief quality of an *énonciation qua énonciation* is its transparency. The *énoncé*, by contrast, is entirely opaque.

The principle of *énonciation* – the existential level of performance – does not only apply to the linguistic context, but to all contexts where meaning, significance, communication, art, images and sounds are in play. To consider the latter domains at the level of *énonciation* is to consider them in their implementation and transparency, much like Ernst considers media in an archaeological sense. If, on the other hand, the medium is considered only as an object, and thus not existentially, then this is potentially equivalent to treating media at the level of the *énoncé*.

Unsurprisingly, to equate the medium exclusively with the level of the *énoncé* is what is implicit in the 'medium specificity' approach. How to do things with words ('I hereby open this meeting', 'I promise to tell the truth') is also to be explained at the existential level of the *énonciation*. It may be that because it must be understood in this sense, a performative statement is open to subversion. In short, a performative statement only works when one experiences it existentially, transparently. To question a performative is not to experience it as such. Is this not similar to the operation of medium – the medium *as* operation?

The victim as medium between the sacred and profane worlds

In the anthropology of the sacred and sacrifice, the victim becomes the intermediary between the profane and sacred worlds. The victim in sacrifice is never there for its own sake, but only to appease the god in the interests of the sacrificer. As Hubert and Mauss explain: sacrifice, '*consists in establishing a means of communication between the sacred and profane worlds through the mediation of a victim, that is, of a thing that in the course of the ceremony is destroyed*' (1981: 97; emphasis in original). The physical destruction of the victim in fact parallels the victim's status as medium. It is as medium that the victim disappears in the process of communication between the sacred and profane worlds.

No doubt because, as medium, the being of the victim disappears it behoves the defender of human rights to advocate, in light of Kant, for the sanctity of the human as an end, where, as such, the human would fully appear.

*

Overall, rather than appearing in an array of objects, the medium disappears in range of contexts. Attempted in the foregoing, then, is a sensitization to the various actual and possible meanings, connotations and nuances attaching to the notion of medium. Not only how to forge a more rigorous approach to the medium is to be learnt from this, but also how to think that which does not appear as such. Just as some will say that it is not possible to think seriously about a spectre because such an entity cannot in fact appear, so it might also be said that one cannot truly think the medium if it does not appear. This conclusion is, in all probability, more readily arrived at by those wedded to a subject–object ontology. For those who are more open minded in this regard, the medium is just the kind of challenge that 'calls for thinking' (Heidegger).

2

Revisiting the 'medium is the message': McLuhan and media specificity

As foreshadowed, this chapter will focus on interpreting McLuhan's classic texts, *The Gutenberg Galaxy: The Making of Typographic Man*, together with *Understanding Media: The Extensions of Man*.

McLuhan and the nature of media

First, it is necessary to acknowledge the apparent plausibility of McLuhan's historical approach to the evolution of communications media.

Macro and micro approaches to the medium

There is no doubt that McLuhan reveals a genuinely macro and fruitful approach that can be taken to the medium (to technics), thus to literacy (the phonetic alphabet, the printing press, cinema, digital recording, etc.). McLuhan's work sits squarely with with that of scholars like Eric Havelock (1986) and Walter Ong (1997) on the impact and transformations of orality, and with that of Jack Goody on the impact of writing on the formation of society (2000), as well as with that of Frances Yates (2001) on memory as mnemonics – which implies the invocation of certain techniques, such as the use of rhythm, rhyme, repetition and invention in mnemotechniques (a system of places) – techniques, Bernard Stiegler would say, that are, like participation, part of technics. It might thus be conceded that, at this macro level, the medium can be observed to change the human – that at a macro level 'media specificity' can be seen to have palpable effects. Walter Ong, for his part, thus refers to the 'democratising' effect of the Greek alphabet (it was easy for everyone to learn) (1997: 90–2).

But are things the same at the micro level? The answer will be that they are not, that while opacity marks the medium at a macro level (i.e. the notion that the 'medium is the message' is palpable), at a micro level, there is transparency – transparency in the sense of Sartre's philosophy of the image, where the image becomes a mode of access to the real. The problem for philosophy is that the macro approach has come, in a majority of cases, to be its default position. This is the one that allows philosophy to treat medium purely as an object.

With regard to the 'medium is the message', McLuhan will be found to replicate in certain ways the 'frog's eye view' of reality (see Lettvin et al. 1959) – a view based on research reported in 1959, three years before the *Gutenberg Galaxy* and five years before *Understanding Media*. Just as the frog sees the environment in terms of its physical needs and not in terms of the way things really are, so, for McLuhan, humans know the world in terms of whatever medium is in play. Like the frog, humans can never know the world as it really is because all knowledge must be filtered through a specific medium, or media. As McLuhan says: '"the medium is the message" because it is the medium that shapes and controls the scale and form of human association and action' (2008: 9). In McLuhan's sense the phonetic alphabet is a medium that changed human consciousness. Or, to cite another example, McLuhan says of lighting that: 'In this domain, the medium is that message, and when the light is on there is a world of sense that disappears when the light is off' (139).

The key point here is to reverse McLuhan's statement that: 'the "content" of any medium blinds us to the character of the medium' (9), so that the content assumes prominence.

To achieve this reversal, examples of media given by McLuhan, such as house, clothes and money, need to be analysed in some depth as, to all appearances, what stands out is their concreteness, the very quality that allows McLuhan to treat the medium as an object. The latter is exacerbated by the notion that the content of any medium is another medium. Indeed, there is no content as such, only media.

And it is no doubt true that the medium of the house is a concrete entity in relation to which its object status is difficult to deny. Moreover, houses are commodities that are bought and sold, something that would seem to consolidate their object status. But what the commodity version of the house conceals is the house as a vehicle for living. And living is the performative experience of the house, the house in its use, the house as the foyer for sleeping, eating, socializing, entertaining and so on. This is the house, then, as transparent medium, not as object, which it will all too readily become once the house is put on the market. Different architectural and design eras, different housing fashions are not a substitute for the notion of the house in its use, as the location for living – as a 'machine for living', as Le Corbusier once said. This interpretation of the house as a locus of living is emblematic of the house as transparent medium, by comparison with McLuhan's notion of medium as concrete object.

But what, exactly, is in the detail of the McLuhan argument?

*

'Hot' media, like radio, are 'high definition' and low in participation, says McLuhan (25). This is because recipients of the radio message receive a large amount of information, or data, and thus do not have to be participatory in accessing information. With a cool medium like the telephone the ear receives only a minimal amount of information so that a significantly greater amount of participation on the part of the listener is required. Presumably, today's interactive media are 'cool' on McLuhan's terms and are therefore more 'progressive'. But this is not McLuhan's view, as it turns out that 'backward countries are cool, and we are hot' (29).

It is perhaps McLuhan's definition of hot and cool media that raises the question of what precisely constitutes the nature of a medium as object. Radio, telephone and language can be invoked here.

McLuhan never considers the possibility that radio, telephone and language as media can equally be inaugurated by the receiver as sender, or vice versa – as in amateur radio. There can be a tin can telephone and language, where receivers can become senders and senders can become receivers of messages.

It can be shown that radio is not reducible to a centralized and bureaucratically controlled network in relation to which there is a mass of recipients of the radio message, but that radio also includes the possibility for each recipient to be a sender of messages, as is instanced by amateur radio operators.

Consequently, McLuhan's notion of medium turns out to be one that is very much imbued with a certain passivity – the passivity entailed in being a receiver. As such, media can then be deemed to have an impact on whole populations. This is when the media becomes mass media. Whether or not this is empirically the case, media are not *essentially* mass media. The latter is only so if the notion of medium is largely modelled on cinema and television, both of which require very significant resources to be enacted. In this context, it is doubtful as to whether McLuhan's *understanding* of media can include the internet and social media.

As opposed to McLuhan, the approach adopted here – to reiterate – is that an active user of language problematizes the notion that 'the medium is the message', which also means that such an active user problematizes the notion of medium specificity.

In the next chapter, we will see that, in the context of Sybille Krämer's work, the medium 'disappears'. With the 'medium is the message' mantra, McLuhan signals the very opposite approach to the medium – the medium as appearing and as entirely explicit. How did McLuhan arrive at this point? And what are some of the consequences for 'understanding media', to cite the title of McLuhan's most important book? And why, after all, re-read McLuhan?

As the media theorist says in the text entitled 'McLuhan's Laws of Media', 'I am talking about "media" in terms of a larger entity of information and perception which forms our thoughts, structures our experience, and determines our views of the world about us' (McLuhan 1975: 74–5). McLuhan claims to have been influenced in formulating his 'laws of media' by the structuralist approach of Saussure and Lévi-Strauss. Hence, the application to the study of media of the terms 'diachrony' and 'synchrony', with special emphasis on the role of synchrony. The range of media specified is vast and includes along with: housing, clothing and money; number, electricity, printing and transport systems. In the wake of McLuhan's notion of the explicit nature of the medium, these examples can be objects of research, as they are opaque rather than transparent.

As we will see in Chapter 6, another theory of technology emphasizes the importance of exteriorization. The latter can be understood to result from a supplement, or prosthesis being employed to make up for a lack. And this employment of the prosthesis can become, in the eyes of certain people, excessive. This is when we are possibly dealing with technophobia. At least the idea of the essential separation of the prosthesis from its user would constitute the precondition for technophobia. For the technophobes and the critics of technology as excess, technical devices are an addition to what is seen – in the fashion of Rousseau – as the essential human, the human conceived as being independent of technics. From another perspective, however, technics are constitutive of the human.

Thus, Bernard Stiegler, commenting on the work of the paleontologist André Leroi-Gourhan, states that 'The movement inherent in this process of exteriorization is paradoxical: Leroi-Gourhan in fact says that it is the tool, that is *teckné*, that invents the human, not the human who invents the technical. Or again: the human invents himself in the technical by inventing the tool – by becoming exteriorized techno-logically' (Stiegler 1998: 143).

So, for McLuhan, the essential human interiorizes a technical medium because the medium is separate from the human *qua* human. This is the significance, as has been said, of prostheses. The latter are added to, then interiorized by, the essentially human. For the paleontologist, and then Stiegler as philosopher of technics, the human is exteriorized in technics such that technics comes to constitute the essentially human.

Typographic man

Before approaching the text that is the main focus of our deliberations, let us look a little more at McLuhan's earlier work, *Gutenberg Galaxy: The Making of Typographic Man* ([1962] 1967). Perhaps the sub-title says it all: typographic man – the product of the printing revolution. The medium of printing, in short, produced typographic man. First of all, note that in the prologue, McLuhan writes that

> Today man has developed extensions for practically everything he used to do with his body. The evolution of weapons begins with the teeth and the fist and ends with the atom bomb. Clothes and houses are extensions of man's biological temperature-control mechanisms. Furniture takes the place of squatting and sitting on the ground. Power tools, glasses, TV, telephones, and books which carry the voice across both time and space are examples of material extensions. Money is a way of extending and storing labor. Our

transportation networks now do what we used to do with our feet and backs. In fact, all man-made material things can be treated as extensions of what man once did with his body or some specialized part of his body. (1967: 4)

In the opening chapter of *The Gutenberg Galaxy*, we encounter a commentary on Shakespeare's *King Lear* and on the transition from people playing roles to assuming jobs. More generally, Shakespeare's plays are taken to be a barometer of the impact of the age of print in the early modern, Renaissance period. This is a reminder that McLuhan was first and foremost a literary scholar, hence the frequency of literary references throughout his writing – in the works of Joyce, for example, as we noted in the previous chapter, the alphabet in *Finnegans Wake* was the focus. Let us argue, then, that it is only because literary forms can achieve transparency that McLuhan, child of Gutenberg, is able to foreshadow the electronic age. Words lose their magic when the written form becomes dominant. Orality gives rise to emotionality and 'living in the present'.

The 'technology of the phonic alphabet'

The medium changes the configuration of the senses. The eye (writing) overtakes the ear (oral). Typographic culture is therefore a 'visual' culture. 'If', says McLuhan, 'a technology is introduced either from within or from without a culture, and if it gives new stress or ascendancy to one or another of our senses, the ratio among all of our senses is altered' (1967: 24).

Oral and literate societies are compared and question arises as to whether the interiorization of the alphabet changes mental processes. In an article published in 1954 on Joyce, Mallarmé and the press (McLuhan 1954), the major innovators of modern literature are seen primarily as prescient as regards the effects of new communications technology. That is, Joyce and Mallarmé make these effects explicit. They foreshadow the arrival at the electronic world that leads to the 'global village'.

As regards culture and the sensorium, we learn that film and images must be learned to be read. Indeed, when a new technology extends one of the senses a new translation of culture occurs along with the interiorization of the technology. Without the interiorization of the alphabet there would be no printing revolution.

The problem with McLuhan's approach to the medium, however, is that it comes across – at least in *The Gutenberg Galaxy* – as largely 'cut and paste' from the research of others. Even Bertrand Russell's *ABC of Relativity* is cited. Indeed, McLuhan's 'method' (also illustrated in the 'Laws of Media') has proved to be an obstacle to grasping the salient points of his theory.

Nevertheless, one should note the following statement: 'any society possessing the alphabet can translate any adjacent cultures into its alphabetic mode. But this is a one-way process. No non-alphabetic culture can take over an alphabetic one; because the alphabet cannot be assimilated; [*sic*] it can only liquidate or reduce. However, in the electronic age we may have discovered the limits of the alphabet technology' (1967: 50).

What, then, needs to be reconsidered in light of *The Gutenberg Galaxy* is the notion of interiorization of technology. Language, for instance, as a technology interiorized is the 'mother tongue'. Can determinism be avoided here? Are there multiple forms of interiorization? Might these be in conflict with one another? If interiorization is equivalent to what goes without saying, how is it possible to become aware of it? Would interiorization be a form of the medium? What about when confronted with the language of the other? – and similar questions? McLuhan thus emphasizes interiorization, whereas we have just seen earlier that another way of interpreting technics is in terms of exteriorization.

'The medium is the message'

In the crucial chapter famously entitled, 'The Medium Is the Message', of *Understanding Media* ([1964] 2008), McLuhan invokes two approaches to media: there is, firstly (and perhaps for McLuhan, most importantly) the notion of the medium not just as technology, but as technological innovation. And because every medium is directly or indirectly an extension of the human, technological innovation has an impact on the lives of people. Electricity, new forms of transport, industrial innovation in relation to work – or the arrival of money in Japan in the seventeenth century – constitute the basis of technological innovations that change the social and physical environment.

The second form of medium is one in which the content is usually thought of as the message: writing, painting, cinema and photography, radio and television and so on. Thus, according to McLuhan, 'Cubism, by seizing on instant total awareness, suddenly announced that *the medium is the message*' (2008: 13). Here, the pertinent question is no longer: what does it mean? But: what is it? Or: How does it work? For, says McLuhan: '[People] never thought to ask what a melody was about, nor what a house or a dress were about' (14).

In responding to McLuhan here, we can argue that he is hardly original in pointing to the effects on society and culture of technological innovation. The early sociologists, such as Émile Durkheim and Ferdinand Tönnies had already done this. As to the idea that technology is essentially an extension of the human – that is, as prosthesis – McLuhan does well to draw attention to this. But, today, rather than being thought of as prosthesis – in which case the human creates the instrument – technics, as we have seen, creates the human. The latter approach to technology – or more broadly, technics – only adds to its invisibility and inscrutability. That is, to the notion of medium as disappearance.

Anyway, to return to our main theme where we find that the medium is the message is reiterated in, of all things, McLuhan's commentary on de Tocqueville's assessment of the differences between England and America: 'Alexis de Tocqueville was the first to master the grammar of print and typography' (14). For its part: 'The grammar of print cannot help to construe the message of oral and nonwritten culture and institutions' (15–16). De Tocqueville – and he alone of the aristocrats – 'understood the grammar of typography' (16) (i.e. how it 'speaks'). And so, in light of Tocqueville, 'any medium has the power of imposing its own assumption on the unwary' (16). Again, the medium has effects, so that we 'need to stand aside from the bias and pressure exerted by any technical form of human expression' (20). Moreover, the medium has enormous influence. In effect: 'Print created individualism and nationalism in the sixteenth century' (21).

McLuhan's point is reiterated (and perhaps refuted) in the example of 'one African who took great pains to listen each evening to the BBC news, even though he could understand nothing of it. Just to be in the presence of those sounds at 7 P.M. each day was important for him. His attitude to speech was like ours to melody – the resonant intonation was meaning enough' (21). But one could respond to this by pointing out that the African's relation to the medium is also essentially McLuhan's. For, it is the medium as such that has an impact – not the so-called content of medium. And yet, if this approach is taken to its logical conclusion, the necessary comprehensibility of the text being writing here would seem to be brought into question.

In summary, then, we have learnt that for McLuhan, the medium, when it is properly understood, is opaque and not transparent, an entity having effects in its own right irrespective of the content.

Hot and cold media again: More and less information

As we have seen, the more information a medium provides the 'hotter' it is. Because it already provides significant information, hot media offer less opportunity for participation on the part of medium users than cool media. In this regard, McLuhan notes that a lecture allows for less participation than a seminar – something that might seem like stating the blindingly obvious! However, as we saw, when it comes to the characterization of societies or cultures, participation is not necessarily a positive feature, as 'backward countries are cool' (29). As we shall see, though, an ambivalence is in evidence with regard to this point when we ask: what might be the point of classifying media in this way?

Perhaps the answer is that the classifications of 'hot' and 'cold' can be applied to different cultures. McLuhan argues – not unlike Claude Lévi-Strauss – that there are, effectively, hot and cool societies. Cool societies require – or offer the opportunity of – greater participation in achieving specific ends. McLuhan cites, in this vein, the effect of offering steel axes to members of Australian Aboriginal culture where stone axes had been the norm and the basis of male prestige. The medium of the steel axe is hot compared to the cooler medium of the stone axe. Here, the hot medium can be interpreted as having a deleterious effect on a culture or society precisely because it reduces – often drastically – the level of participation by members of a given group or culture. As McLuhan remarks: 'The hot radio medium used in cool or nonliterate cultures has a violent effect' (33).

Clearly, McLuhan works with the idea that a society or culture can be insightfully analysed according to the type of media that are extant in it. Sociologically speaking, city and urban life is made all the more frenetic by the hot media that tend to be predominant in it, whereas the lifestyle of pre-industrial and rural societies tend to be characterized by cool media that call for a high degree of participation. This to imply, no doubt, that the more highly mechanized a society is – that is, the more sophisticated the technology, by which is meant the more technology begins to replace the human or nature – the greater the dominance of hot media to the detriment of human participation.

Is there not a paradox to be acknowledged here? It is that when media are addressed in terms of different cultural forms – when the form of the lifestyle is what first strikes the researcher – then the medium as such would seem to fade into the background – would seem, indeed, not to appear, or to disappear.

'The electric light', says McLuhan, 'ended the regime of day and night' (57). From this we could conclude that technological innovation separates the human from nature, that there is the world of technics and the world of nature. In a manner evocative (as we shall see) of Kittler's theory of media – where every medium can now be translated into a digital format – McLuhan claims that 'the message of the electric light is total change. It is pure information without any content to restrict its transforming and informing power' (57). However, the electric light, as opposed to electricity in general, is a modality of electricity, so that while we see the light, we do not see electricity (the medium) as such. This point remains unrecognized by McLuhan in the entirety of his ruminations on media. Thus, contra to McLuhan, there is no appearing of radio in general – only particular instances of radio. There is no cinema or photography in general, but only specific instances of films and photographs. In short, the medium as such never appears, even as it is the condition of possibility for the appearing of modalities of the medium.

Media as translation

'Media', claims McLuhan, have the power to 'translate experience into new forms' (2008: 63). As such, media are designated as 'metaphors' – no doubt in the sense that metaphor, etymologically, means 'to transport'. On this basis words become 'a kind of information retrieval … Words are complex systems of metaphors and symbols that translate experience into our uttered or outered [*sic*] *senses*' (63; emphasis added). More broadly, in the 'electric age' we find ourselves translated into information. Again, following the principle of 'modal ontology (rather than Shannon and Weaver), information (the medium) never appears as such and its existence can only be deduced from what it makes possible.

The Greek alphabet as a medium

What is the difference, McLuhan asks, between and actual instance or 'token' of the American flag and the words: 'the American flag'? Surely, the difference is difference between media. Moreover, as we said with reference to the message written in blood, at the level of connotation, the message here would seem identical with the materiality of the medium. Thus, blood, like the material form of the flag, 'says' something. In what sense, therefore, can the thesis of the disappearance of the medium still be maintained? Indeed, in what sense can it be denied that the medium always appears at the level of connotation?

A response to this question derives from a consideration of the notion of connotation itself. Thus, someone speaking a foreign language is not just making a statement but is at the same time connoting: I am a foreigner. In writing in English, I am also connoting the English language. That is to say, connotation implies that something is uttered on two levels: the first level could be called, after Freud on dreams, the manifest content, while the second level (not necessarily second in terms of significance) could be designated as the implicit level. The point over all, though, is that to connote is the act of stating at the second degree. It is not the appearing of the medium as such.

We can turn now to the issue of the phonetic alphabet (perfected by the Greeks) that has become the cornerstone of Western writing and language. As we have seen, one of the notable features of the phonetic alphabet is its democratizing aspect in that, as Walter Ong has noted. By comparison, 'all pictographic systems, even with ideographs and rebuses, require a dismaying number of symbols. Chinese is the largest, most complex, and richest: the K'anghsi dictionary of Chinese in AD 1716 lists 40,543 characters. No Chinese or Sinologist knows them all, or ever did. Few Chinese who write can write all of the spoken Chinese words that they can understand' (1997: 87).

In such circumstances, literacy can become a form of power. Clearly, to a non-Chinese, Chinese characters must appear in their very materiality. But this does not mean that they appear in their role as medium, which, as we have come to see, is a non-appearing.

To reiterate Ong's general point: writing is a technology that has perceptible effects. Hence, the sub-title of Ong's best-known work is: *The Technologizing of the Word*. Simply put: for Ong the invention of writing (a technology) changes consciousness. If this is accepted, then, surely, we are once again in McLuhan territory, where the medium would show itself through the changes it brings about to human consciousness. Ong proposes that 'writing (and especially alphabetic writing) is a technology' (81). And: 'Technologies are not mere exterior aids but also interior transformations of consciousness, and never more than when they affect the word' (82). Here, there is an echo of the principle of 'medium specificity'. Writing (medium) will therefore result in a literate view of the world, just as an 'oral' view of the world will be the condition of non-literate cultures. On this basis, technology – the medium – colours my world. Ong's reference to the 'internalisation' of the medium can also be noted as he is in agreement with McLuhan, his former teacher, on this point.

Ong further informs us, in invoking his own experience, that, 'in composing a text, in "writing" something, the one producing the written utterance is also alone. Writing is a solipsistic operation. I am writing a book which I hope will be read by hundreds of thousands of people, so I must be isolated from everyone' (101). Yet, when Ong refers to the conditions writing imposes in order for the book being written to be read, are we to conclude that it is precisely these conditions that the writing as read brings to the fore? Surely not. As Ong acknowledges, writing presupposes a reader (even if the first reader is the author), and for reading to be possible writing must be transparent; the medium cannot appear as such, even if, at a broader historical level there is a supposed difference between societies with and societies without writing.

In today's conjuncture, the transparency of scientific discourse has been brought into question, so that reference is now often made to the 'scientific' view of the world. This, I am saying is an off-shoot of the principle of media specificity, of the view that I am opposing in this study.

Writing history, writing technology

The chief characteristic of Ong's and McLuhan's (and of many others in their wake) historical approach to technics is the equating of changes to the material incarnation of the medium with the effects of medium in concrete reality. In other words, the historical approach privileges the medium as opaque and thus tends to obscure the medium's essential quality of transparency. What needs to be recognized is that no matter how extensive or fine-grained a history of a medium might be, it fails to get to the essential aspect of the medium, which, *qua* medium, is its invisibility, its transparency. This is no doubt to imply that the medium should be equated with its ontological, rather than historical or epistemological status. In this light the glibness of the following statement by McLuhan cannot be overemphasized: 'War is never anything less than accelerated technological change' (McLuhan 2008: 111). As such, the sentiment represented here would be an extreme version of the thesis of the medium as essentially historical. The medium/technology comes to intervene in social and cultural life bringing about the fundamental changes with which we are now all familiar.

It will be objected, perhaps, that technological (therefore, media) developments *were* an issue during the Second World War. Whether the German Messerschmitt Bf109 fighter plane was more effective than the British Spitfire is surely of some moment. Again: the dam-buster technology of the bouncing bomb was no doubt a crucial technical achievement. There are thus old and new, effective and ineffective technologies. History would seem to be fundamental after all! The question is, though, whether the nature of technology and the medium can be distilled from a limited number of historical examples.

Once the wartime situation is examined in terms of the *results* actually achieved (Messerschmitt planes shot down; dams breeched), the focus on the medium as material object disappears. Moreover, war, as Clausewitz saw, is an 'art'. And, furthermore, 'war is never an isolated act' (Clausewitz 1985: 106), nor does it 'consist of a single instantaneous blow' (106). Nor yet again is the result in war ever 'absolute' (106). How many planes need to be shot down? How many dams breeched? How many ships sunk and soldiers killed before the result can be determined as victory? The art of war (neglected by McLuhan) comes to intersect with the art of politics therefore presaging Clausewitz's famous dictum that 'war is politics by other means'.

Consequently, what initially seems to present a problem for the invisibility of the medium thesis – namely, McLuhan's comment on war – turns out to be based on a flawed argument; weaponry as the medium of war still, in the end, does not appear as such when war as whole is considered.

Technology gives rise to a POV

That technical objects are formative of a point of view is reiterated by McLuhan in the following passage: 'What we have today, instead of a social consciousness electronically ordered ..., is a private subconsciousness or individual "point of view" rigorously imposed by older mechanical technology' (2008: 117). This is no doubt an instance of the technological determinism seen to be endemic in McLuhan's theory. What is less often reported on is the fallacy of the 'media specific' approach, such as one finds in Herta Wolf's comment on the image: 'What causes this blind faith that "a picture says more than a thousand words?" ... doesn't the greater evidence attributed to the horrific pictures from Abu Ghraib result from their being produced by photographic procedures? Is this evidence not based on photography's media-specific referentiality' (2007: 68).

It is this mode of thinking about the image that McLuhan's 'the medium is the message' sets in motion. Technological determinism there may or may not be, but who could dispute the fact of the advocacy of media-specific referentiality? Thus, photography in *Un art moyen* (1965) is defined by the sociologist, Pierre Bourdieu, as the 'system of rules for the reproduction of the real which animate popular photography' (Bourdieu 1965: 111). Ultimately, for the sociologist, it is not the medium-based view as such that is in play, but the medium (photography) that reinforces the conventional, mimetic view of reality. Bourdieu thus states that 'it is not surprising that photography can appear as the recording of the world most in keeping with this vision [of the traditional view of the world as natural], that is, the most objective' (112). Photography supposedly reinforces the myth of the objectivity of a certain 'realist' view of the world, which dominates popular culture. The realism that photography is charged with actualizing is deemed by Bourdieu to be a 'naïve realism', and that, ultimately, photography owes its 'realism' not to an agreement with the reality of things, 'but rather to conformity to rules which define its syntax within its social use' (113). In other words, photography confirms the socially instantiated vision of objectivity.

Even though photography is viewed here through the prism of a social definition, where photographic objectivity becomes a reinforcement of socially consecrated objectivity, it is clear that the social view is itself influenced, at least in part, by photographic objectivity.

While Bourdieu – and with him, the sociological view in general – does not explicitly lay claim to a 'media specificity' view, it is clear that with a modicum of theoretical adjustment, the media-specific view will come to take a more notable place in a sociology of the medium. That is to say that although photographic realism is a socially derived phenomenon – and not immediately a photographic view of the world – further investigation is likely to show that in fact, photography, from its earliest days, informed a socially based realist view rather than the reverse. It is easy to claim that photography is embedded in (a specific) society; but it is also possible to argue that a certain society is also embedded in photography.

Electronic media

From McLuhan's point of view, the telegraph, and electronic media more generally, have rendered the 'point of view' redundant. Now, the medium can be everywhere at once, limited only by the speed of light. The 'point of view' – in a nineteenth-century newspaper, for example – is characteristic of the mechanical age when everything moved at a much slower speed. Perhaps the ultimate feature of the electronic age as far as the medium is concerned is, as Bernard Stiegler has indicated, the simultaneity between the event and its reporting. Once, a sailing ship took at least seventy days to travel from England to Australia with mail, so that, clearly there was a massive time lag between the time of writing a letter and receiving a reply. Now, communication can take place electronically, a fact that led McLuhan to coin the phrase 'the global village'.

With electronic media, the McLuhan dictum of 'the medium is the message' would seem to be almost irrefutable. Here, the medium engenders changes, such as the following: the 'human interest' story dominates news media because '"human interest" is the electronic or depth dimension of immediate involvement in news' (2008: 275). Moreover, 'the electronic [*sic*] gives powerful voices to the weak and suffering, and sweeps aside the bureaucratic specialisms and job descriptions of the mind tied to a manual of instruction. The "human interest" dimension is simply that of immediacy of participation in the experience of others that occurs with instant information' (275). Let us say, in this regard, that McLuhan's point is that, in principle, the electronic age is one that enables immediate involvement. Whether this occurs in practice is another matter. On another level: 'dialogue', says McLuhan, 'supersedes the lecture' (278). In effect, there is no longer any need to have a centralized point of dissemination of information. 'There is a collapse of delegated authority and a dissolution of the pyramid and management structures' (268). In fact, all forms of centralization are brought into question in the electronic age. The 'centre-margin' pattern is dissolved. With regard to meteorological reporting, the 'telegraph, by providing a wide sweep of instant information, could reveal meteorological patterns of force quite beyond observation by pre-electric man' (280). Linear sequencing then becomes redundant.

We reach the point, then, where McLuhan's indications of the features of the electronic age merge into a description of the effects of digitalization. In the early 1980s, the argument was put forward that computerization (the medium) was essentially 'labor displacing' (see Jones 1982). Have we not arrived now at a point where McLuhan's position becomes unassailable? – a position where the medium in its form has an impact that far exceeds the content it supports? McLuhan, as we have noted, scorns those who attribute primacy to the content of the medium. In discussing the telegraph and the electronic age, McLuhan observes that the writing of John Crosby of the *New York Herald Tribune* 'well illustrates why the "content" obsession of the man of print culture makes it difficult for him to notice any facts about the *form* of a new medium' (McLuhan 2008: 272). Clearly, the form of the medium appears over against content. The medium is not what disappears. As Graham Harman aptly says: 'The meaning of McLuhan's famous slogan, "the medium is the message" is precisely this: it makes no difference whether we make "good" or "bad" use of television, fingerprinting, or nuclear weapons. In each case, it is the medium itself that is decisive' (Harman 2019: 99).

Against the tenor of this position, I have argued that the medium that appears, appears as an object and that the medium is invisible – even undetectable – in its *performance*. The first person to receive the Mazarin Bible that came off the Gutenberg press of moveable type in 1455 would quite possibly have been amazed by this Bible as object before engaging in a reading of the text. After the initial 'shock of the new', such a person might have said: 'In all the illuminated manuscripts, the first words of the Book of John 1:1, seem to say: "In the beginning was the act" – now I see that it is: "In the beginning was the Word."' In reading the text, and the word, 'Word', in particular, the Bible as book does not appear as such; that is, it disappears as object and becomes transparent as medium. Thus, even if the medium is new as an object, this ceases to be relevant when the medium functions as medium.

Initially, as McLuhan proclaims, radio as medium object created interest. But when radio enabled a ship at sea to send distress calls, radio ceased to be an object, became transparent, and raised the key question: did anybody get the message?

If, via their cell, or mobile phone, someone accesses his or her savings bank account and finds that the balance is zero, or even that the account is in deficit, the likely response will not be: 'to be able to access the account so quickly is truly amazing!' Rather, the almost certain response will be: 'I had better transfer some funds into my account, otherwise I'll be in deep financial trouble.' The bank account holder is not interested – or is no longer interested – in the technical *object*, and is engaged with the medium in its transparency.

But it might be asked: is not McLuhan's point that technology – the medium – has an impact independently of the individual performance of a medium? In response, it might be said that digital technology, despite the unconcern of users, can have a definite effect on them and thus on social and psychological life. Let it be acknowledged that what has been set out regarding the unconscious effect of technics, or media, is part of an ongoing debate, so I am not (or at least not yet) making any claim to a definitive insight as to the true state of affairs. I would say, however, that claims about the impact of digital media on users should be weighed up by considering the position of the analyst/critic vis-à-vis the medium that is the object of reflection. In other words, we need to become aware of the fact that the critic of the digital also invokes this medium precisely when pointing to the deleterious (or even positive) effect of digitalization. Here, one can think of an earlier time when Jean-Jacques Rousseau *wrote* in order to criticize writing. Is there, then, really a position external to the medium as transparent? And so, to be dazzled by the medium as object is to be unconsciously led astray when it comes to understanding the true nature of the medium.

More than this, perhaps, we now know that it is not at all necessary to know anything about a medium as object for it operates perfectly as a medium.

Thus firstly, it is unnecessary to know how a medium (as object) works in order for it to work as a medium. This is to reinforce the 'medium as transparent' thesis.

But to claim that one knows how pens and typewriters work, as Kittler does, is also to evoke a McLuhanesque conception of the medium. Indeed, in this vein the question arises as to whether it is really necessary to go any further than an analysis of the title of McLuhan's most famous book to know the key to McLuhan's position on the medium. Media, on this basis, cannot really be appreciated unless they are *understood*. In effect, then, McLuhan presents with a 'pen and typewriter' view of the medium. For it is with digitalization that the true invisibility of the medium becomes thinkable.

So, what are we to think of McLuhan's understanding of media when he speaks of the effects of radio, of television, of the telephone, the phonogram and the cinema? The effects he is talking about are the effects of media generically understood and independently of their content. On this basis, radio as such, and not Nazi propaganda, would be the key to McLuhan's understanding. What eventuated, however, was that through Goebbels's initiative, the *Volksempfländer*, or 'people's radio', was distributed from 1933 onward. In hindsight, it is true that this medium object was the condition of possibility for the dissemination of Nazi propaganda. But it should be said and underlined that it is the latter that the listener engaged with, not the object, which, as object, fades into the ether. Consequently, in this context in particular, radio is a medium because it brings to presence, propaganda – or any content, for that matter. The risk in going down the path opened by McLuhan is that the medium as object becomes extant to the detriment of politically charged content.

The War of the Worlds 1938 broadcast by Orson Welles, mentioned by McLuhan in his discussion of radio (2008: 327),[1] surely, forces one to acknowledge that radio as medium has an impact to the extent that the broadcast content has an impact, and not radio (medium) as the message. Of course, McLuhan might respond by invoking the argument that what he is referring to at the macro and broad historical levels of media technology – is the 'completely involving scope of the auditory radio image' (327) – not just to specific examples of the medium in action. The argument I put is that the medium in action is the only manifestation of the medium. Or, indeed, as we can say by way of a model ontology – the medium as action is the only form of the medium that can be experienced.

---

1 For a detailed outline of the events and a description of the traumatic impact of Welles's 'War of the Worlds' broadcast, see Holmsten and Lubertozzi (2001). The opening paragraph of this text summarizes the event as follows: 'On October 30, 1938, Orson Welles took Howard Koch's adaptation of H. G. Wells' classic, *The War of the Worlds*, and convinced more than a million Americans that a Martian army had come to Earth to annihilate the human race' (xi).

The medium as 'disappearance':
The work of Sybille Krämer

In Chapter 1, the various meanings attaching to the term 'medium' were considered. What was notable was the string of connections between medium and 'middle'. This link is continued in the media theory of the German philosopher, Sybille Krämer, whose work is the subject of this chapter. After indicating the scope of Krämer's research, we will undertake an interpretation of methodological considerations discussed in the book, *Medium, Messenger, Transmission: An Approach to Media Philosophy*. It is here that Krämer sets out her thesis of the 'disappearance' of the medium.

*

In one of her 'introductions' to various thinkers whose work engages with the medium, Krämer refers to the ideas of Jean-Luc Nancy and his concept of *Mitsein* – 'being with'. It is appropriate to refer to Nancy here because he places community and the collective at the forefront of thought, so that the question arises as to what the significance of medium might be in the overall being of the collective as *Mitsein*. Like Nancy, Krämer also wants to come to an appreciation of the medium as it operates in the community and society. She shows, however, that as community is an original 'being-with' (*Mitsein*), Nancy does not concede a place for the medium or for mediation, since community/society is not derived from isolated individuals coming together (the social contract thesis) and who thus seek to develop means of communication. Rather, community – sharing – amounts to a *subsequent* separation into individuals: 'it is the separation that makes communality itself possible; community *is* being separated into many' (53). Ultimately, then, we see that 'Nancy thus transforms the question: "What is a medium?" into the question "Where is a milieu?" And such a 'milieu' can be found whenever a being is constituted as being-with' (2015: 54).

Nancy's philosophy of community is significant for Krämer as it is the *ne plus ultra* of a theory of medium and mediation. Thus, the apparent non-existence of mediation in Nancy implies that *Mitsein* entails pure immediacy in the relation between individuals given that it is also individuality that constitutes community. However, it is also in the essence of mediation and of the medium to be invisible and thus to give the impression of immediacy. Immediacy becomes, in effect, the mode of being of mediation.

A more conventional point of departure for Krämer is Shannon and Weaver's theory of communication as the attempt to produce something that is not anticipated (new information) and is a signal – or message – that 'is not perturbed by noise'. In other words, if the channel is the messenger, the aim is to bring about a successful transmission (or to make the probability as high as possible that there will be a successful transmission – we are, after all, referring to 'the mathematical theory of communication') of a message that is sent (normally by a sender, whether mechanical or not) and is received (normally by a receiver, or addressee, whether mechanical or not). It is worth noting the work of Shannon and Weaver in particular here because the issue of transmission is fundamental to their theory of communication. Noise, by contrast, is the enemy of transmission. Regarding noise, the authors write that when 'a signal is perturbed by noise' it 'means that the received signal is not necessarily the same as that sent out by the transmitter' (Shannon and Weaver 1998: 65).

The controversial aspect of what Krämer calls, in light of Shannon and Weaver, the 'technical transmission model' is that it is based around the mathematically defined notion of information and not meaning, which is affected by context. Nevertheless, transmission for Krämer takes place, or does not take place, whether one is dealing with information or meaning.

Krämer points out that, until recently (1990s), the medium remained a marginal theme in philosophy. That it would eventually become the focus of attention, Krämer suggests, is predicated on the fact that language (hitherto thought of as a medium) becomes the object of inquiry both in analytical philosophy (cf. Austin, Ryle and Wittgenstein) and in semiotics (cf. Saussure, Peirce, Jakobson, Benveniste and Lévi-Strauss). Perhaps we could say that McLuhan makes the medium an object of thought, just as language and signs had become objects of thought. Transparency of language and the medium thus give way to opacity and what I have been referring to as 'media specificity'. Michel Foucault, in the *Order of Things* (1982) notes the emergence of language as an object. Initially, in the Classical Age (seventeenth and eighteenth centuries), 'it was only by the medium of language that the things of the world could be known' (296). Moreover, the very modern concern with language as object rather than as medium is signalled by the fact that: 'From the nineteenth century, language began to fold in upon itself, to acquire its own particular density, to deploy a history, an objectivity, and laws of its own. It became an object of knowledge among others, on the same level as living beings, wealth and value, and the history of events and men' (296).

And so, initially, language becomes an object and philosophy participates in this development. If one's specialty was logic, then it became a matter (as with Russell) of finding the way that logic was in language. A philosophy of language thus becomes eminently possible.

Then, with the advent of McLuhan, the medium becomes fully objectified, but philosophy is apparently not interested in following up on the principle of the 'medium becoming the message'. Krämer summarizes the situation as follows: 'The strategic goal of McLuhan's identification of the medium with the message was to take away the transitory transparency and neutrality of the media and make visible their autonomous opacity and instrumental shaping power. This is precisely the central theme of the "medial turn"' (Krämer 2015: 28).

If philosophy was slow to be interested in the medium as object, would it ever be ready to consider the medium as transparent, as that which 'disappears'? This will subsequently be Krämer's question.

Language had, however, also been conceived as the vehicle of thought and ideas, where thought and ideas would be prior to language. Or again, speech was considered to be prior to writing, or prior to all that would materialize speech and language. Derrida's work brings into question the whole conception of the a priori with respect to language. Is a similar approach appropriate for the medium? The answer would be in the negative if the medium is the very condition of possibility of its content. Prior to the emergence of a consideration of the role of the medium, there could, hypothetically, be thought without language. If the medium is transparent, there is nothing prior to it.

Krämer's return to Plato

Krämer sees herself returning in a sense to Plato because for her, media are 'below the surface of visibility' and animate what is visible. Thus, in a key passage that goes to the heart of her approach, our theorist affirms that:

> We hear not vibrations in the air, but rather the kettle whistling; we see not light waves of the yellow colour spectrum, but rather a canary; we hear not a CD, but rather music; and the cinema screen 'disappears' as soon as the film grips us. The smoother media work, the more they remain below the threshold of our perception. (2015: 31)

Krämer thus illustrates the idea that the medium is transparent. Or, as we read: 'A medium's success thus depends on its disappearance' (31). Again, '*The implementation of media depends on their withdrawal. I will call this "aisthetic self-neutralization"*' (31; emphasis in original). Krämer is, however, quick to point out that the 'disappearance' of the medium applies only to its use: 'The invisibility of the medium – its aisthetic neutralization – is an attribute of media *performance*' (31; emphasis in original). (In passing, we should note that there is an echo of Wolfgang Ernst's approach here; for Wolf, too, emphasizes performance, or implementation.) This qualification needs to be made so that the concrete, material aspect of media can be acknowledged. There can, in other words, be a history of concrete media support apparatuses. McLuhan is not wrong in this regard.

Aristotle, as we have already indicated, was an early proponent of the medium's transparency, and Krämer elaborates on this. She also acknowledges the work of Niklas Luhmann's work in relation to media in the context of communication, where he affirms the medium's necessary transparency. Krämer then refers to the work of a pioneer of German media theory, Fritz Heider, who, in *Ding und Medium* (Thing and Medium) (1925) pointed out that medium was not a thing to the extent that was essentially transparent. Krämer summarizes the approach of Aristotle and Heider as follows:

> a medium always occupies the position of middle and mediator, and it is thus fundamentally non-autonomous. Media are not sovereign, and heteronomy is their defining feature. Aristotle's idea of the 'diaphanous' as distinctive of media of perception and Heider's concept of the 'false unity' of the media event represent two different ways of conceptualizing this heteronomy. To condense this into a catchy formula: *There is always an outside of media.* (34; emphasis in original)

Note here the importance of the term 'middle'. And in a neat turn of phrase that alludes to the necessary material and immaterial nature of media, our author states that 'Media are bodies that can be disembodied' (34).

Signs and media

The relation between signs and the medium, Krämer suggests, is – at least initially – one of inversion. Here, it is necessary to assume that part of the nature of a sign is its material attraction. A road sign has first to call attention to itself before it can successfully be the vehicle of a message ('No Left Turn'). But, at the second degree, the sign has to become invisible as a purely material entity.

The materiality of a medium is always invisible in its performance. It is only subsequently that the material aspect might be brought to light. On reading the message, the materiality of the sign disappears. With the medium, only after reading the message does the materiality of the medium appear.

Of course, the aspect that Krämer does not pursue is that things become interesting, if not more complicated, when it becomes difficult to decide whether a sign function is ever entirely absent in relation to any message, image, icon, and so on. No text, one might argue, is entirely disembodied. The material book draws attention to itself as a sign before it is read. I read because I see the book. In other terms, we see the messenger before the message. When the message is delivered the messenger disappears. Thus, the marathon messenger dies after delivering the message that all wanted to hear, namely, that the Athenians had defeated the Persians.

It would seem that Derrida is possibly the first thinker to argue against the primacy of the material, sign aspect of the message. For he talks, it will be recalled, about the 'end of the book and the beginning of writing'.

The syllogism

Krämer points out that the syllogism is also evocative of the medium via the latter's strategic importance in that it 'refers to the middle term in a syllogism' (36). Thus, in the following famous example:

All men are mortal;
Socrates is a man,
Therefore, Socrates is mortal.

Everything hangs on the middle statement: 'Socrates is a man'. 'The conclusion', says Krämer, 'lies in connecting the terms that are not middle terms, but this only happens in the act of effacing the middle term' (2015: 36). Perhaps some will say that this only works if it is self-evident that Socrates is a man, then the statement effaces itself. Otherwise, the middle term might be seen to call for a substantial amount of verification work. It is nevertheless true to say that once the middle term (*terminus medius*) is verified it then becomes superfluous and the deduction can be enacted.

To this, we could add that the middle tends, in many contexts, to be treated with suspicion, if it is not entirely rejected. For middle can imply, not just 'both-and', but also 'neither one nor the other', as connoted by the notion of 'middle road', often seen as the inglorious path of compromise. Much more heroic – because more clear-cut? – is to be uncompromising, on one side or the other, whether this be in politics or morality.

Clearly, then, Krämer introduces a different way of appreciating the notion of medium than is to be found in the majority of media studies, which tend to take a McLuhanesque approach to the medium. Rather than being a figure in its own right, the medium largely acts as a catalyst to events while not itself being an event. As our author explains in a chapter on the medium as encapsulated in the 'messenger model', 'The primary function of media is transmission. Media do not directly produce anything; they do not possess any demiurgical power. Methodologically it makes more sense to describe them as middle, mediator, and milieu rather than [*sic*] an instrument or a medium' (2015: 75).

The messenger mediates in five dimensions

Krämer goes into illuminating detail about the five dimensions of the messenger model. But we shall only follow her part of the way, while nevertheless leaving the way open to draw some tentative conclusions about the status of the messenger.

The messenger that Krämer has in mind is a pre-electronic entity, an entity in relation to which the materiality of the body (for one thing) still counts when analysing the messenger's status. According to our theorist, the messenger mediates in five dimensions:

1. *Distance as heterogeneity*: The key point here is that pure otherness (in the message, for example) is the messenger's concern rather than homogeneity, which would tend to go without saying. Levinas's notion of 'trace' approximates what is being evoked (and, as we noted previously, Derrida's notion of trace also evokes the medium). For, if, as Levinas proposes, Western philosophy is an 'egology' (i.e. is ultimately based on sameness), then a breakthrough is necessary in order to appreciate otherness and difference. The messenger *qua* messenger must be concerned with otherness and difference – that is, with the message as radical heterogeneity.

2. *Heteronomy as speaking in a foreign voice*: In light of the previous point, we can expect the messenger to be heteronomous not autonomous and to be subject to foreign directives. This is to presuppose of course that the messenger and the message form an indissoluble identity, which could be problematic. Apart from what Krämer says, it might be instructive for a moment to think of the messenger as distinct from the message. In the marathon incident, the messenger's exhausted body is also a sign of something, whether this be victory or defeat. The body *connotes* something: courage, self-sacrifice.

3. *Thirdness as the nucleus of sociality*: The messenger occupies an intermediary position between the sender and the addressee of the

message and is the key to intersubjective relations. The third is also a mark of neutrality and thus the mark of the sciences. As shown in Serres's work (see Chapter 5), the third is also a figure of interruption.

4. *Materiality as embodiment*: Here, the message belongs to a continuum of materiality that 'encompasses the corporeality of the messenger' (83). The earlier point I made regarding the messenger's body and connotation is responded to here. It is now a matter of thinking this through.

5. *Indifference as self-neutralization*: Predictably, it is said that the messenger '*behaves indifferently towards the content of his message*' (83). As the occupier of the middle ground the messenger is neutral. There is an aspect of self-withdrawal upon which the mediality of the message is based. Now, the body of the messenger seems to have become transparent.

It may be that the phrase, 'kill the messenger' only makes sense in certain periods of history. Of course the phrase can still be invoked metaphorically and actually in any historical period. The absurdity emerges when the call goes out to 'kill the internet'. Krämer is, then, referring to a situation where the physical being of the messenger is involved in the mode of communication – a mode of communication where the body should remain transparent. Perhaps the truth of the messenger mode is revealed by way of the digital revolution, rather than the reverse.

The messenger philosophy

According to Krämer, the messenger contradicts philosophy's view of communication and language. Indeed, our author claims that philosophy is repelled by the messenger; for the latter is not a worthy moral or political being, since this messenger-being lacks autonomy, disappears into the message for which he or she is never the author. He or she occupies the morally dubious middle ground, has nothing to say in his or her own name and panders to foreignness. Moreover, the messenger speaks in the purely mechanical manner that Descartes attributes to birds. And birds and other animals can never fully have language because they behave, mechanically – like messengers!

Transmission: Viruses and contagion, transference and witnessing

The theme of transmission brings the character or individuality of the messenger/mediator into focus. The task of transmitting messages can fall to angels, gods, viruses and infection, transference (in psychoanalysis), witnessing, translation and money. Also of note is violence as contagion, the key theme of the work of the literary theorist and philosopher, René Girard.

In her discussion of 'Angeology' as an instance of transmission, Krämer makes a remark, in light of the work of Massimo Cacciari, concerning the nature of the image that I profoundly agree with:

> However, the angel thus becomes 'the exact image of the problem of the image' [Cacciari and Vedova 1989: 16], for an image is always different from and more than a symbol: Images also contain something magical in the form of a real effect of the depicted; they are at the same time both distinguishable and indistinguishable from that which they represent. They are the living presence of a distance, the projection of the absent in the present. For this reason, 'every true image is never only a simple representation'; rather, it is one with its own state of being-distant – *'it is one with absence'* [Cacciari and Vedova 1989: 20]. (2015: 94)

When interpreted in collaboration with Cacciari and Vedova the angel is, in a certain sense, the incarnation of the image as the presence of what is absent – in this case, God. Whether or not one believes in angels, the point is that they are essentially a means of transmission. Or, to put it another way: only an angel can transmit the word of God. In Agamben's terms, God needs angels as the administrators of His Kingdom. Paradoxically, God's autonomy can only be realized or be transmitted through angels.

In this regard, angels do not really exist; in any case, they cannot be perceived. However, this is the key feature of the medium: that it cannot be perceived even though it exists.

For Michel Serres, one of the key thinkers in angeology, 'Hermes, the Greek messenger god [is] the forerunner of the angels' (Serres 1995: 45). It is a matter, then, of everything from aircraft and the postal service to modern computers that function as messengers and facilitate transmission.

As already mentioned, in the context of transmission, Krämer considers, along with angels, viruses and contagion; money; translation (from one language to another); psychoanalysis and the transference, as well as witnessing. After a brief summary of the main line of inquiry in each of these domains, I will focus in more detail on viruses and contagion, and then on psychoanalysis and after that, on witnessing.

To turn firstly to viruses, it is to be noted that 'What constitutes a medium in the course of infection is *relative to and dependent on the position of the observer*. It is nevertheless clear that an infectious transmission is impossible without a (transmitting) medium' (Krämer 2015: 98). The key feature of virus transmission is that a virus is not autonomous: it must first occupy a cell that it needs in order to replicate. A virus, then, is essentially a parasite. For transmission to occur, the virus must take on features of the messenger even if it is not a messenger itself. This reminds us that the nature of the messenger is a key element in the possibility or otherwise of transmission. The First World War saw the following used as messengers at Gallipoli and elsewhere: animals such as camels, dogs and horses as well as pigeons. Humans, of course were messengers in the form of dispatch riders, and used signal flags and semaphore, but there were also significant electronic forms, such as wireless telegraphy, field telephones and telegraphic equipment. And electrical signal lamps were used to send morse code messages. As such, transmission success may well vary according to the messenger form enacted.

The transmission of something – the virus or pathogen – will then depend on a 'transmitting medium': air, blood, saliva, skin, food, water and so on. The pathogen requires a receptive milieu (body or organism) and not a milieu of immunity. All of this applies in the field of bacteriology. Viral transmission, as has been mentioned, assumes a different hue because a virus is not autonomous. This feature also applies to computer viruses, which only become disruptive when a user activates an infected program.

Contagion, as is commonly recognized, is the unpredictable and rapid spread of something, such as a virus. But violence could also be contagious. And Krämer cites the work of René Girard, for whom violence as a contagion occurs in the context of the logic of revenge killing. In societies where a judicial system does not exist, a scapegoat is sacrificed in order to bring a halt to violence. Here, the meaning of sacrifice is that the entity marked for execution did not initiate the violence. Without this sacrifice, Girard argues, certain societies risk being torn apart by violence, due precisely to the latter's contagious nature. In Krämer's terms, violence takes on features of virus transmission, and sacrifice takes on features of an immunizing strategy. Disease epidemics are contagious (and, metaphorically, 'viral') because ultimately it becomes impossible to determine exactly what is cause and what effect. Like violence, the disease seems to spread out of control.

Krämer also refers to 'aesthetic infection', first of all in relation to Aristotle's notion of catharsis, where the audience members are 'purified' of certain emotions (particularly pity and fear), and, secondly, in the context of theatre more generally. By way of a theatrical performance the audience member becomes 'infected' by what is happening on the stage. On this basis, it is a wonder that audience disruption is not more frequent than it is.

Also, the notion of mimesis (that can take place in theatre) is a feature of Girard's theory of violence, not just in archaic societies, but also in modern society. Mimesis, for Girard, is to be explained by the fact that human desire is – as Lacan put it – the desire of the other. More colloquially, I desire what the other desires; therefore, there is an inevitable contest over the desired object.

Money as medium

Krämer is less interested in money as a symbolic form, and more interested in money as a medium. As such, money in its functioning 'disappears' as an autonomous object. In its mediator function money facilitates the exchange of goods and services and anything else that might need to be exchanged. As is commonly noted by economists and journalists, money is a *medium* of exchange. Money, indeed, becomes a good example of the difference between money, or the medium, as an object (gold coin, notes, bank statement, etc.) and the medium as such, which comes to fruition in its activation. Those who take a 'media specificity' approach to the medium have difficulty distinguishing money as an object, from money as a medium. But, with regard to money, was it not ever thus? The figure of the miser, the Scrooge persona, greed as a feature of immorality, each attributes a fundamentally object status to money. Krämer thus reminds us of this aspect of the conception of money.

Money has also been negatively perceived because of its essentially abstract nature, and the fact that it is indifferent both to what is exchanged and to those who make the exchange, a feature that potentially makes an understanding of it more difficult for those of a more empirical, or moral, bent.

Krämer cites Georg Simmel in his *Philosophy of Money* referring to the link between money, sacrifice and debt. At the same time, money can be what mediates between competing desires, a fact that pushes up the price – if not the value – of things. Does the fact that money is a measure – that is, is quantitative – have any bearing on it being a medium? If quantity can have a medium, is this also true of quality?

From this angle, we can evoke the art market, which clearly embodies money as a measure of quantity through price. But a painting, for example, as reference to the theatre has also shown, can transmit value for a given viewer, who may or may not agree that value can be translated into price. In this instance, the painting (or work of art) is what assumes the role of medium, and not money.

Walter Benjamin's view of translation

In speaking of translation, Krämer refers to Walter Benjamin's argument that language is a medium and not a means. The translator, because he is situated not in language but between languages, becomes, Krämer says, 'a kind of messenger figure' (2015: 125). Translation, as Benjamin understands it, is a form of transmission. This is based on the notion that the original can include within it the quality of translatability and also that there is a 'kinship of languages', which implies not that they are the same, but that they are all engaged in allowing language as such to appear. So, for Benjamin – following Rudolf Pannwitz – the translator allows the foreign language to have an impact on the language into which it is translated. Consequently, to translate French into English would entail English becoming more French, rather than the reverse. While more traditional approaches view translation as ultimately impossible, and therefore as non-transmissible, Benjamin views translation as eminently possible and therefore as a form of transmission. To translate, then, is 'to translate *languages* and not texts' (119).

What, for Benjamin, constitutes a form of 'noise' in relation to translation as transmission is the attempt by traditional translators to reveal the meaning of the target text and to assume that language was only a means for uncovering meaning. It is only by breaking free from such a utilitarian understanding of language that translation can become a genuine form of transmission.

Psychoanalysis and the medium

The question that guides Krämer's deliberations on transference as medium in psychoanalysis is whether the analyst is, in the process, a neutral medium or an actor (126). Crucial to giving a satisfactory answer to this question, Krämer believes, is the fact that: 'The psychoanalytic concept of transference is interesting because it promises to reveal new aspects of the phenomenon of medial mediation. Paradoxically, however, the notion that the analyst is a medium and a mediator in the transmission event is precisely *repressed* or represented as a problem to be *overcome* in psychoanalytic literature' (126).

There are, then, Krämer believes, two competing views of the transference: one, where the analyst remains steadfastly neutral and impassive in relation to the analysand's discourse and actions; and the other, where the analyst, of necessity, becomes an intersubjective entity in the transference process, often taking on the characteristics of a person in the analysand's past. Traditionally, the doctor, analyst or other health professional is a medium to the extent that they maintain their neutrality. However, it is well known that psychoanalysis brings into question the view of the analyst as entirely passive in the transference, the latter being the point at which the analyst is most visible in the overall trajectory of the analysis.

Krämer does not say so, but the fact is that psychoanalysis was, and remains, controversial. There is controversy stemming from the theories of the psyche that psychoanalysis presents to the figure of Freud himself as the originator and then contested leader of the psychoanalytic movement. The controversial aspect is only heightened by the 'baroque' theorizing of Jacques Lacan, the one-time surrealist who claimed to have returned to the true meaning of Freud's text. 'Desire is the desire of the other'; 'the unconscious is structured like a language'; 'man thinks, therefore, but it is because the symbol has made him man'; 'the signifier is what represents the subject for another signifier'. In less aphoristic mode, Lacan, under the influence of Saussure and Lévi-Strauss, implicates the signifier in the transference function. He thus claims that: 'For in the *Traumdeutung* it is in terms of such a function that the term *Ubertragung*, or transference, which later gave its name to the mainspring of the intersubjective link between analysand and analyst, is introduced' (2006: 434). If the signifier is implicated in the transference, then it is also implicated in how the analyst becomes a medium in the transference and counter-transference. Lacan, some have claimed, privileges the symbolic order – the order that includes language. Even so, the spoken word has always been a founding element of the psychoanalytic session; so, to lay emphasis on this is not unwarranted, the point being that for some analysands analysis is an entirely verbal or symbolic affair, while for others transference will culminate and is termed the 'abreaction of affects' (see Laplanche and Pontalis 1988: 460), where affect/emotion will be prominent.

Whatever the case, it is true that in the transference the figure of the analyst assumes for the analysand a prime importance. And it does so not because of the analyst *qua* analyst, but because he or she becomes a figure in the analysand's past. It would seemingly be on this basis that one can speak of the analyst as medium. As such, the person of the analyst fades to the extent to which he or she becomes a medium. This, at least, is what Krämer is gesturing towards without some of the finer detail being invoked to clinch the point.

In any case, another more affective if not bodily mode of the transference is presented by the psychoanalyst, Julia Kristeva, who writes that:

> I write [in theoretical works] the facts/effects of my transference onto the texts. Neither philosopher nor writer, nor sentinel of repression, nor hostess of pleasure, the analyst maintains herself on the crest. She wagers on the meaning of the transferred word. Without end, but not without unease.
>
> The decentering of the conscious subject that Freud explored in the intimacy of the transference (which is also revealed in modern literature) supports my interpretation. (Kristeva 2020: 502–3)

If Lacan's approach to the transference privileges the signifier, Kristeva's approach includes affective involvement. If, for Lacan, the symbolic is primary, for Kristeva the semiotic (love, affect) also comes into play. What happens to the analyst's neutrality if love/affect is involved in the transference? Freud's answer was that such a situation must be strictly limited to the domain of the analytic session and not be otherwise exploited. Transference, in short, must be clearly oriented towards a cure for symptoms and thus towards the 'success' of the analysis.

But maybe it could be argued – especially in light of Kristeva's approach – that the analyst never occupies a position of absolute neutrality because to do so would entail the analysand being unreceptive to the analyst's interpretations. In the best of all possible worlds, transference love is never to do with anything more than the ability of the analyst to have the analysand engage seriously with his or her interpretations or with the ability of the analysand to recall (or to be 'acting out') crucial memories on their own account. In other words, meaningful analysis (meaningful neutrality) entails transference love, or a certain lack of neutrality, but within limits.

Paths to the transference can thus be very different in their emphases with regard to language and the body. Indeed, some would argue that psychoanalysis enables a range of approaches to the transference because it is not a dogmatic science.

Whatever the case, it is, in effect, the role of the unconscious that is crucial in the transference. To reject the plausibility of the existence of the unconscious is equivalent to rejecting psychoanalysis *tout court*. Again, to reject the reality of the unconscious is to reject by default the role of the analyst as medium in the transference; for it is also via the transference that the unconscious comes to be revealed and a cure for psychic pain embarked upon.

As this chapter is not, per se, about explaining the nature of the unconscious and the psychoanalytic theory pertaining to it, let us simply take note of the way that Krämer links the transference to the notion of medium.

> My method now consists in drawing together aspects of the classical and the post-classical theories, as the question arises: Would it not be possible to combine what Freud constructed as a kind of exclusive relationship between the analyst as, on the one hand, an observing, reflecting, and interpreting medium and, on the other hand, an emotional person acting out his own subconscious feelings? (2015: 139–40)

So, in a manner similar to what has already been outlined regarding transference neutrality, rather than being a medium as a completely neutral entity, the 'post-classical' analyst accepts that, via counter-transference, the analyst will be an active participant in the analysand's treatment. On the basis of this situation, Lacan's theory of speech (the relation between the 'je' of desire and the 'moi' of the ego) forms the basis of the psychoanalytic session as dialogical rather than monological. In sum, 'According to the post-classical perspective the physician is an interactive partner who always also has an emotional and not only interpretive relationship to the patient' (139).

In my view, Krämer also needs to underline the point I made earlier, namely, that the analyst in the transference is not there in his or her own person but as a surrogate from the analysand's own life – whether past or present. Only, then, I would say does the analyst fully become a medium.

If we followed Krämer's view, it would appear that the intersubjective, dialogical nature of the newly conceived notion of transference that the theorist proposes rules out a strict view of the analyst as medium. However, it is because the analyst's involvement with the analysand must be limited, both for deontological and analytical reasons, to the analytic session the analyst can become a medium. Only as medium – that is in taking one's distance from the situation – can the analyst bring the treatment to a close, thus confirming the transference as the key element in the whole psychoanalytic schema.

Witnessing and the epistemological nature of 'the testimonials of others'

We turn, now, to Krämer's treatment of witnessing and its status in relation to the medium and transmission.

After establishing the key aspects of witnessing as: (1) the creation of evidence, (2) perception, (3) speech acts, (4) the audience and (5) credibility, we come to what is crucial: the credibility of the witness and the issue of trust. Witnessing thus contains an ethical dimension that impacts on the possibility of uniting witness and medium, thus ensuring the successful transmission of information or knowledge. Only if the witness speaks truly can genuine transmission occur.

Krämer's approach can be elaborated upon by asking the following question: how can the role of witnessing be understood with regard to what happened in the Nazi death camps? As related in the writings of Primo Levi and Giorgio Agamben, those who died in the camps cannot be witnesses. Those who survived risk not being believed, so horrendous were the crimes committed. But also, a true witness is one who is present at the event they are deemed to witness, which implies that the only true witness to the horror would be someone inside the gas chamber – that is, only the inmates themselves could be witnesses.

Notoriously, the death camp gas chambers became an issue in the 1970s and 1980s in relation to revisionist history represented by David Irving in Britain and Robert Faurisson in France. The question arose as to what would count as evidence of the reality of the gas chambers and the Nazi death camps. The thinker and linguist, Noam Chomsky, attempted at one point to make revisionist history into a matter of freedom of speech, and somehow a text that he had written on this became the preface of Faurisson's book, *Mémoire en défence* published in 1980. The embarrassing thing for Chomsky is that, in the preface, he does not just speak about freedom of speech in a generic sense, he refers explicitly to Faurisson and the injustice of the critics. Due to the way that he used documents (e.g. Ann Frank's diary), most serious historians and Faurisson critics, such as Pierre Vidal-Naquet, saw Faurisson as a complete charlatan with clear anti-Semitic views.[1]

For his part, Agamben – notoriously, for some – takes the figure of the *Muselmann* to be of great significance. The *Muselmann* is the one in the camps who is equivalent to the 'walking dead'; the one who is in a state of pure survival and nothing more. When considering the witness as medium, we can profit from Agamben's clarification of the status of a witness.

Agamben points out, for example, that 'witness' derives from both the Latin for *testis*, the origin of 'testimony' and which etymologically evokes the third party (**testis*) in a trial. The other Latin source is '*superstis*', which 'designates a person who has lived through something, who has experienced an event from beginning to end and can therefore bear witness to it' (Agamben 2002: 17).

---

1 See, for example, Pierre Vidal-Naquet (1981) 'De Faurisson et de Chomsky', *Esprit, Nouvelle série*, 49 (1): 205–8.

In passing, we note that the French word for witness is *témoin*, which again evokes testimony. Testimony is what one gives as a witness in a court of law. The idea of witnessing is contaminated by law, according to Agamben. Law is only interested in making a judgement, not in truth or justice. Trials, which are the basis of law's judgement, have only confused issues when it comes to what happened at Auschwitz. Trials give the impression that there is no longer any problem with regard to witnessing. In fact, says Agamben, 'the very problem is so enormous as to call into question law itself, dragging it to its own ruin' (20).

Interestingly, Agamben notes that the Greek word for witness is *martis*, thus connoting, 'martyr'. 'The first Church Fathers coined the word, *martirium* from *martis* to indicate the death of persecuted Christians, who thus bore witness to their faith' (26). Krämer also draws a link between witnessing and martyrdom. But, Agamben argues, the victims of the camps were not martyrs (2002: 26).

Witnessing in the Greek sense nevertheless has to do with remembering. 'The survivor's vocation is to remember; he cannot *not* remember' (26). However, with regard to the camps, the '"true" witnesses, the "complete witnesses", are those who did not bear witness. They are those who "touched bottom": the Muslims, the drowned. The survivors speak in their stead, by proxy, as pseudo-witnesses; they bear witness to a missing testimony' (34). To put it another way, the survivors bear witness to the impossibility of bearing witness. If you are inside the event, you are dead and cannot bear witness; if you are external to the event, you cannot be a credible witness. You cannot be a medium.

For Agamben, it is necessary to designate a witness to the extermination camps. And it is the *Muselmann*, poised between 'the human and the inhuman'. 'Simply to deny the *Muselmann*'s humanity would be to accept the verdict of the SS and to repeat their gesture' (63). Again, the *Muselmann* is the '"complete witness"', the only one for whom testimony would have a general meaning. But, Agamben asks: 'How can the non-human testify to the human, and how can the true witness be the one who by definition cannot bear witness?' (82).

Thus, we reach the ultimate point of the paradox. Does paradox 'save' Agamben's position with regard to witnessing when the event is death in the gas chambers of the Nazi camps? Let us leave this question in abeyance for the moment and return to Krämer on witnessing.

If, with Agamben, we seem to bypass speech and testimony to focus uniquely on the body of the survivor, who, *qua* survivor, becomes a witness, the question is: does this constitute a valid instance of witnessing? Krämer refers to Agamben on witnessing, but does not elaborate on the paradox of the *Muselmann*. For Krämer, when faced with the survivor accounts as witness, 'what matters most in these accounts is not the testimony of facts but rather the *performance* of witnessing itself. It is an act that precisely does not obey the logic of a "demonstrative speech act"' (2015: 159). Be this as it may, there is a sense that Krämer does not grasp the gravity of the survivor situation, which has, after all, given rise to intense debate, as is indicated in part by the revisionist history affair. If Agamben goes to one extreme in resorting to the paradox of witnessing through the medium of the inhuman, Krämer and others are situated at the other end of the continuum, where witnessing becomes largely a personal matter for the survivors – a matter that might be addressed, for instance, by psychoanalytic therapy.

On the other hand, Krämer is illuminating when she argues in part that the key to gaining insight into transmission from the angle of witnessing is to examine closely the relationship between testimony and audience. Thus, testimony is only effective to the extent that the audience believes and has faith in, the witness. This is significant because the focus is moved from the quality of information or knowledge received to the quality of the medium. Krämer does not pursue the point in this way, but it is evident that if witnessing draws attention almost exclusively to the quality of the medium, in the human sense, '*who* says something' takes precedence over 'what is said'. A religious inflection now appears in witnessing. Consequently, the statement: 'I am the truth and the light' is true *because* Christ says it. Krämer also evokes this religious dimension, but we will not be able to follow her further here. Martyrs become trustworthy witnesses to the extent that they are prepared to die for the cause. Here we can recall the Greek *martis* as cited by Agamben.

Is witnessing part of the scientific method? It is possible to argue that, in principle, it is not. That is to say, even if human consciousness comes into play in the results of scientific experiments, human perception as such is not part of the method of science. Rather, instruments are. We do not say: the results of the experiment must be true because I trust Prof. Einstein implicitly.

Nevertheless, because scientific work is organized and initiated by humans, human intervention can figure in science by default.

In an everyday sense, we can note that witnessing takes place in a variety of contexts, each with its own specific elements: thus, witnessing through direct perception would occur in witnessing a road accident (like the victim[s], the witness might also be traumatized by the event); in sport, the umpire witnesses an infringement on the rules of the game. Here he or she lays claim to a neutrality of perception. In law (and Krämer also deals with this) the witness offers testimony, so that it is not only perception that is invoked, but also, and even primarily, the manner in which perception (of an event, a personality, a situation) is translated into discourse. Moreover, witnessing is at stake in the victim's discourse. What does it mean to be a victim? It can mean that the victim is one who bears witness to – is the medium for – an injustice.

The witness as medium – or, in Krämer's terms, as the means of transmission – is the one who is believed, the one in whom one has faith and that, as a result, whose discourse is transparent or, whose very being (cf. the *Muselmann*) leaves no room for doubt. This, however, is not to rule out the category of bearing 'false witness', a category that complicates the notion of witnessing still further.

Maps as medium

In a definitive case study on maps, Krämer is able to put profoundly in question a McLuhanesque, medium-specific view of the medium (see 2015: 187–209). The question guiding Krämer's analysis is: in what sense is a map transparent or opaque? This question invokes the ongoing debate about the map and the territory – Jean Baudrillard having claimed, for example, that the map precedes and creates the territory; it is therefore effectively opaque (Baudrillard 1989: 166).[2]

Rather than deny that it is possible to understand maps as opaque (as, for instance, culturally or socially constructed in history or as a representation, not

2 In the wake of Baudrillard, Christian Jacob, whose work is cited by Krämer as an exemplar of the view of maps as ultimately opaque, writes: 'The power of maps lies in the way they communicate knowledge and implicitly reinforce the social and political order through their efficiency as symbols. Maps are didactic devices for the socialisation of individuals' (1996: 195).

reality), Krämer simply argues that this is not the point if one is to grasp the true nature of the map, which is the map in practice – the map as a pragmatic and practical device. Indeed, to treat the map as an opaque object presupposes one also knows that it is as transparent, that is, as it is enacted: 'the map can be regarded as a trace in the narrative of opacity only because and insofar as it functions as a messenger in the narrative of transparency' (2015: 190–1). The map, viewed as cultural artefact, as a representation in the framework of mimesis or as a simulacrum in Baudrillard's sense, implies treating it as a particular type of decontextualized object in relation to which the intellectual imaginary has no limits. This, then, is the key insight that one can derive from Krämer's astute analysis.

From Krämer's study, it becomes clear that bias in geographical representation (e.g. the land masses skewed towards Europe in Mercator's globe) should be distinguished from the map function. Maps, unlike geography, are not mimetic. In this respect, Krämer points out that 'The map does not become a medium until it is situated in practices that at the same time assume its representational transparency, such as when someone uses the map to orient himself' (193). To reiterate, a map is only truly a map in its use and not as it is as an object. Is the latter not the principle that might be invoked in a critique of McLuhan's version of the medium, namely, that the medium is only truly the medium that it is in its use? Of course, there was the invention of the printing press, and it has effects; of course, radio, television and the internet have emerged in the modern era and have certain specific qualities. But a medium only truly exists in its enactment. This is the conclusion that is reinforced by Krämer's study of maps.

Just as the errors of the chronometer referred to in the introduction to this study do not disqualify this technology as a transparent mechanism for the calculation of longitude, so, in Krämer's words, we can say that "Every critique of distortions must *nolens volens* invoke the narrative of the representationality of maps, as this narrative establishes the criterion necessary to diagnose something as a distortion' (197).

To claim that the medium is its enactment should not steer us away from the fact that the medium is only 'present' in its 'absence'. This, as will be further explained in the latter sections of this study, is what is implied by the medium as a modal ontology.

4

Discourse networks, time and materiality: Kittler, Ernst, Krauss and the 'post-medium'

What have we learnt so far?

In the introduction, we saw that there were a number of different contexts in which the medium emerged: for example, in relation to immanence and the environment, in Heidegger's view of time as temporization, and in the context of OOO and the work of art, where the materiality of the work is distinct from the content as medium.

Chapter 1 focused on the etymological significance of the term 'medium', particularly as this brought up the connection with the notion of middle and the middle voice. Different logics, such as 0–1 of contradiction and 0–2 of the carnival were highlighted, as was the significance for understanding the medium of the notion of the excluded middle. We also looked at the term, medium, when used to refer to a séance and the attempted communing with deceased persons. This led us to Jacques Derrida's consideration of 'spectre' as medium and the idea of 'hauntology', which evokes that which both does and does not appear, as in the manner of the spirit of Hamlet's father.

In Chapter 2, we examined in some detail McLuhan's theory of media and his take on media history in order to establish whether or not it is justified to conclude that McLuhan's media theory is based on the notion of media specificity.

Chapter 3 addressed the work of Sybille Krämer and her theory of the medium as disappearance illustrated by the process of transmission and the work of the messenger. We also looked at Krämer's take on the status of the analyst in the transference as well as the status of the witness as medium.

Finally, with regard to Krämer on the medium, we focused on the nature of maps from the perspective of opacity and transparency. Despite the possibility of looking at the map as object, a map is only truly a map, we found, in its activation, in which case it is transparent. What was also revealed is that any *theory* of maps (and of the medium in general, for that matter), necessarily obscures the status of the map as practical. In short, 'Like a Husserlian "*epoché*", a theoretical approach requires dispensing with the practical use of maps' (Krämer 2015: 209).

Throughout the trajectory, then, there has been a continual attempt to outline the significance of the difference between the medium as transparent and the medium as opaque; the medium as that which does not appear but is the condition of possibility of that which does appear; or, to put it another way, what matters is the medium as pure materiality in contrast to the medium as implementation or performance.

Medium as immaterial and material object

Now, in this chapter, we bring to the fore and examine aspects of German media theory that highlight the materiality of the medium. Even though the argument of the preceding chapters has been that the medium *qua* medium disappears, or is transparent, the way that Kittler and Ernst, for example, approach the medium is of strategic interest. After addressing key aspects of German theory, our attention will turn to the work on the medium of art theorist and critic, Rosalind Krauss. Krauss's approach, in focusing on the obsolescent medium, also raises the issue of the relation between the medium and materiality.

A strand of German media theory that explicitly promotes the medium as concrete object thus effectively challenges the notion that media are to be characterized by their disappearance. And it is necessary to address this. Indeed, despite appearances to the contrary, with the approach inaugurated in the modern era by Marshall McLuhan, the study of the medium in many quarters remains dominated by the claim that the material support, historically inflected, *is* the medium *qua* medium.

This implies, as we have seen, not only that the medium appears as such (often within a constructivist paradigm), but also that it is essentially found in the historical evolution of technics, culminating with the digital revolution and the dominance of computers. Hence, we should recall again Kittler's famous claim that digitization puts an end to the need for individual media, as 'a total media link on a digital base will erase the very concept of medium' (Kittler 1999: 2). Crucially, Kittler also says that 'Media *determine* our situation' (xxxix; emphasis added). Despite Kittler's words, the virtual materiality of the digital image might mean that focus must now rest on the image as such and not on the medium as material support. This, at least, is a key aspect of the thesis we have pursued in this investigation where the medium is understood as that which does not appear vis-à-vis what does appear, namely: images, meaning, messages, information, knowledge, feeling/sentiment, idea, space, time, personality, memory, music and so on.

Mark Hansen claims that 'Kittler's work announces ... the digital obsolescence *of the image as such*' (2002: 69). As noted earlier, Hansen's statement implies that a change in the material support is equivalent to bringing a change in the medium. Kittler's notion of medium is thus still in keeping with the age inaugurated by McLuhan.

To gain a fuller picture of medium as object, a reading of two of Kittler's key texts will follow, the first being *Discourse Networks, 1800/1900* (1990), and the second, *Gramophone, Film Typewriter* (1999).

And, in the wake of the putative dissolution of media *tout court*, Rosalind Krauss speaks of a 'post-media' reality. As a critique of 'post-media', Krauss, inspired by Benjamin, endeavours to rehabilitate obsolescent media – in effect, media as object – the better to gain a deeper understanding of that which in its operation went more or less without saying (see Krauss 1999a). Obsolescent media can, Krauss proposes, come to assume a 'redemptive' role by bringing to light the 'necessary plurality of the arts' (305). How then, we ask, does Krauss's approach compare with that of Ernst? A response to this question will be the focus of the final section of this chapter.

Kittler: *Discourse Networks*

The work under consideration here does not, in the first instance, engage with the medium *qua* medium. However, Kittler's focus on 'alphabetization' as mastery of language through sounds (phonics), in Germany in 1800, the role the mother assumes in this process and the consequences for poetry and the literary scene more generally are underpinned by a certain notion of mediality. Kittler addresses the elements that impinge upon a life in the republic of letters, especially the respective roles of women and men. Men are the writers, but their 'success' depends on the response of readers of taste – predominantly women. Thus, 'around 1800', Kittler remarks, 'a new type of book began to appear, one that delegated to mothers first the physical and mental education of their children, then their alphabetization' (1990: 27). With regard to the latter, the mother's voice becomes crucial in pronouncing the sounds of the language: 'The Mother's Mouth thus freed children from books. Her voice substituted sounds for letters' (34).

Writing, in the sense of literacy – a literacy that is evocative of the scribe – by contrast, is linked to success in the public sphere, where men are dominant, especially in the bureaucracy. Poetry, and what makes it viable, together with a demonstration of the way Goethe's *Faust* was appropriated around 1800, also figures in Kittler's effort to expose the rudiments of discourse networks in 1800. The true significance of the 'word' in *Faust* is focused upon – the word that also evokes the beginning. In the beginning was not the word, but the act. All of *Faust* is ultimately to be understood as an indication of the position of the scholar in 1800. And so, we read that 'After 1800, professors, especially in chairs of philosophy, made a career of free translation – of *Faust* in particular.

The discourse network as the condition of possibility of scholarly, educational, literary, philosophical work and much more is the medium – although Kittler never uses the word – through which the sociocultural milieu assumes its mode of being.

But let us return to the mother, or to the 'Mother's Mouth', as Kittler's subheading puts it; for here is an explicit instance of the medium, since, strictly speaking, the mother's mouth, so fundamental in the process of alphabetization at the turn of the nineteenth century, never appears as such. Even though Kittler refers frequently to the 'mouth', what is really being evoked are the sounds (vowels) that the mouth articulates and that children listen to: 'The Mother's Mouth thus freed children from books. Her voice substituted sounds for letters, just as in the course of his Scholar's Tragedy Faust substituted meanings for words. ... And when later in life children picked up a book they would not see letters but hear, with irrepressible longing, a voice between the lines' (1990: 34). Because the medium is in play, what would be heard 'between the lines' would be the sounds of letters, syllables and vowels. This, then, is how language acquisition in the discourse network of 1800 takes place through the medium.

We will now leave the discourse network of 1800 as Kittler portrays it, but not before making a final reference to the medium. At the turn of the nineteen century (1800), Kittler argues, the book was consolidated as the only form of 'serial storage of serial data. They [books] had been reproducible since Gutenberg, but they became material for understanding and fantasy only when alphabetization had become ingrained' (116). To put it in terms of the approach adopted in this study, the book, in giving access to serial data, is the medium and is thus the transparent vehicle of knowledge and information.

With the emergence of the discourse network of 1900, rather than alphabetization, the materiality – or the physiology – of words and writing comes to the fore. And this cannot be more evident than in Nietzsche's approach to writing. At least, this is Kittler's claim. More specifically, 'The logic of chaos and intervals was implemented as a technology by the discourse network of 1900 – through the *invention of the typewriter*' (192; emphasis added). With the typewriter, writing 'became selection from countable, spatialized supply' (194). Supposedly, Dionysus 'is a typewriter myth' (196). Moreover, 'script, instead of continuing to be a translation of a Mother's Mouth, has become an irreducible medium among media, has become the typewriter' (199).

To the extent that, in this context, what is at issue in Kittler's thought can be discerned, it would seem that the typewriter draws attention to the physical nature of words. The point is reinforced by our theorist's reference to Mallarmé's advice to Degas that poetry is made with words – not ideas, as Degas had assumed (cited at 184).

Memory, too, is essentially a physiological affair, where, if one is Nietzsche, it is pain that drives memory, or, if one is Hermann Ebbinghaus, memory is about physically applying oneself and learning by rote. Thus, as Kittler reports from Ebbinghaus's research into mnemic techniques, 'Lines of seven syllables can be learned instantly, lines of twelve syllables have to be read sixteen times, and lines of twenty-six syllables have to be read fifty-five times before the mechanism of reproducible memorization clicks on' (208).

Whether or not it is possible to authenticate Kittler's claim that the art of language and thought in the discourse network of 1900 comes to assume an entirely physiological and material form, it is clear that the medium (as the word in poetry or as the typewriter in the production of poetry and thought) is presented as an entirely material entity – as an object, in short. The following line – evoked by a student's dream of hearing Goethe's recorded voice – sums up things precisely: 'no engineer can stand having women love not the invention itself but its output' (231).

All that is implied by focusing on the physicality of words and letters and these in comparison with film and the photograph no doubt cannot be given here. Let us, however, note the following: the typewriter became the material object as machine and tool for producing typefaces and operated as the model illuminating the bases of perception – 'there are sensory and motor, acoustical and optical language centres linked to nerve paths just as the working parts of a typewriter are connected by levers and rods' (251). The putative materiality of the word is thus inextricably linked to physiology and psychotechnology, such as is instanced with the tachistoscope used for presenting objects to the eyes for very brief periods of time. Thus, not ideas, not meaning or interpretation, not symbolism – but rather *asymbolia* becomes the focus of attention in Kittler's version of the discourse network of 1900.

The typeface of Stefan George's poetry

It is, Kittler observes, the arrival of new technological media (such as the cinema and photography) that leads to the visual poetry of Apollinaire with his calligrams, and Mallarmé with *Un coup de dés*. Already, we know that for Mallarmé, words as words were the key constituents of poetry, and Apollinaire is similarly oriented, but doubly so. With Apollinaire words are the constituents of poems; but the words also connote the importance of words as such through the images they form on the page. The poem, 'The Eiffel Tower' is in the form of the tower. As we will confirm in light of Kittler's commentary on Stefan George's poetic typography, it is, despite all, because the words *exist* that typographical configurations become a focus of interest. In short, it is only because a medium is involved that the said configurations attract attention.

Thus, in the first edition of George's *Collected Works*, artist Melchior Lechter fabricated the 'Stefan George script', a script that was 'adapted from George's handwriting' (259). But, according to Kittler, 'any handwriting that can be transposed into reusable typeface functions fundamentally as *mechanized* script' (259). But whether it is a question of letters or words, handwritten or printed, it *is* a question of *letters* and *words* – not of objects. All of the techniques of printing that might be intended to have an effect on reading from a physiological perspective cannot erase the distinction between word and object. If the word is in play, an object is not and, consequently, we are dealing with the medium, and therefore with something transparent. All this is so even if detailed attention is given to a typewriter typeface. Kittler thus pronounces that 'Whereas the physiologist Messmer counted 270 letters above or below x-height in an ordinary text a thousand letters long, I find in George an average of only 200 extended as opposed to 800 small letters' (260). While there is nothing to stop such detailed attention being given to the typeface – to treating the typeface as object, whether aesthetic or not – it does not change the fact that for a word to be a word and thus to be constitutive of a typeface it cannot simply be a physical phenomenon. The typewriter is an object, but it is also a medium because the word is a medium. As an addendum it can be said that any physiology of *reading* – where for example the elimination of ascenders or descenders might affect reading speed – must take account of words *as* words, not just words as physical objects.

But the argument is that the *material* nature of letters has an impact on reading. How letters and words are presented (whether by tachistoscope or not) is consequently deemed to be a key variable in the reading process. And, of course, the latter is essentially to do with words as words. I, however, persist in saying that while the mode of objectification of the medium can facilitate or inhibit reading (Nietzsche's handwriting had, after all, to be deciphered), the rationale of decipherment is to allow the reader to go beyond the materiality of the medium. To become ensconced in the materiality of words is to cancel reading. One of Stefan George's key poems – studied by Heidegger in his thinking on language – is entitled 'Das Wort' (The Word), the last line of which reads: 'Without the word no thing can be' (264). Just what this line means is open to interpretation, but one meaning that can be proffered is that the word as medium is necessary to allow access to what is beyond the word.

There can be a transposition of media – so the discourse network of 1900 proclaims.

The dream is a medium. But more than this, the images (one medium) have to be translated into another medium: words. Again, a word can be an image. This, then, is the basis of Freud's dream as a rebus.

Later, after talking about Freud, President Schreber and literature as a simulation of madness, Kittler states that: 'The typewriter brought about (Foucault's *Order of Things* overlooks such trivialities) "a completely new order of things"' (1990: 352). In what sense (if at all) is a form of technological determinism infused in Kittler's thinking about the medium?

Kittler and the impact on the human of media technologies

A key passage from one of Nietzsche's letters cited in *Gramophone, Film, Typewriter* (1999), is one Kittler had already cited in *Discourse Networks*, namely: '"Our writing materials contribute their part to our thinking"' (1990: 196). In *Gramophone, Film, Typewriter* Winthrop-Young and Wutz translate this passage as: 'Our writing tools are also working on our thoughts' (1999: 200). Again, Nietzsche is quoted by Kittler as saying that the writing tool '"is a thing like me"' (206). And our theorist does not fail to provide an elaboration here. In using the typewriter: 'Nietzsche, as proud of the publication of his mechanization as any philosopher, *changed from arguments to aphorisms from thoughts to puns, from rhetoric to telegram style*. That is precisely what is meant by the sentence that our writing tools are also working on our thoughts' (1999: 203; emphasis added). Again, in *Discourse Networks*, Kittler had claimed that, in light of Nietzsche's purchase of a Malling Hansen typewriter, 'Dionysus (like Dracula several years later) is a *typewriter* myth' (1990: 196. Emphasis added). The discourse network of 1900 – of which Nietzsche was a part – gives rise to writing in its materiality. Is this why the typewriter is so significant? But how is the typewriter instrumental in creating the Dionysian myth? Kittler does not himself explicitly piece together the evidence. The context, however, is the Nietzschean theory of the instantiation of memory through pain. Memory is the result, as it were, of what is stamped on the body – the more painfully the better if the memory is to be retained. With regard to Kittler's claim, one can only surmise – recalling the emphasis on the materiality of writing – that the Dionysian myth with its focus on the body resulted, for Nietzsche, from the stamping of letters on paper with the typewriter 'plungers'. As Malling-Hansen put it in his application for an improved version of his invention, 'The writer, using his ten fingers, depresses with one of them one piston after another onto the paper.'[1] Or, in Kittler's words, proffered in his discussion of the discourse network of 1900: 'Type hits paper, leaving an impression, or sometimes even a hole' (1990: 195). We are yet to consider whether it is plausible or implausible, but 'typewriter became act in the dithyramb. The rhythm of the lyric has, of course, the "advantage" of "better impressing" words "into memory"' (199).

Whatever one makes of Kittler's thesis that the Dionysian myth is a product of the typewriter, and his acceptance of the claim that the mode of technology determines the mode or style of thinking, there is little doubt that the technical objects – or the medium – assume a certain opacity and are thinkable and representable as a result.[2]

Reflection on the typewriter – so pivotal in *Discourse Networks* – constitutes the third, concluding section of *Gramophone, Film, Typewriter*. Why does the typewriter occupy this strategically significant place in Kittler's text? We will return to this question, but can tentatively say that the typewriter is crucial because it forms (via the Turing machine) the transition to the computer and, secondly, even if more speculatively, because the typewriter evokes the symbolic in Lacan's three registers of the real (gramophone), the imaginary (film) and the symbolic (typewriter).

---

1 Malling-Hansen, Patent 158,071, 11 December 1873, page 3: https://books.google.com.au/books?id=0bLFMPHiXpMC&pg=PA38-IA87&lpg=PA38-IA87&dq=malling+hansen+writing+ball+patent+125,952&source=bl&ots=Bj6y64dq78&sig=ACfU3U2a-ItUNZBC_H7U7cnMwdNsKXkOsA&hl=en&sa=X&ved=2ahUKEwi8jqGq35n2AhVKUGwGHdI6DRg4ChDoAXoECA8QAw#v=onepage&q=malling%20hansen%20writing%20ball%20patent%20125%2C952&f=false (accessed 25 February 2022).
2 See photographs of Nietzsche's Malling-Hansen's typing ball in *Discourse* (1990: 194) and in *Gramophone* (1999: 204).

Gramophone

In his second key work, into which we shall now delve, Kittler's attention turns initially to the medium of the gramophone.

In July 1877, Edison's 'Hullo' reverberates from his analogue phonogram '81 years before Turing's moving paper strip'. Perhaps despite Kittler, and as a reminder of what we have already stated, this 'hullo' has to be understood as the epitome of transparency. All the more so when it happens for the first time. From Edison's point of view, success is equivalent to transparency and failure equivalent to opacity. Were things to remain there, however, we would be left in the realm of the symbolic, whereas Kittle wants to direct the results of Edison's achievement towards the real. Indeed, as has been pointed out by Winthrop-Young in Kittler (2006) and Schmidgen (2019), the Lacanian psychoanalysis (cf. the approach to paranoia) and thus the registers of 'real', 'imaginary' and 'symbolic' are as close as one will get to glimpsing a structure that would determine the outcome of Kittler's thinking.[3] In any case, our author moves to a consideration of sound as a physical (therefore real?) phenomenon and the object of scientific research, and the evolution in musical history from Wagner's demonstration of 'the physical overtone series' to Schoenberg's analysis of harmony. In short, we are now encouraged to confront the opacity of the medium. Or, in Kittler's words: 'The real takes the place of the symbolic' (1999: 24), and this in turn is interpreted as the 'Old European alphabetism' being overtaken by 'mathematical-physical notation' (1999: 25). Here, the impression arises that what is crucial is the appearance and effects of the medium *as such*. Whether, and if so in what sense, this is a justifiable impression, remains to be seen.

That, for Kittler, the sound – at least subsequently – of the voice emanating from Edison's machine was imperfect, goes without saying. However, it is not only a matter in this context of understanding how the machine might be improved, but, equally, how the brain reacts in relation to sound. Might the operation of the phonograph throw light on the way the brain, hence perception, works? Such is the question that Kittler uses to guide his analysis.

---

3 The problem arises when gramophone, film and typewriter are entirely equated respectively with 'real', 'imaginary' and 'symbolic'; for it is likely that each medium participates in more than one register.

As a result, it is found that in its functioning as both recorder of sounds, or noises, and the mechanism of their consequent reproduction, the phonogram resembles the way that the voice performs in the human body: the act of speaking is 'no more than the physiological filtering of breath or noise, and the entry and exit of band-pass filters are interchangeable, the larynx will admit only those frequency mixtures which once escaped from it' (73).

Ironically, after Freud had a telephone installed in his study, he described the work that went on there, 'in terms of telephony' (89).

The final pages of *Gramophone* are devoted to the way sound engineering, made all the more sophisticated for having derived directly from war time experience, gives rise to simulations that more than satisfy a yearning for the real. For instance, 'Laurie Anderson's voice ... simulates the voice of a 747 pilot who uses the plane's speaker system to suddenly interrupt the ongoing entertainment program to inform passengers of an imminent crash' (111). What the Second World War has bequeathed to the world is the development of sound recording and transmission that takes on a veritable life of its own, a fact no more notable than in the context of rock music, where 'sounds' rather than voices have become the mainstay of the industry. Kittler tells us, in sum, that 'rock songs sing of the very media power which sustains them' (111). With rock and other forms of popular music, voice (natural sound) and gramophone (manipulated and engineered sound) become entirely confused. For Kittler, like McLuhan, the truth is in the medium, not the message.

Given that electronic storage systems have the capacity to capture (code), store and then re-present the previously stored material, and given that this can occur with sounds or images from nature, it would seem that the issues of transparency and opacity become extremely significant. In this regard, Kittler makes much of Turing's and Shannon's invention of the 'vocoder' (voice coder). To prevent Churchill's messages to Roosevelt being intercepted by the enemy during the Second World War, the war leader's voice was transformed by the vocoder into 'white noise'. Then, on receipt, the latter was transformed back into Churchill's articulate voice. In the end, Kittler claims, it is a matter of the physics and codification of sound and not one of the actual voice of the – or a – speaker. And the same pertains for the genre of post-1950s rock music. In principle, 'hi-fi stereophony can simulate any acoustic space, from real space inside a submarine to the psychedelic space inside the brain itself' (103).

Let us say more about this after having considered Kittler's approach to film and (again) the typewriter. For only then will we be in a position to illuminate successfully Kittler's approach to the medium.

Film

In his foray into the nature and influence of film as a medium, Kittler states that 'The age of media (not just since Turing's game of imitation) renders indistinguishable what is human and what is machine' (146). In psychiatry, film makes it possible to capture in images forms of behaviour that patients fail to produce in the lecture theatre. The result is that 'films are more real than reality and that their so-called reproductions are, in reality, productions' (145). Moreover, 'It is precisely this indistinguishability between framed and framing, between insanity and psychiatry, that does justice to film technology' (147). And the foregoing is illustrated by feature film itself in the form of 'Dr Robert Wiene's *Cabinet of Dr Caligari* (1920)' (146), where framing and a visual style evocative of madness pertain.[4] In other words, we are encouraged to believe that it is film as such that leads to the confusion between sanity and madness, fantasy and reality, the true and the false, freedom and confinement. We shall come back to this.

Of equal importance is the capacity of film – in true narcissistic fashion – to present the exact double, or 'doppelgänger', of a character. In the *Cabinet of Dr Caligari*, for instance, the one who controls the somnambulist, Cesare, and the doctor in charge of the asylum, become reflections of one another in a manner only made possible by the film medium itself. As Kittler recounts:

> the doppelgänger trick is nothing less than uncanny. Half of the lens is covered with a black diaphragm while the actor acts on the other half of the picture frame. Then, without changing the camera's position, exposed film is rewound, the other half of the lens is covered up, and the same actor, now in his role as doppelgänger, acts on the opposite side of the frame. (153–4)

The technical possibility of the doppelgänger in film opens the way to the technical possibility of actualizing phantasy and, more generally, of

---

4 On this, see Kracauer (2019).

presenting an incarnation of dreams and the fantastic. This is, then, the basis
of the essential link Kittler detects as existing between film and the psychic
apparatus. Or, in Kittler's words, 'film presents its spectators with their own
processes of perception – and with a precision that is otherwise accessible
only to experiment' (161). On this basis, film and the Lacanian imaginary are,
for Kittler, inextricably linked. With regard to the aforesaid imaginary, it is
important for Kittler that the technical mechanism – the mirror, as in Lacan's
famous text[5] – is formative of and not simply reflective of the ego-subject. It
is a matter, as Lacan states in his remark on Daniel Lagach's 'Psychoanalysis
and Personality Structure' of the '*construction* of the subject' (2006: 564;
emphasis added). Of key significance in the 'mirror stage' is the fact of 'The
Mirror Stage as *Formative* of the *I* Function' (2006: 75; emphasis added). Even
if Lacan also acknowledges that identification on the part of the infant is also
involved, it is a 'formative' identification.[6] The key for Kittler to this formation,
we can intuit, is the technical object, in this case the mirror. But, clearly, film,
qua technical object, also becomes a potentially formative mechanism from
Kittler's perspective.

To recall again Mark Hansen, 'What Kittler's work announces ... is not
(simply) the obsolescence of the cinematic image in the age of the digital, but
the digital obsolescence *of the image as such*' (2002: 69). Hansen's statement
implies that a change in the material support is equivalent to bringing a
change in the medium. And so, despite apparently updating media theory
in light of digitalization, Kittler's notion of medium is still in keeping with
the age inaugurated by McLuhan – the McLuhan for whom media were
the concrete, historical objects and artefacts (codex, book, electricity, film,
computer) that appeared as such and ultimately supposedly constituted the

---

5 See Lacan (2006: 75–81).
6 Compare with

> It suffices to understand the mirror stage in this context *as an identification,* in the full
> sense analysis gives to the term: namely, the transformation that takes place in the subject
> when he assumes [*assume*] an image – an image that is seemingly predestined to have an
> effect at this phase, as witnessed by the use in analytic theory of antiquity's term, 'imago'.
> (2006: 76)

To be noted, too, is the following passage from a study of Lacan and cinema by Pietro Bianchi: 'The
image seen in a mirror, far from being purely a *reflection* of something that is supposedly already
there in the development of the child, should rather be understood as *constitutive*, its effect being
productive and not merely *passive*' (2017: 7).

message. Another way of putting this is to say that what McLuhan inaugurated and what Kittler continues to confirm is the dominance of *media specificity* in relation to meaning, message, image and so on. Thus, time presented by the clock becomes 'clock time'; orality produces an 'oral' (non-literate) view of the world; the printed word opens out on to a 'bookish' view of the world; a photograph presents a photographic view of the world; the computer would produce an essentially virtual world and so forth. Or, as Hansen says regarding the digital and time, 'time has changed in the wake of the digital computational revolution' (Hansen 2009: 295). Moreover, in the wake of the dominance of the technical artifactual, digital medium, 'we cannot but recognize the extensive temporalizing power wielded by technical artifacts that function autonomously or quasi-autonomously in relation to narrowly human regimes of temporalization' (304). Hansen goes on to note 'the ways in which *media objects* function to capture human time' (306. Emphasis added.) He also proposes that 'representation is a process *that takes time*' (306). But this is the issue: is there 'time beyond its mediatic capture' (307)?

Typewriter

As noted, Kittler's discussion of the typewriter is an elaboration of the analysis begun in *Discourse Networks* in relation to Nietzsche and the typewriter. Some points are repeated, as if to emphasize the insights already set out.

Generally speaking, machine writing, according to Kittler who here invokes Lacan, is an incarnation of the symbolic. The typewriter machine not the female typist (doppelgänger), who was also called a 'typewriter' and presumably the Morse code machine and semaphore flags along with aeroplane skywriting must all be, by analogy with the typewriter, incarnations of the symbolic. Brail and stencil printing could perhaps be added to the list. In any event 'Lacan's three registers cannot possibly be demonstrated more effectively: the real of the writer, the imaginary of his doppelgänger, and, finally, as elementary as forgotten, the symbolic of machine writing' (1999: 214).

Nietzsche serves as the model for demonstrating that the typewriter changes the style of writing and mode of thinking. For instance, when using a typewriter, T. S. Eliot (like Nietzsche) gives up his long sentences in favour of a more aphoristic, 'staccato' style (229).

The typewriter changes male–female relations. The typist ('Minnie Tipp') is available to type up the dictated word or the handwritten script. Pressure is then on the writer to come up with a script. With a typist available, the writer must write.

Heidegger's well-known critique that the typewriter effaces the character and style of handwriting – or, more generally, the hand as such, a hand that distinguishes human from animal – is addressed by Kittler, who quotes the philosopher: 'The typewriter veils the essence of writing and of the script. It withdraws from man the essential rank of the hand, without man's experiencing the withdrawal appropriately and recognizing that it has transformed the relation of Being to his essence' (1999: 199; Heidegger 1992: 85). Nietzsche writing *with* a typewriter that changes his thoughts is thus the counterpart to Heidegger who writes *about* the typewriter. In Kittler's eyes. it, nevertheless, remains to be seen as to whether Heidegger's thinking is unaffected by the typewriter. Nietzsche exhibited a truth (the impact of the typewriter on thought) that Heidegger, in his refusal to accept it, could still have become influenced by it.[7]

Kafka's relation with his fiancée and stenographer, Felice Bauer, is also typewriter-inflected. To bridge the distance between them, Kafka types letters and post cards that he sends to Felice, at the same time bemoaning the fact – à la Heidegger – that the letter in general and the typed missive, *qua* typed, even more so, is a form of distancing. Moreover, the anonymity of Kafka's main literary character is reinforced by being reduced, in *The Castle*, to a single, typed upper-case letter: 'K'. In a sense, the typed text is also Kafka's way of hiding.

The presence of the typewriter is thus quite evident, as it is with Nietzsche's 'writing ball', or with the Turing machine that is an extension of, and even resembles, a typewriter. But what of Nietzsche's theory of memory as torture? What of the diarists in Carl Schmitt's satire, 'The Buribunks: A Historic-Philosophical Mediatation' (Schmitt 1918 and 2019) – how are these strands linked to the typewriter?

The answer to the first question is that Nietzsche's proposition of torture giving rise to memory evokes the human body as the place of inscription,

---

7 On Heidegger and print, see the introduction to this study, note 7.

where, in keeping with 'Beyerlsen's technical observation that in typing, everything is visible except the actual inscription of the sign' (Kittler 1999: 211), early typewriters 'did not even have types and a ribbon. Instead, the writing paper was perforated by needle pins – inscribing, for example, in a rather Nietzschean manner, the proper name of the inventor' (211). Early typewriters thus imitate a form of inscription that evokes pain, the pain that, for Nietzsche, is the basis of memory.

With regard to Schmitt's Buribunk text, the following passage, included in Kittler's lengthy citation, links it to the typewriter:

> The basic outline of the philosophy of the Buribunks: I think, therefore I am; I speak, therefore I am; I write, therefore I am; I publish, therefore I am. This contains no contradiction, but rather the progressive sequence of identities, each of which, following the laws of logic, transcends its own limitations. For Buribunks, thinking is nothing but silent speech; speech is nothing but writing without script; writing is nothing but anticipated publication; and publication is, hence, identical with writing to such a degree that the differences between the two are so small as to be negligible. I write, therefore I am; I am, therefore I write. What do I write? I write myself. Who writes me? I myself write myself. What do I write about? I write that I write myself. What is the great engine that elevates me out of the complacent circle of egohood? History!
>
> I am thus a letter on the typewriter of history. I am a letter that writes itself. …
>
> At each second of world history, the letters of the typewriter keyboard leap, impelled by the nimble fingers of the world – I, onto the white paper and continue the historical narrative. (Schmitt 1918, cited by Kittler 1999: 241)[8]

Publication – the ultimate goal of Buribunks – presupposes typing. Keeping a diary of every second of the day – something that is intimate, or private – even if handwritten, will become typing, will be published.

The Buribunk text is then used by Kittler by way of transition to Turing and the latter's statement that 'I will learn to compute on my typewriter'. Thus typewriter (a process of discontinuous, discrete functions) foreshows the discrete functions of the computer – of the Turing machine, a machine that 'was never built but is mathematically conceivable' (1999: 249).

---

8 For a complete and recent English translation of this text see Schmitt (2019).

There are, to be sure, philosophical issues raised by Schmitt's story – such as how 'writing oneself' might relate to 'being' oneself. Or, one could linger over the references to Leporello's effort at diarizing Don Juan's 'conquests'. But, for the moment, all this is beside the point, the latter being how the medium appears or disappears in Kittler's discourse.

And in a certain sense, as has been repeatedly stated in this study, it may be in *not* appearing that an instance of the medium emerges as what it is. To find it impossible to track exactly the genealogy of what for Kittler is a concrete medium artefact is to imply that the medium is not reducible to the (in Mark Hansen's terms[9]) 'media artifactuality' composed of the gramophone, film and typewriter trilogy. When the non-German-speaking reader is confronted with the German text of a facsimile of Kafka's 'postcard to Felice Bauer' (Kittler 1999: 227), what he or she is confronted with is not an instance of the typewriter medium, but with a pure object – that is, with the pure opacity of artifactuality. Kittler's detailed and technically informed analysis of the nature and articulation of technical objects might seem like a way of directing attention away from the potential aporias of attempting to 'understand' media. What does the nature of medium – its ontology and its form – really matter when we are being led to an appreciation of the medium from the inside, from the position that, due to a lack of technical literacy, seems to present the medium *as it really is*?

Sybille Krämer (2006) has endeavoured to set out the general lines of inquiry that appear to govern Kittler's theoretical trajectory in relation to the medium. For her, a crucial distinction is to be made between 'alphabetical writing' (which can be the object of semiotics and interpretation) and 'technological media', or media beyond the purview of signs. The former is deemed to be dominant prior to the nineteenth century, while the latter emerged with the phonogram after 1877 – after the emergence of Edison's phonograph.

The city as medium

Within Kittler's framework, the city (to focus on it for a moment) is a medium because it not only 'centralizes the flow of energy and information' (Kittler

---

9 See Hansen (2006: 301).

1996: 725), but is also a node or hub of 'information processing'. This is true as much for the pre-modern as for the modern era. Thus, 'part of the greatness of ancient Florence consisted in having erected with the Uffizi, the first office building – a central bureau for data processing' (721–2).

But then, how does the city as a node of information flows and processing accord with the following definition of media? – to wit, 'MEDIA record, transmit and process information – this is the most elementary definition of media. Media can include old-fashioned things like books, familiar things like the city and newer inventions like the computer' (722).

Kittler's city, then, is not equivalent to the built environment – the city that is the subject of Mumford's famous history – but is the result of media events and processes. However, what is disarming about this approach is that media also tend to appear as such, as is evident in the example of the Uffizi in Florence. To be sure, this is not the end of the story, but it is worth remarking that the city could be a medium in a more familiar sense, the sense of an environment or milieu in which things take place, the sense of an environment that *enables* events but does not itself appear. Even as an information-processing hub the city exudes a physical presence for Kittler, as the following passage demonstrates:

> The railway stations, which have (in the words of Napoleon III) ascended by the middle of the nineteenth century to the status of city gates, could not so readily give, as Joseph II did to Austria's cloisters, a new function to the old portals, which had been up until that point the incoming/outgoing point for a postal system whose coaches transmitted people, goods, and news, that is, addresses, data, and commands. (723)

In a sense – and it is in a sophisticated sense – Kittler aims to reveal the presence of the medium even where it was hitherto thought that the medium was absent. As such, one sees how a railway network – its stations, carriages and passengers – in fact becomes a medium and, for Kittler, a very concrete one, in certain respects. And so, when it comes to the appearance or disappearance of the medium, Kittler's theoretical odyssey raises the stakes to the highest degree.

Rather than seeking the underlying theoretical and historical coherence of Kittler's endeavour, the foregoing account has taken each medium dealt with at face value, the better to determine how transparency and opacity or disappearance and appearance play out with regard to individual media. Surely, in this regard, it has been shown that for Kittler there is an era of the phonograph or gramophone, an era of film and, finally, the era of the computer. Does this not mean in short that for Kittler, like McLuhan, transparency is of little or no account once technological, storage media are concerned? This may well be true, but what Kittler's detailed, technically informed approach enables is a deepening of our understanding of how the medium is transparent even in the wake of Kittler's highly sophisticated media materialism. It is just that, against Kittler's claim, it is not at the material level that the medium *qua* medium exists. Rather, the latter exists in its non-appearing or disappearing.

Wolfgang Ernst and the medium as immaterial and material object: 'Post-medium'

It has been pointed out that Ernst sees media as essentially measuring instruments. This implies two things: first, that media transcend human capacities – most notably perception – in providing a knowledge of the world. That is, measuring media have an epistemological function. Second, the notion of measuring media raises the question (already asked) as to whether or not a machine view of the world must inevitably prevail. In this regard, Ernst tends to be ambivalent, so that what remains unclear is whether measuring by the machine provides a machine view of things, or whether the machine, like a good prosthesis, provides access to the world *as it really is* – a point that will be received by many current media aficionados as being quite heretical. This is because, as the following argument will endeavour to confirm, the 'media-specific' view is held dogmatically. As an initial indication, one can point examples of technics where the claim that a specific piece of technology produces a particular view of the world is demonstrably problematic – as, for example, with the microscope or the telescope, or with medical instruments, such as the ophthalmoscope (to examine the retina) or the otoscope (to examine the ear cavity). With each of these technical instruments, there is maximum transparency (a result can be produced that is not medium specific) as opposed to opacity (the result is medium specific).

As far as the medium as object is concerned, media archaeology, especially as formulated by Ernst, whose work in turn has been influenced by Foucault's archaeology (see Ernst 2011), is exemplary. For Ernst, Foucault does not write narrative history, but rather sets out the conditions of possibility for writing (narrative) history.[10] Indeed, media artists inspired by an archaeological approach, can appropriate 'old' media in creating 'new' art (see Parikka 2012: 2). The key concern of media archaeology is to emphasize the supposed essential materiality of the medium. Such materiality is emblematised by the items in the cellar of media archaeology organized by Ernst at the Humboldt Institute of Media Studies (Berlin), where old, if not obsolescent, forms of media are collected (c.f., Parikka 2011: 63, Figure 1), but only in order to be made operational again. As Ernst explains:

> Archaeology, as opposed to history, refers to what is actually there: what has remained from the past in the present like archaeological layers, operatively embedded in technologies ... 'Historic' media objects are radically present when they still function, even if their outside world has vanished. Their 'inner world' is still operative. Both classical archaeologists and media archaeologists are fascinated by the hardware of culture, its artifacts – from ancient marbles up to electromechanical engineering products. (Ernst 2011: 241)

In other words, the idea of the medium as object is again reinforced and with it – at least implicitly – the dominance of the principle of media specificity. Ernst, then, does not subscribe to a narrative history of media as represented by historical forms of media. In this vein, the media archaeologist writes: 'Rather than being a nostalgic collection of "dead media" of the past, assembled in a curiosity cabinet, media archaeology is an analytical tool, a method of analyzing and presenting aspects of media that would otherwise escape the discourse of cultural history' (2011: 240). Moreover, media for Ernst are not just objects,

---

10 Ernst defines Foucault's concept of the archive as 'the law of what can be said' (2016: 175). But also, in his effort to distinguish an archaeological from a traditional history approach – especially from the history of ideas approach – Foucault gives precedence not to the document as text to be interpreted, but as a material entity to be described (see Foucault 1974: 7). Similarly, discourse is for archaeology, 'not a sign of something else' (138), but something to be analysed 'in its own volume, as a *monument*' (138–9). It remains to be seen to what extent this also describes Ernst's approach.

but are equally subject, to the extent that 'the machine is the better media archaeologist of culture, better than any human' (2011: 245). The medium, then, is an entity in its own right, with its own characteristics: 'Media technology thus emerges from culture as an autonomous entity' (Ernst 2013: 137). On this basis, there is no denying that media archaeology is object focused (or subject focused, if one accepts Ernst's claim that the machine performs in the manner of a subject). Does this mean that media archaeology is medium specific? Is it the machine that determines the communicative outcome? In this light, the following statement by Ernst is pertinent: 'With a cool archaeological sense for signals (instead of semiotics, as in cultural semantics), the machine registers all kind [*sic*] of electromagnetic vibrations – and thus comes closer to the real world than any alphabet can' (Ernst 2011: 245). The idea that the vibrations in question come close 'to the real world' can be read as suggesting medium transparency. But Ernst oscillates (apparently not always with insight) between a position that presents the machine medium as transparent, and one where the machine *is* the message, as the following passage suggests: 'The noise, the scratch of the wax cylinder, is the pure message of the medium; in between, the human voice is literally incorporated' (250). Furthermore, although not referring to the machine, Ernst makes it clear that he tends to take up the cudgels for media specificity: 'The obsession with an unmediated representation of the past is itself a media effect; the apparent shift of emphasis in nineteenth-century historiography from describing to showing can be deciphered as an effect of the new optical media' (Ernst 2005: 592). Again – and more interestingly – 'With the emergence of photography, the idea of the theatrical gaze literally staging the past is displaced by the cold mechanical eye, a technologically neutral code rather than a subjective discourse' (592). The question is, does the 'neutral code' present reality? Or is it the message? Moreover 'The experience of an authentic existential link with the past through photographs is media-critically (if not ironically) undermined in current media art works on memory, such as Christian Boltanski's photographic installations' (592).

Here, photography is presented as being on the cusp of transparency, with Barthes on photography being clearly evoked:

Photography brings the past back to the memory not by means of some mnemic energy but through a physical event: rays of light which once emanated from a real object touch the viewer upon regarding the picture. Apart from any rhetoric of metonymy or synecdoche, the chemical essence of photography simply registers the physical trace of light beams which have illuminated the photographic plate. (593)

Then, it seems to be the case that media transparency is an illusion (implying that the truth is media opacity – that the message is the medium):

> Of course, no representation is ever un-mediated. Like the rhetorical *dissimulatio artis* in Ranke's historiography, which aims at the apparent self-expression of history, the technological media have to make their recipient forget their technical operation at the machine-to-human interface in order to create the *illusion* of pure content: only at a moment of technological breakdown will the medium become visible. (593; emphasis added)

'Technological breakdown' or course reminds us of Heidegger and the broken tool as present-at-hand. Indeed, Heidegger's presence is pervasive in Ernst's archaeology. But now we find that transparency becomes technologically true: 'The desire to achieve historical transparency in historiography is metaphorical, whereas in photography it becomes technologically true' (594). This could mean (and probably does) that the technological object 'speaks', and not something like reality as such. On the other hand, transparency as the task of the medium seems to be recognized here: 'the secret of technological media is precisely that they usually hide their mechanisms *in order to let the message appear in pure form* (on the cinema or television screen, for example)' (598; emphasis added).

But then, a final oscillation: 'Media irony (the awareness of the media as co-producers of cultural content, with the medium being evidently part of the message) is a technological modification of Hayden White's notion that "every discourse is always as much about discourse itself as it is about the objects that make up its subject matter"' (White 1978: 599).

In an earlier text, media specificity is confirmed thus: 'media of electronic transmission, whose message will have been the medium, not man' (Ernst 2002: 626). And, to reiterate, 'In the hissing we hear the medium itself' (630). Could there be a clearer declaration of media specificity? Again, 'The catastrophic, however, is what is closest to the medium itself, from the point of view of media archeology [*sic*]' (630). But we should note Ernst's reference to media and literary theorist, Samuel Weber, and the fact that it is now impossible to tell the difference between a live broadcast and its reproduction (633). Does this not mean that there is media transparency? With regard to television and other media, it is still the defects of transmission (the hiss, etc.) that, for Ernst, reveal the medium.

Overall, Ernst's media-archaeological approach shows that media supports are *in* time, while, as a medium, they become forms of temporalization. This can be difficult to negotiate when different modes of time are in play: for example, chronos (continuity), *kairos* (the right moment), instant/messianic time, the issue here being whether time is always embodied, technically as well as biologically.

What is of particular pertinence in Ernst is the question – already indicated – of whether the medium as such 'speaks', or whether, alternatively, the medium is the condition of possibility of all forms of communication. In the interest of developing a deeper understanding of the issues, if not of finding an answer to this question, Ernst's key text, *Chronopoetics* (2016), will be the focus of the following analysis.

Ernst's vision of time and technical media

After a detailed consideration of time-measuring media across the nineteenth and twentieth centuries, and effectively culminating with Heisenberg's insight into the uncertainty of measurement, Ernst says in summary that 'A theory of measuring media is thus always a also a theory of time' (2016: 5). And again 'Time is a crucial criterion for media theory, as it provides insight into the being of technical media' (63). In light of Ernst's survey of time-critical media instruments (e.g. in electronics and informatics), we are led to conclude that rather than being *in* time the medium of measurement is constitutive of time. In short, time does not exist outside its measurement or recording process. The measuring process goes far beyond unaided human consciousness and perception. Indeed 'Ultra-microscopic objects, like electrons and photons, can be described not as isolated objects, but only as time-critical events' (46). Thus 'time-critical analysis focuses on the genuine event-like nature of media' (3). Even at a more common-sense level, it is clear that a perception of time is inseparable from the measurement of time. At this point, my question is: are we to be satisfied with the conclusion that time is the time of the measuring instrument and not time as such? In other words, are we dealing with another version of media specificity? Is this how we should interpret the following statement: 'the discovery of time-critical moments as specific objects of knowledge *was a direct function of highly sensitive measuring media*' (2016: 38. Emphasis added). Here, the following arises: is time event based (cf. discrete images in cinema, or chronophotography) and thus susceptible to measurement; or does time become a series of discrete moments because this is what instruments can measure and record?

Bergson, as we know, and as Ernst acknowledges, was vehemently opposed to time as discrete moments in favour of time as duration. Although not agreeing with the notion of time as duration, Heidegger, too, opposed the idea of time as a series of discrete moments. In Ernst's media-based approach neither philosopher – nor philosophy in general – has an adequate grip on the nature of time. According to Ernst, the 'etymological core of "time" itself' is 'partitioning' (2016: 67).

Ernst's method as a concept of time

As has been noted, Ernst's media archaeological method must be distinguished from a media history approach. Whereas the latter relies on narrative for its viability, the former refers to the actual media objects that existed in time. Like orthodox archaeology, Ernst examines the physical media objects in the present that derive from the past. In light of Foucault's appropriation of archaeology, Ernst takes up the challenge of establishing 'the law of what can be said' as this applies to an understanding of media and time. Ernst's point of departure that 'technological media always take place in the temporal dimension, regardless of whether they are understood through epistemological reflection' (2016: 3). The alert philosopher is of course going to pose the question of the meaning Ernst gives to the nature of time. And the answer is that the notion of what time is emerges progressively from Ernst's conception of the ancient Greek term, *kairos*, as the 'right' or 'critical' time, a time that relates to the actual, timely or otherwise, operation of technological media. Overall, Ernst does not engage in an extended meditation on time as such, but there are significant references to *Being and Time*, especially with regard to the question of how an entity from the past can also be in the present, which implies that it is not entirely present or past. But for Ernst, care is necessary when thinking about media technology in a philosophical way (à la Heidegger) lest one fails to take into account 'the actual technical conditions of the apparatus' (2016: 149), something that an archaeological approach no doubt succeeds in doing better than other competing methods (such as phenomenology). Ernst makes the observation that 'The power of media is that their temporal process becomes imperceptible' (11), hence again the need to engage in an archaeological method that takes this into account and does not privilege consciousness, an insight that can be derived from the Heideggerian object as 'ready-to-hand', where technical tools, in their operation, 'never appear as such' (224). This is essentially the case because rather than being *in* time, technical media constitute time. Thus, we read that 'As an alternative to the discourse of history, technical media themselves *create* presence' (214). Such is the case because technical media exist only in their operation, not simply as objects whether past or present. Nothing is more important for Ernst's notion medium than this. It links up with the whole character of the media museum: the latter in Ernst's hands is a museum of *working* media from the past, not simply a storehouse of superseded objects.

A 'time-critical' approach to media thus focuses on the 'event-like nature of media', media in their functioning and operation. On this basis, we could say that all media – *qua* media – are live. This may be a key difference between Ernst's approach and that of Rosalind Krauss for whom the presence of a now obsolete media object seems to be sufficient to prompt a knowledge of its historical significance. Indeed, *metaxy* – already commented upon by Kittler – the Aristotelian term for 'middle', or 'in-between', is given a dynamic and thus temporal twist through being associated with delay (2016: 4). To think the time-critical character of technological media is to move away from a static, ontological approach towards a dynamic, temporal approach, something that is inherent in the media themselves and which affects media users. In photography and cinematography, the time-critical basis of image production is clear cut, while for other media this is less so.

Technological media, as we have observed, are to be understood in terms of their operation or performance. With the television image, for example, which

Ernst spends a good deal of time analysing, time is '*crucial* for the realization of the image, as the individual image lines must succeed one another so quickly that the entire image surface is recorded in fractions of a second' (2016: 128). This distinguishes the television image from the iconic, cinema film image. The latter, for its part, as is well known, is also time sensitive in that the film must be projected at twenty-four frames per second in order to create the impression of natural movement. Here, the debate with Bergson is resolved in favour of the movement of the still frames actually replicating time as differential and event-based, as opposed to the Bergsonian notion of duration. This is again captured conceptually by the notion of time as *Kairos*. *Kairos* also allows Ernst to claim that technological media create time: time does not pre-exist the medium in some ontological sense, but is the direct outcome of the operation of the medium. This puts Ernst's notion of time in direct opposition to the time of historical narrative, as well as to time understood semiotically and culturally.

Not only Bergson's notion of time is brought into question, but the whole notion of the 'now' – so scorned by Heidegger – and the moment are effectively rehabilitated within the frame of time as event-based and differential, the latter includes the notion of delay and thus evokes the Derridian neologism of '*différance*'. In being time-based, what technological measuring media enable is the confirmation of 'infinitesimally small temporal moments' (2016: 39). As a result, 'The anthropological narrative of time … comes to an end, and is replaced by the concept of the human as an ensemble of computable numbers' (39). On this basis, the chronophotography (movement of individual frames) of Étienne-Jules Mary and Edweard Muybridge takes on a new significance with regard to an understanding of time. Miniscule 'leaps' take place in what Ernst calls the 'discretization' of time, leaps that are required for the perception of movement. Instead of this being an illusion, it is now to be appreciated in terms of how time is.

What we have just remarked upon is based on the most intricate and complex aspect of the Ernst project, which is his consideration of the technical measuring of time, where time is 'generated', particularly in the domain of physics. (37–61). When it comes to measuring the 'smallest fractions of time', time 'below the perceptual threshold' (52), 'physics shifts from direct measurement to models' (52) because measurement in itself (in Heisenberg fashion) changes what is measured. Thus, if media theory is destined to invoke other disciplines, they would be mathematics and physics. This implies that the measuring device is as much time-based as the object of measurement. The issue of the relation of measuring media and what is measured is perhaps insightfully summarized by Ernst's reference to Goethe's statement that ' "If the eye were not sun-like, it would not see the sun" ' (57) – to which Ernst adds that 'it is also true of measuring media that they themselves have a time-critical sense, and in order to grasp the temporal beings (or modes) of nature they must be time media' (57). In short, the medium of measurement and the measured are united by time.

It should be noted in passing that the event, or discrete nature of the way time functions, also gives renewed scope to the phases of rhythm as instances of time. In this context, we note Ernst's observation in relation to the computer that 'The more complicated the algorithms, the more rhythmic they are' (80).

The clock of the computer makes it time-based, precisely in the sense that it coordinates changes in the computer itself. In light of the example of the computer, Ernst proposes that 'digital media are fundamentally time-critical, as the basis of binary signal processing – the flip-flop circuit – divides time and thus recalls the etymological core of "time" itself: partitioning' (67). On–off, 0–1, thus becomes emblematic of time as non-linear, another reason that Ernst's approach to time is at odds with time as narrative in written history, based as it is on the arrow of time. Let us remark here that the written history of events is driven by a desire to smooth over discontinuities in the interest of free flow of time based on cause and effect. On this basis the past is invoked to explain the present. Needless to say, Ernst's approach is removed from this.

Although more analysis is required, we might tentatively conclude that time as such is of the form presented – to cite Ernst's most important example – by the computer. Is time computer-like because time is always technologically – thus, medium – inflected, or is the computer the best vehicle for presenting time because time is essentially discrete, rhythmic, event-based? I leave an answer to this question in abeyance for the moment because I want to refer to another segment of Ernst's study, one that deals with recorded voices and the electronic ' "time image" '.

The medium as transparent?

In discussing the impact of experiencing the recorded voice, Ernst clearly comes down on the side of the transparency of the medium. With radio in the 1930s, the real voice of the speaker was brought into the home. In this regard, radio broadcasting, Ernst observes, 'creates the impression of real presence when nobody is actually present' (104). But it is in citing Samuel Beckett's play, *Krapp's Last Tape*, that clinches the point. For it is crucial that when Krapp listens to a recording of his voice from the past he, like the audience, will be convinced that it is really Krapp's voice that is heard, and not the noise of the medium. Krapp's last tape is, in short, transparent as far as the medium is concerned. Indeed, it is not too far-fetched to say the whole tenor of the approach adopted is to emphasize the essential transparency of recording in the recording process. Moreover, in keeping with his overall theme, Ernst notes that, with Krapp, two distinct times are in play: the time of the voice in the past and the time of listening in the present. The tape thus becomes time critical.

The point of transparency is also important from a museo-archaeological point of view, since with technological media being archived in their operative mode, it is the 're-enactment' of Edison singing into the phonograph, 'Mary Had a Little Lamb', that constitutes an archaeological, as opposed to a museum, approach to media. That we can hear Edison's voice today and that the phonograph is operational, is an indication that 'It is the essence of operative media that they only occur as media during their implementation and thus they not only exist *in time* but also consist *of time*' (210). Such would be the way that the medium always transcends its materiality.

With regard to the electronic 'time image', as manifest in television, not only is the image time based, as we have already indicated, but also the time of the 'live' programme and the time of its replication or reproduction become indistinguishable. In other words, there is no trace of the medium as such and only the 'content' that the medium makes available for consumption, so that the 'authorising information must be given outside the image' (150). In effect, the old sense that space is being traversed or condensed by the medium is deemed to be as nostalgic as 'technomathematics makes the traditional medial concept of the channel itself obsolete' (186).

Ernst's emphasis on the implementation and operational status of media is what ultimately makes the medium and time coalesce. As such, media as time would seem to become transparent. However, Ernst also speaks at various points in his trajectory as though he were intent on making time as such – thus the medium as such – explicit. Thus, after invoking Heidegger, on ' "unconcealment" (*aletheia*)' we read: 'Media archeology [*sic*] is an attempt to conceptualize this concealed temporal mode of technomathematics' (2016: 251). Is Ernst's effort therefore ultimately geared towards making time *qua* time – and thus the medium – entirely present to view? And is such an effort compatible with the notion of the medium as implementation? Such are the questions that remain to be pursued in a future reflection.

From Kittler and Ernst to Krauss's theory of the post-medium

As already noted, the key point about the medium made by Rosalind Krauss is that the obsolescence of the technical support can lead to the redemption of a specific medium like photography, which, Krauss claims, has now been superseded by digital technology. In this vein, Krauss writes that 'one must follow Benjamin's example by addressing particular instances in which the obsolescent could be said to have a redemptive role in relation to the very idea of the medium' (Krauss 1999a: 296). Clearly, such a position is at variance with that of Ernst, for whom 'old' media, if they are rendered perfectly functional, remain the media that they always were, regardless of the era.

In her 1997 essay on the artist James Coleman – an essay intended for a Coleman exhibition catalogue – Kraus introduces the issue of the medium while focusing more particularly on Coleman's aesthetic strategy (Krauss 1997). In making her case in the article, 'Reinventing the Medium' (1999a), Krauss repeats a point made in an earlier essay on Coleman, namely, his 'drive to invent a medium' (1997: 302)[11] with, amongst other formats, the

---

11 Krauss also says in the 1997 essay that 'Artists do not, of course, invent mediums. Carving, painting, drawing were all in full flower before there was any socially distinguishable group to call itself artists' (1997: 5).

now 'outmoded' technical support of the 'photo novel'. The 'photo novel' is an example of Barthes's 'third' or 'obtuse' meaning, a meaning that evokes Kristeva's notion of *'signifiance'*, a meaning that can be experienced but cannot be described. The film still, embodiment of the filmic for Barthes, is equated with the third meaning. The point, no doubt, is that the 'third meaning' corresponds to the medium: what does not appear but is the basis of appearance. It would be oversimplifying to say that the third meaning can be *created*; yet, this is what Coleman – at least as interpreted by Krauss – seems to be endeavouring to do. He seems to be creating a medium using old media, namely, the photo novel. Whereas the third meaning (as medium) is what cannot be described – as what disappears, in fact – Krauss sees it as her task (which is also the artist's) to make the medium visible, to present it, indeed, as something that *can* be experienced. The medium as physical support, as object, thus becomes confused with the medium as 'third meaning', as that which disappears.

In her essay on the post-medium – which features, amongst other things, the art of Marcel Broodthaers and Richard Serra – Krauss writes that 'in order to sustain artistic practice, a medium must be a supporting structure, generative of a set of conventions, some of which, in assuming the medium itself as their subject, will be wholly "specific" to it, thus producing an experience of their own necessity' (1999b: 26). Nevertheless, Krauss's main interest is the constitution and dissolution of 'medium-specificity'[12] – by which Krauss means 'intermedia'. The collector's object, Benjamin claimed, defies utility.

Broodthaers's focus on 'the filmic medium' in its origins prompts Krauss to point out what the artist saw therein – 'If the medium of primitive film resisted structural closure in this sense, it allowed Broodthaers to see what the structuralists did not: that the filmic apparatus presents us with a medium whose specificity is to be found in its condition as self/differing (1999b: 44). More than this, though, it is, we are told, the 'redemptive possibilities encoded at the birth of a given technical support' (46) that is most significant. 'Redemptive' evokes Benjamin's view that obsolescence might well provide a real insight

12 See, for example (1999b: 30, 32–3).

into the nature of the medium, one that is foreclosed when the medium is fully operational. Here, it is difficult not to see the medium as objectified, even if it is also 'self/differing'. In short, the medium becomes a kind of *presence*. Predictably, the question arising here is whether a non-operational medium is truly a medium. The answer already indicated in terms of Ernst's work is that a non-operational medium is not a medium.

On the other hand, in light of reproducibility (Benjamin), Krauss claims that art not only loses its 'aura', but also the specificity of its medium (46). However, this implies that the medium is equivalent to the materiality of the artwork and that this disappears when, through the mechanism of general equivalency, the artwork becomes a commodity. But if the medium enables the content of the artwork to appear (let us recall here Picasso's *Guernica*), then reproducibility does not result in the loss of the specificity of the medium. What would considerably complicate things in such a situation is if mechanical reproduction were also a medium – even an ideal medium. For, surely, reproduction *qua* reproduction disappears in the art object that is reproduced. In effect, an experience of *Guernica* reproduced can only be experienced via the content of the reproduced artwork. Perhaps, therefore, in reproducibility we have the clearest reaffirmation possible of the medium as that which does not appear. Krauss, however, fails to notice this.

Unlike other theorists of the medium (e.g. Wolf 2007), Krauss does, for the most part, endeavour to distinguish the medium from its physical support, as the following passage indicates: 'the specificity of mediums, even modernist ones, must be understood as differential, self/differing, and thus as a layering of conventions never simply collapsed into the physicality of their support' (1999b: 53). When the physical support is privileged in defining the medium, the result is a 'media-specific' view of the world.[13]

Despite this Krauss's turn of phrase lets her down at times – as is exemplified by the following passage on the artist Richard Serra, where medium is equated with a 'supporting structure': 'For, in order to sustain artistic practice, *a*

---

13 Ji-hoon Kim is thus mistaken when he writes that 'In a series of articles since the mid 1990s, the renowned art critic Rosalind Krauss has striven to maintain the *legitimacy of medium specificity* and of the notion of medium as such in order to individuate forms of artistic practice in the contemporary new media environment' (2009: 114; emphasis added).

medium must be a supporting structure, generative of a set of conventions, some of which, in assuming the medium itself as their subject, will be wholly 'specific' to it, thus producing an experience of their own necessity' (1999b: 26; emphasis added).

What makes things difficult for a thinker intent on doing justice to the subtlety of the notion of the medium is the field of aesthetics itself where different media invariably constitute the precondition of commentary and criticism. It would thus seem mandatory to refer to painting in general, to sculpture in general, to architecture in general and so on, even if, at the same time, the content of the artwork is also in focus. Would it be, then, that the field of aesthetics gives the lie to the non-appearing of the medium? Krauss ultimately seems to respond in the affirmative to this question. And all the more so given her notion of the illuminating, or 'redemptive', qualities of obsolescent media, since an obsolescent medium is surely, above all, a physical object.

In this regard, I would argue that the issue could at least be partially resolved by elaborating on the distinction Krauss signals between art in general and the specific artwork. Although Clement Greenberg might have tried to unite medium (flat canvas) and artwork, Krauss enables us to see that medium here only becomes (albeit in an illusory fashion) explicit when it is a question of the nature of art in general. When attention is turned to the specific work of art, content can then occupy the whole of the commentator's attention, as is surely the case with Picasso's *Guernica* already referred to. And it is with regard to content that the medium disappears.[14]

What, then, is the relation of a specific artwork to art in general? This is a question that also arises within Krauss's reflections on the medium. While conceptual art might be said to unite art and artwork, so that (theoretically) the content (an idea) of the artwork becomes art as such, it is more illuminating to follow Heidegger's lead and say that, just as Being cannot be reduced to *a* specific entity (Dasein), so art as such cannot be embodied in a specific work. Rather, while art appears in works of art, art in general is not reducible to a

---

14 We will see in Chapter 7 that Graham Harman with his Object-Oriented Ontology disputes the importance of content in art.

particular work of art. Conceptual art is thus misleading here. And so, like the medium, art as such appears only in disappearing (into the work of art).

In the end, Krauss's work enables us to appreciate the point just made without herself always following the same path.[15]

---

15 Thus Krauss says, apropos of Benjamin, that 'In becoming a theoretical object, photography loses its specificity as a medium' (1999a: 292). Moreover, 'Photography has, then, suddenly become one of those industrial discards, a newly established curio, like the jukebox or the trolley car' (296).

5

Michel Serres and communication as medium: Is it possible?

In Michel Serres's five-volume series entitled *Hermès*, the issue arising is whether a figure resembling the messenger of the gods actually appears. In other words, does the medium appear? What are we to make of this statement regarding the messenger? Serres thus writes 'As the bearer of the message, the messenger appears ... but he must also disappear, or write himself out of the picture, in order that the recipient hear the words of the person who sent the message, and not the messenger' (1995: 99). Sybille Krämer has alerted us to Serres's recognition that angels, as messengers, must also disappear (Krämer 2015: 60). Hence, the statement in the dialogue in Serres's book on angels that, just as '"the body and voice of the teacher disappears in relation to the text that he's expounding"' (1995: 102), so we can conclude that, in general, '"The body of the messenger appears or vanishes. The intermediary writes himself out of the picture. He must not present himself, or dazzle, or please ... or even appear.

"That's why we don't see angels"' (102).[1]

Ostensibly, therefore, Serres does not hold to a medium-specific view where the message *is* the medium. It remains, now, to follow up on the notion of the medium as disappearance as this plays out in Serres's Hermes series. Although in the latter, the medium is rarely explicitly thematized, there are numerous insights – such as abstraction as a means of transfer – that indirectly illuminate the nature of the medium. In fact, my aim will be to determine whether Serres's actual trajectory is in keeping with the medium as disappearance.

---

1 As a media theorist (who thus needs to objectify the medium), Timothy Barker, although citing Krämer, completely misses this point (see Barker 2021).

Hermes as the medium

In the first volume of the *Hermès* series, the notion of structure is presented as an instance of a formal method that, like modern mathematics, treats symbolic content as secondary: 'In a formal system it is not at all a matter of meaning; signifying content is never referred to either implicitly or explicitly' (1968: 31). Structure as a formal mechanism enables it to be transported into a wide range of different contexts. In fact, it could be said that Serres presents structure as a decontextualizing phenomenon.

By introducing structure as a strictly formal feature, Serres is able to transition to the theme of the abstract nature of modern mathematics in relation to communication. Formalism – the abstract – excludes 'noise' (the inexact, the empirical, the material), or, more generally, the third element ('le tiers exclu') in the dialogue. But unlike Plato and other formalists, Serres argues for the necessity of noise in the communication process. Thus, 'the act of eliminating the cacography [errors in a text], the attempt to eliminate noise is at the same time the *condition for the apprehension of an abstract form* and the *condition for the success of communication*' (1968: 43; emphasis in original). By drawing (imperfect) triangles and circles in the sand the passage to the ideal is realized. The material, empirical world, rather than being a permanent obstacle to the ideal (the abstract, the material world as the excluded third overcome), as Plato thought, is the necessary way to the ideal. Idealization, formalization, abstraction, while being the result of a dematerialization, are nevertheless indebted to the material world. Or another way of putting it in terms related to this study is to say that the material becomes the medium of the ideal. In short, the material disappears in the emergence of the ideal. Whereas Régis Debray's 'mediological' and ultimately conventional materialist approach views transmission (of ideas, of the exegesis of sacred texts, etc.) as inseparable from its material incarnation (Debray 2000: 2), Serres shows that transmission occurs through the, as it were, *overcoming* of the material dimension – of the excluded third. In effect, successful communication is all about '*rendering a form independent of its empirical realisations*' (1968: 44; emphasis in original). The fact that noise, or the empirical, needs to be overcome does not mean that it cannot be productive. Indeed, as chance effects, noise can be the basis of new forms, whether in mathematics or philosophy.

Mathematical truths, Serres proclaims, are given once and for all. The history of mathematics is thus not cumulative, linear or continuous. Historians of a conventional stamp, for whom history is cumulative, thus have difficulty coming to terms with the history of mathematics. Mathematical 'language' is univocal, transparent and immediate in its impact.[2] Even though mathematics might well be formed out of a certain background of 'noise', there is no noise – in principle, no opacity or impurity – in mathematics.[3] Moreover, mathematics communicates universally, or not all (96). There is no 'local' mathematics that would then have to be translated into other local idioms. In this regard, to the extent that Meno, in Plato's dialogue, 'recalls' mathematical truths, these are true universally, so that Meno, mathematically speaking, far from remaining a local Greek slave, becomes a figure of universal significance. We should rather say, no doubt, that Meno becomes a *medium* of universal significance.[4]

Interference

When he comes to consider the sciences (including mathematics), Serres finds not only that it is a matter of the relations between the sciences, but also that one science blurs into – or 'interferes' with – another science. The encyclopaedia, rather than the dictionary, is the figure for the totality of sciences. Each science has 'multiple liaisons' with other sciences, and other sciences link up with it (1972: 62): 'The fact of unity', Serres explains, 'resides in a complex game of referred and referrer (référé et du référant), that [Serres] would name, as it were, interference' (62). In this regard, 'The notion of interference has the advantage of including at a single stroke the play of relations that open up the regions to each other' (63). As one of number of examples that Serres offers, we find that 'astrophysics is a region based in part on optics, on electricity, on thermodynamics, none of which is a simple region in itself' (65). And, Serres, the traveller, elaborates: 'I can travel from crossroad to crossroad in the labyrinth, from interchange to interchange, but I cannot grasp the totality of

---

2 Compare with 'mathematics furnishes the example of an almost perfect communication, of univocal information in its emission and reception' (Serres 1968: 95).
3 See Serres (1968: 90–6).
4 Some of these points have recently been elaborated upon by Thomas Sutherland (2021), but not with an emphasis on the medium.

the journey in a static map. In the place of interferences, I lack a reference to the global: it is essential that I am deprived of it' (65).

Playing on the notion of interference in French as 'conjunction', our author proposes that 'interférence' is 'inter-reference' (157) – that is, interconnection and translation and not just intrusion or disruption.

Here, the focus is very much on the prefix 'inter-', meaning 'between' two or more entities. Hence, the importance of *inter*ference, *inter*actions, *inter*mediaries (Serres 1974: 51), as well as *inter*disciplinarity – 'The astrophysical revolution, as important as the formalist one, has two results: it opens up new spaces and new times; it also opens up the sciences to each other and brings about the triumph of interdisciplinarity' (1974: 167).

Translation

'To translate' means that one set of terms, or entities, and another set are deemed to be equivalent. This is the principle that Serres investigates in *La Traduction* (Translation) in the context of four categories: sciences, philosophy, painting and the Earth.

In the history of science, three elements of method can be enumerated – elements that give rise to outcomes and thus can be considered equivalent to a medium: deduction (as in logic and mathematics); induction (as in experimental science) and production (as in practical domains). Clearly, common to each of these domains in both French and English is the suffix 'duction', evoking 'leading' or 'bringing' – as in 'duct'. '*Translation* ('Traduction'): the history of genetics – respectively, the history of sciences in general' (1974: 16). What changes in history with regard to life runs parallel with what changes in science as the logic of life. The foregoing gives rise to a 'tree of knowledge' or of 'knowing' (*connaissance*), where the issue turns around the appearance of continuity or discontinuity (detour).

Serres engages in a reading of François Jacob's *La Logique du vivant – Une histoire de l'hérédité* (1970). Here, let it be recalled (following Krämer as outlined in Chapter 3) that as the *messenger* of the gods, Hermes does not appear. Serres is thus justified in not making the messenger the object of his discursive perambulations.

In light of the foregoing, we can surmise that to engage with Jacob on life is also to engage with the history of science. In part, how the human body and genetics in biology are understood follows from both nineteenth-century thermodynamics, where entropy equals the breakdown of order and the twentieth-century theory of information, as pioneered by Léon Brillouin, where the possibility exists for a certain negantropy, or increase in the amount of information and thus of order.[5] Entropy is incarnate in the irreversibility of time compared to the Newtonian and mechanical notion of reversible time. Biology, then, can be further translated into a hidden structure of phenotype and genotype. The hidden part of genetics is discovered via certain 'characters': figures (chiffres), letters, signs, an element of a code. In effect, the history of genetics consists in passing from the reproduction of animals to the reproduction of a text. Reproduction and its significance is *translated* into a text (Serres 1974: 20).

Genetics further raises the issue of a 'pro-gramme' and the universality of the code. The figure most in play is the topological form of the tree – the genealogical tree (23). Metaphorically, '*Genesis* begins, it is true, in a garden of plants' (23). Darwin is at the pinnacle of the arborescent cone (24). Biology becomes 'protean' in that its arborescent structure is susceptible to appearing in multiple contexts. In Serres's book, *Genesis*, Proteus is an array of 'intermediary states' (*Genesis* 2002: 15). Proteus never appears as such but disappears into one of his states. Proteus, then, exemplifies translation.

In the history of heredity[6] as the reproduction of generations ('*reproduction du semblable par le semblable*'),'the interlocking (l'emboîtement) of germs [of one germ within another] is the translation, in another language, of the iteration of homothetic forms in a given space' (1974: 35). Serres's thesis is that 'the form of interlocking is a projection, a way of designating a tree' (37).

Hermes is everywhere in the informational network, the latter being a battle against disorder. Hermes is there to distribute messages. There is no longer any primary 'station', no centre or hierarchy: 'the cone or pyramid are at an end' (40). Negantropy enters the picture: 'Thus order re-emerges in the

---

5 The exact extent to which information can also exemplify negantropy is contested, most notably by Brillouin himself. The key debate has consisted in differing interpretations of 'Maxwell's demon' and the possibility of overcoming entropy (disorder). For a key discussion, see Brillouin (2013: 162–71).

6 This history will not be treated in detail here, the focus being on Serres's approach to translation and the notion of medium in relation to Jacob's text, and, subsequently, in relation to Jacques Monod on chance and necessity. The latter introduces in more detail the question of information theory and negantropy.

order of more or less complex systems and networks' (40). Cybernetics and the mathematical theory of information emerge in the twentieth century along with the notion – according to Serres – that 'contemporary knowledge, in its totality, *is* a theory of communication (41). Translation is tied to the history of texts: 'There is only one history and only one science' (41). Such a view presupposes that there is no translation without a translator as the figure who does not appear – a figure who is the medium.

Life and Information: on Monod and Chance

Whether one agrees or disagrees with Serres's form of ontology, the medium nonetheless appears. Thus, we are told that for the philosopher – 'shepherd of multiplicities' (Serres 2002: 23) – the multiplicity of the possible (e.g. the multiplicity of times) is also '*intermediary* between the phenomena' (2002: 23–4; emphasis added). Given that negantropy is the emergence of order – of life – out of chaos, the genome (genesis and order) is the secret code of phenomena (1974: 47). Entropy, by contrast, leads to death (47).

For his part, French biochemist and Nobel laureate Jacques Monod[7] activates the logic of '*inter*ference: *inter*actions, *inter*mediaries' (51). He raises the notion of communication to a new level: 'Here is a complete network of circulations: messages and code, translation and transduction, mediators and transfers, executions and cancelations, feed-backs and enslavements, responses to threshold effects, transitions, direct and indirect circuits, homeostasis and omnipossibility, self-regulation, writing and reading, etc.' (51).

Notable here is that translation (traduction) evokes – or even becomes – 'transduction'. But translation, we will say, is one thing becoming manifest in another, or quite simply becoming another. Translation and code thus go together, given that a code is what becomes manifest in an arrangement that is other than the code: letters, numbers, signs – that is, in diverse media. Recalling the function of RNA in genetics, Serres states that 'Hermes is the god of biochemists, who know better than others, … what a messenger is' (51). Thus, ' "life" is communication' (51).

---

7 Jacques Monod (1910–1976) shared the 1965 Nobel prize with François Jacob and André Lwoff for discoveries in genetics.

With Monod, chance and necessity[8] are translated into 'islets of negentropy' (61): 'When there exists a chain, a tree or a network, a code and a translation are needed' in relation to the identity of the code and chance (hazard) (63). Chance opens up – interpolating Serres – translation. Chance (disorder) is translated into order. Clouds as chaos, as stochastic phenomena, give rise to order – to the face that I can see in the cloud. 'Chance', Serres remarks, 'is not something and it has no dimensions, just like heat and information' (66). Again, 'chance is number, the play of numbers' (66). Chance also appears in the code. Serres asks, 'What is an object in general?' And he answers, 'A message as a cloud plus transportation over the interlaced networks of communication' and 'Hermes only sends a cloud of figures' (67). It is disorder to be translated into order. But is there a translator here? Not necessarily. For what is evoked is something akin to 'natural' processes: transformations for which chemical reactions would be the model.

With Leibniz, the focus is on 'system'. Leibniz shows that 'everything is deducible from a small number of definitions' (Serres 115). The main figure/concept Leibniz invokes is *mathesis*. Thus, the individual, for Leibniz, is translated 'immediately' as '*mathesis*' (128). Consequently, the world is written in mathematical terms (137). To be noted is the fact that the original meaning of *mathesis* is 'science, learning, especially mathematics'. Leibniz's arithmetic triangle raises the issue of number in relation to translation. Monads are the simplest elements. Every text 'is a monodology' (136). Finally, Leibniz searches for another word that would translate the notion of the biblical *Genesis*. He finds it in the term, 'origin' (137).

Things emerge stochastically – by chance: 'The foundation of being is aleatory and combinatory' (148). In other words, being is translated as aleatory – as non-determined, as disorder. Let us deduce from this that for Leibniz, the believer, God is the translator. Thus, mathematics must bring order to the world – must translate disorder as a certain mode of order. As a result, 'science in its entirety is everywhere in the entirety of the world. The order of science is the order of the world' (151). Furthermore, 'The order engendering the sciences is parallel to the order engendering things themselves' (151). As such, science, in its transparency, becomes a perfect medium of the world.

---

8 The title of Monod's best-known and much discussed book is: *Chance and Necessity* (1972).

Again, 'History and prehistory of beings is isomorphic with the history and prehistory of forms of knowledge' (151).

Turner Translates Carnot – Or: Painting Translates Mechanics and Thermodynamics

When considering how principles in the history of science are, for Serres, translated into art, the following passage contributes to setting the scene:

> At stake here is a tableau, in the sense of 'tabulation'. The point is to lay out the set of tools and to omit nothing, to tabulate all the products of mechanics, static and dynamic: from the framework to the derricks, from the wheel to the sail. All this makes a world, a world that is drawn, drawable. It is a world in which chains trace motion (the ropes and hawsers) and in which arms and masts trace rest (the truss and the axles). Lines, points, circles-geometry. (1982a: 55)

George Garrard (1760–1826), whose works Serres is describing, the painter/tabulator of the 'products of mechanics' through, in particular, the use of lines and points – through the use of drawing, in short – can be compared with the works of J. M. W. Turner (1775–1851).[9] With Turner there is a change from a world dominated by Newtonian mechanics to one where thermodynamics is in the ascendency. It is the path, as Serres explains, that runs from Joseph-Lagrange (1738–1813) and his treatise on mechanics to Sadi Carnot (1796–1832) and the emergence of thermodynamics. Or, we move from wind and water to fire and the forge. Thus Turner

> enters into the boiler, the furnace, the firebox. He sees matter transformed by fire. This is the new matter of the world at work, where geometry is limited. Everything is overturned. Matter and color triumph over line, geometry, and form. No, Turner is not a pre-impressionist. He is a realist, a proper realist. He makes one see matter in 1844, as Garrard made one see forms and forces in 1784. And he is the first to see it, the very first. No one had really perceived it before, neither scientist nor philosopher, and Carnot had not yet

9 The works of Garrand and Turner are not the only artists to have captured the attention of Serres. One can note, for example, the discussions of Poussin and Vermeer in *La Traduction* (1974: 189–202) and of Georges de la Tour, who 'translates Pascal' (203–31). My focus, however, is on Turner, as this links in more clearly the theme of thermodynamics and translation.

been read. Who understood it? Those who worked with fire and Turner – Turner or the introduction of fiery matter into culture. The first true genius in thermodynamics. (1982a: 57)

Turner paints rain, hail, snow and fog. He paints 'disorder' and chance effects – the entropy of thermodynamics and the Industrial Revolution to which it gave rise. Even though Serres seems subsequently to revise his theory of Turner's relation to the Industrial Revolution,[10] it is still a matter here of translation: of painting as the translation of scientifically based principles. Thus, two contrasting styles of painting 'translate' two different scientific principles: mechanics on the one hand (Garrard) and thermodynamics (Turner) on the other.

There is, perhaps, a double translation at play. In the first place, scientific principles are translated into the medium of painting, and then paintings translate the specific principles in question. For this reason, Mike Shortland's translation[11] (another meaning of 'translation') of Serres's essay in the art journal, *Block* (1982b) adds weight to the argument being mounted as it includes visual images of key paintings described by Serres. With regard to the aforementioned text, reproduction now exists three times over, as the accompanying visuals are themselves translations (reproductions) of the paintings referred to by Serres. These reproductions thus translate scientific principles. A media-specific approach, however, would propose that it is a painterly view of things that emerges, not scientific principles.

If we reconsider the medium in relation to Turner's entropic paintings, we become immersed in the question of how it is possible to understand Turner's *relatively* ordered presentation of disorder. Perhaps, as will be mentioned later in the text, Paul Klee provides a clue here.

Distribution

'Quantitatively' speaking, Serres registers the predominance of disorder compared to order. As he repeats in *La Distribution*, 'What exists, and it is a tautology, is the probable. Now the most probable is disorder' (1977: 10).

10 See Serres (1997).
11 I will refer to the more accessible translation of Serres's essay by Marilyn Sides (1982a).

And what is disorder? A distribution is disorder, as Serres later specifies in *Hermès V: Le Passage du nord-ouest* (1980: 101). But also, the universe is in disorder. Disorder is, furthermore, exemplified by 'clouds or the sea, storms and noise, a mixture and crowds, chaos and tumult. The real is not rational' (1977: 10) and 'disorder precedes order' (37). Mythically, as in Plato's *Timaeus*, the *khora* exemplifies disorder (61). It is the (primitive) appearing of disorder being prior to 'nomination and form' (61). If we equate the rational with order, it is said that 'the rational is a rare island' (11) in a sea of disorder. The latter constitutes the 'beginning' of everything. It is also a 'distribution. Of atoms, of points, or of everything no matter what. Disorder, noise, rags, fairs, crowds, moors in pieces, decompositions or mixtures, ovens, chaos, black boxes open or closed, storms, the undifferentiateable and uproar' (13). At the beginning are distributions analogous to a throw of the dice or the deal of cards. Distributions are therefore aleatory.

In his preface to *La Distribution*, Serres says that he now regrets the use of the term, distribution, firstly, because it hints too much of order, and, secondly, because Hermes is not a postman. He does not distribute, nor does he share or divide messages. 'He does not even bear messages. He is the deal itself' (14) Indeed, the message is not an instance of order. Rather it is 'chaotic, a cloud of letters' (14).

Chaos

At the beginning of his *The Thinking Eye* notebook, in a section entitled 'Towards a Theory of Form Production', Paul Klee points out that true chaos can never be put on a scale (Klee 1973: 2–3).[12] If, for Serres, existence begins in a cloud – let it be defined as disorder – what are the possible implications for the notion of medium? Perhaps only an astrophysicist or a mathematician can answer this question. The neophyte might say that the fact that disorder,

12 As Katherine Hayles indicates in the introduction to her edited book, *Chaos and Disorder* (1991), there is a difference between the scientific and colloquial meaning of chaos. Whereas, traditionally, 'disorder was allied with chaos', now, chaos is 'conceptualized as extremely complex information rather than an absence of order' (1991: 1). The science of 'chaos' has discovered that 'hidden within the unpredictability of chaotic systems are deep structures of order' (1). Even though a section of *La Distribution* is entitled 'Chaos', Serres refers more frequently to disorder than to 'chaos'. To be recalled, however, is the fact that the science of chaos turns out to be the science of ultimate order, not ultimate disorder.

entropy and death exist – just as a cloud or chance in general exists – is paradoxical if to exist is to exhibit some sort of order.

In her commentary on Serres's work, the theorist of AI and information, N. Katherine Hayles, points to a possible error in the foregoing by saying that

> In physics its epicenter is the emerging interdisciplinary research front known as the science of chaos; in mathematics, fractal geometry; in literary theory, deconstruction. Although these projects are all very different, they share the belief that chaos is not simply the opposite of order, but its precursor, partner, and (for deconstruction) supplanter. From this changed perception of the relation between order and disorder flow multiple implications. The most important for Serres's project derives from formal results within information theory that demonstrated noise in a communication channel need not destructively interfere with the message, but rather could become part of the message. (1988: 3)

By following Hayles, we can begin to understand how it is possible that complex, chaotic systems can exhibit a form of 'order'. In effect, disorder gives rise to a certain mode of order. The notion that there is order in disorder ceases to be paradoxical. As orderly systems are always subject to chance effects, they become unpredictable, that is, they become chaotic or disorderly. On the other hand, what might first appear as disorder can, as in fractal science, emerge as perfectly orderly: the structure of a snowflake is one, now famous, example.

In referring to Kant's cosmogony – which deals with the origin of the universe – Serres notes that the 'original *distribution* is a dissemination, a dispersion of atomic elements in the manner of Democritean chaos' (1977: 117; emphasis in original). Indeed, it is difficult not to see in Serres's approach a reiteration of the (classical) movement from chaos or disorder to order. Here, a distribution is not cloud-like because it has the features of a system, features that are to a certain extent predictable (122). For Kant, however, God is the medium that does not appear as such. Only the order of the world appears. Not that this is referred to by Serres. For him, Nietzsche's 'Eternal Return' is cosmological: it is concerned with the nature of the universe as it is now as well as its origin. Eternal Return, it is implied, becomes the medium par excellence in the era of the Enlightenment because the focus is on time and its impact on the world. The system does not produce time, but is produced by time (116). Distribution (the unpredictable outcomes of an event) becomes system, then breaks down again into a phase of distribution. This is the basis of 'the Eternal Return' for Serres, which is 'the operator, and motor of the expansion' (123). This 'Eternal Return' is hardly that of Nietzsche, for whom it is a question of what returns exactly eternally; rather, what is eternal is the movement from disorder to order, then back to disorder. Indeed, as one says, the universe is chaotic. As Serres proclaims, if there is a 'Return', it is cosmogonal (to go with actual movement of planets and stars) rather than cosmological (to do with a vision of the world). This issue of entropy only features in cosmogony; cosmology, by contrast, is negontropic. The latter, for Serres, characterizes Nietzsche's thinking in the Eternal Return and thus renders such thinking closer to that of eighteenth-century mechanics than nineteenth-century thermodynamics. On this basis, we are led to consider that Kant's 1755 text on cosmogony might be closer to being a medium for thermodynamics than is to Nietzsche's thought.[13]

In light of the foregoing, it is clear that, for Serres, the key chapter of Kant's *Cosmogony* (1900) is the one dealing with an expanding universe because 'creation is not work of one moment' (1900: 145). Such a universe has a universal centre of attraction, or fixed point, in relation to which creation takes place. As God is the author of creation, the process is necessarily infinite because God is omnipotent. Not only are there millions of stars in the Milky Way, but there are, Kant proposes, probably many Milky Ways. 'Creation is never finished or complete' (145), he says, and it has a Phoenix-like structure (154). Worlds come into being, then gradually die and new worlds are born. It is this phoenix structure that Serres translates into the principle of the Eternal Return.

As Serres presents it the notion of the Eternal Return (is it the return of the same or of difference?) does not address the primary element in Kant's treatise, namely, the fact that the plurality of worlds is evidence of God's existence. Worlds, for Kant, thus become a *medium* allowing God's omnipresence to reveal itself. Unlike Newton, for whom the universe was fixed once and for

---

13 This, to be sure, is a controversial point to make in light of the literature on Nietzsche's Eternal Return (for an overview, see Loeb 2013) and even on the relation between Serres and Nietzsche. Large (1997 and 1999) argues, for instance, that the Eternal Return is in no sense a 'vision of the world', as Serres proposes (1977: 115), or a cosmology, or a *Weltanschauung*. Indeed, it is, at best, says Large, 'a provisional hypothesis' (1997: 38). But the nature of a hypothesis (e.g. whether or not it makes provision for entropy) can still be addressed.

all, Kant foreshadows thermodynamics and irreversible time along with the notion of an expanding universe[14] now seen to be evidence that the Big Bang really happened. And so, instead of God being at the origin, we have the Big Bang, for which the universe is the medium.

Serres treats Nietzsche's texts as a 'chemistry of sensations and ideas'. Thus, the organizational principle is chemical, whereas it is claimed that, for Marx, the principle is a 'mechanics', while for Freud it is a 'physics' (1977: 190). The chemical metaphor, as it were, is also seen to be working in *The Anti-Christ*, now viewed as a discourse against corruption, illness and epidemics transmitted by viruses. It becomes a matter of 'circulation': 'Nothing other than circulation. Nothing other than the object of circulation' (187).

The virus[15] – 'the virus of decadence, the virus of decomposition' (187) – must be 'hunted down'. 'Decomposition and decadence' are the enemies, and both are hastened by Christianity (although Serres says that *The Anti-Christ* is not an antireligious treatise (189)). It is well known that Nietzsche believed that war must be waged against Christianity. Repugnance for what is unclean; 'hatred of the impure' – such also is the mark of European Fascism (189). But Nietzsche refers as well to the harmfulness of 'sympathy for the ill-constituted and weak' (Nietzsche 1974a: 116). The weak are those who lack an instinct for power and who experience life as a kind of sickness. In an effort to prove that Nietzsche's references to viruses, impurity, the unclean and so on foreshadow Pasteur's work (Pasteur was a chemist and microbiologist), Serres neglects to acknowledge that Nietzsche despised those for whom Pasteur's work was destined to help, namely, 'the ill-constituted and the weak'. As is well known, through vaccines, Pasteur's work became a medium of salvation of the ill constituted, those susceptible to disease.

Nietzsche's invocation of chemistry has not gone unnoticed (see Large 2016). And in *Human All Too Human* (1989), Nietzsche refers to 'a *chemistry* of the moral, religious and aesthetic conceptions and sensations, likewise of all the agitations we experience within ourselves in cultural and social intercourse and indeed even when we are alone: what if this chemistry would end up by

---

14 This is mentioned by Serres along with the 'big bang' (see 1977: 120).
15 On viruses and infection as forms of transmission, recall Krämer (2015: 96–105).

revealing that in this domain too the most glorious colours are derived from base, indeed from despised materials?' (12).

What is the import of the chemical metaphor? In this regard, thermodynamics is not excluded. We have, then, 'Two chemically opposed conditions; either mixture or separation. Two thermodynamic conditions: either a lowering of force [puissance] or its elevation; either a devaluation or a trans-valuation; either decadence or transmutation' (Serres 1977: 191).

For Nietzsche, says Serres, infection 'poisons the world' (192). Infection becomes equivalent of theology spreading to philosophy, of Christianity spreading to the furthest reaches of Western culture. Theology is also parasitical (thus, of the 'third') as it is borne along by philosophy and thought more generally.

What passes without comment in Serres's reading of Nietzsche is the way that Christianity is a medium for the dissemination of a certain morality, one that is opposed to 'life'. Even though it would seem that Christianity as such is the *object* of Nietzsche's ire, it is in fact the content of Christian beliefs that is at issue. Or, to put it differently, Christian morality claims, according to Nietzsche, to be morality as such, whereas it is only one version of morality. Morality, then, is the medium through which Christianity is articulated rather than Christianity being the medium through which morality is articulated.[16] And, of course, it is the modality of the medium that is of key importance here as far as this study is concerned.

Myth, literature and science

Myth – and especially the myth of a journey, or 'circumnavigation' (Odysseus/Ulysses) – is, if we accept Serres's presentation, not just the forerunner of science, but also the means by which the themes and problems of science first make their appearance. Thus, chaos and order, the expressible and the inexpressible, space and the void, reason and the irrational first become visible through myth.

16 As Nietzsche specifies in *Beyond Good and Evil* (1974b), morality in Europe is 'herd-animal morality' (section 202, 106) – read: is Christian. Further, 'this morality defends itself with all might: it says, obstinately and stubbornly, "I am morality itself, and nothing is morality besides me!"' (106–7). Even more specifically, it is as though 'the morality of *mutual pity*' – central Christian tenet – 'were morality itself' (107).

In the Oedipus myth, the crossroads as 'bifurcation' become the first intimation of geometry. The Odyssey and the image of the weaver (Penelope) bring things together, evoking a bridge between things, and providing a foretaste of geometry as place, as topology. With regard to the latter, it is again through Plato's *khora* that 'we recognise a topological space, the Same and the Other, separated, are rejoined by the Demiurge in the figure of chi' [X] (Serres 1977: 205). The crossroads, so decisive in for Oedipus because he unknowingly kills his father there, serves to highlight a topological figure: the crossroad is also a point of bifurcation – a topological figure being one that can transform – or be transformed – into something else without any change in the materials involved.

Myth, then, is not opaque. Indeed, the myth as such is transparent and is thus a medium that facilitates knowing. And so, mythic discourse need not be separated from scientific discourse. It is a matter of accepting that one flows into the other. Indeed, 'The best contemporary myth is the idea of science purged of all myth' (Serres 1998: 128). Literature, similarly, ceases in Serres's hands to be an object in its own right and becomes a medium. Philosophy then can learn from science just as science can learn from philosophy. The medium is, therefore, the condition of interdisciplinarity. It is the basis on which Serres voyages between the past of science and its present, between art (Turner) and science (thermodynamics), between natural and social science. Reference to the medium – reference to Hermes – means that no continent of knowledge or experience can remain closed in upon itself. There is, in effect, no fixed source for ideas, knowledge, insights and inspiration.

In his quest to show that fictional writing is multifaceted, Serres engages with the work of the influential nineteenth-century writer and critic, Jules Barbey (1808–1889). Barbey's fiction is set in Normandy, and evokes historical events (such as the 'war of the Chouans'[17]). Indeed, the point made is that fiction often encapsulates a dynamism that is lacking in conventional historical writing. Given the topological relation between 'discours et parcours' (discourse and journey), if time is change historical writing should change with it.

For the rest, Serres finds numerous illustrations in Barbey's writing of the relation between order and disorder, reversible time and irreversible time, noise

---

17 Chouans were peasant band members that, in 1793, rose in revolt against the Republican government and in support of a restored monarchy.

and message, between metaphor, which 'is reversible', and metonymy, which 'is not' (1977: 253). A constant figure throughout Serres's analysis of Barbey's stories is the windmill (le Moulin). Topologically, the windmill is a clock and a clock is a windmill (213). The windmill is also a metaphor, and is therefore reversible. Fiction poses questions that should be asked by historians – about the nature of time, for example (233). Finally, 'the time of narrative (récit) is the time of the world' (253).

Mathematics is time neutral. The time of mechanics is reversible, and that of thermodynamics is irreversible. This is the significance of entropy. With information comes negentropy, the opposite of entropy. But the background of information is noise, that is, disorder. We have seen that Serres's wager is that each of these spheres can be found exemplified in a range of different contexts, contexts that are undetermined by time or space. This is the sense in which Hermes plays his part as medium. Consequently, Epicurus and Lucretius are as relevant today for science and literature as they were in former times. In short, with Hermes as medium, the 'arrow of time' is no longer operational.

'Two cultures': *Le Passage du nord-ouest*

The notions of order and disorder – and thus of mechanics and thermodynamics – also feature in *Hermès V: Le Passage du nord-ouest* (1980). Here, Hermes takes us to Descartes and to Balzac and to Musil's *Man Without Qualities*. Serres refers to Musil's description of the weather in the opening paragraph:

> There was a depression over the Atlantic. It was travelling eastwards, towards an area of high pressure over Russia, and still showed no tendency to move northwards around it. The isotherms and isotheres were fulfilling their functions. The atmospheric temperature was in proper relation to the average annual temperature, the temperature of the coldest as well as of the hottest month, and the a-periodic monthly variation in temperature. The rising and setting of the sun and of the moon, the phases of the moon, Venus and Saturn's rings, and many other important phenomena, were in accordance with the forecasts in the astronomical yearbooks. The vapour in the air was at its highest tension, and the moisture in the air was at its lowest. In short, to use an expression that describes the facts pretty satisfactorily,

even though it is somewhat old-fashioned: it was a fine August day in the year 1913. (Musil 1982: 3)

For Serres, the north-west passage is the straight between literature and the exact sciences. Musil's novel perhaps shows the way. It is open-ended, ready to receive new information. It does not consist of closed, self-contained narrative, or intrigue. Thus, rather than being modelled on mechanics, where time is reversible, the text more closely resembles an event in thermodynamics where time is irreversible. All this, even though the main character, Ulrich (like Musil himself), 'abandons the sciences'. Here, it is not only a matter of what the novel *says*, but also one of what it objectively *is*. Or better, what it says connects with what it objectively is.

A road accident is described early in the novel. Serres refers to this 'local' occurrence of chance in the manner of Lucretius's 'clinamen' (1980: 57). The issue of the relation between the local and the global emerges. Indeed, through the novel, we learn about scientific issues, which enable Serres to refer here to an instance of the north-west passage (59). The road accident in the novel then is the incidence of disorder that will give rise to a re-establishment of order. But then again, the question is, 'How is the border between order and disorder to be established?' (57). Moreover, are we dealing with 'a road accident or a collective crime? Can this be determined?' (57). What is certain is that someone died, this death being, says Serres, 'the point where disorder becomes order' (58).

Similarly, how can the passage between the exact and the human sciences be established? And what relation does this question have to the actual north-west passage sea route between the Atlantic and Pacific oceans, a passage that was finally established by Roald Amundsen in the early twentieth century? Perhaps, as some have said, the difficulty of establishing the actual passage in question is analogous to the difficulty of finding a way that connects the exact and the human sciences. What we could expect from Serres's perspective at least is that the human sciences including literature might have played a role in finding the original passage, while the exact sciences would offer insight into literary forms. The coastline along the north-west passage, when subjected to fractal analysis, becomes infinite. In effect exact borders are difficult, if not impossible, to establish. A cloud's borders, similarly, are difficult to establish.

Any attempt will turn out to be an approximation. The inexactness here is pervasive. Predicting the weather is of the same order of inexactness. Thus, the opening of Musil's text describing the weather of the day brings together the exact and the inexact sciences.

A description of initial conditions can never be absolutely exact. Therefore, prediction (e.g. meteorological) can never be exact. Inexactness is not then only a feature of the inexact sciences, but also exists in the so-called exact sciences. Musil's meteorological description at the beginning of *The Man Without Qualities* would constitute initial conditions in relation to which the future cannot be foretold exactly. Norbert Wiener also begins his (scientific) work in cybernetics with a discussion of clouds and the question of the possibility or otherwise of meteorological prediction. Regarding the latter, Serres (1980: 36) cites the following: '"Boston: January 17, 1950: Sky 38% overcast: Cirrocumulus."' (Wiener 1961: 31).

For his part, Balzac describes Paris, globally, as a large steam engine ('it is the era of Carnot' (Serres 1980: 54)), while Musil describes the 'Vienna-hothouse' locally (54), and thus in terms of 'complicated, turbulent and numerous events' ('It is the era of Boltzmann and Gibbs' (54)). What is more, 'Musil, like Boltzmann, following Turner, enters the boiler (chaudière): his machine is aleatory. Here and there order and rhythm begin to form, and from this normal pulse something ensues' (54). Thus, the writing of both Balzac and Musil is an incarnation of aspects of the science of their day. Order and disorder in Musil derive from a focus that is local in orientation. Indeed, it is from a local perspective that order and disorder become amplified.

The north-west passage is a combination of imagination and harsh reality. Imagination played a role in speculating that a north-west passage was a possibility. The harsh reality was that few vessels or commanders (including James Cook) were up to the task of conquering the pack ice, extreme cold, fog and snow with which every voyage – until the age of global warming – was confronted. The narratives of previous voyages became a vital resource in contemporary efforts to conquer the challenging terrain. The renowned historian of the Artic, Glyn Williams, captures the sense of what was at stake by comparing the imaginary aspect of conquering the north-west passage with the physical aspect of the tides:

> The story of a search for a passage in the eighteenth century is one of credulity
> and some duplicity, of hopes raised and dashed, of the misdirection of those
> 'closet navigators' or armchair geographers much reviled in explorers'
> journals. It has a rhythm similar to that of the tides on whose rise and fall
> believers in the existence of a passage pinned their hopes. Slowly a surge
> of support for a discovery voyage gathered momentum, only to break and
> collapse as the venture failed; but before long a groundswell gathered once
> more and the process was repeated. (Williams 2003: xviii)

As we have already observed, in Serres's terminology, 'discours est un parcours'
(discourse is a journey) – or: the text is tangential to reality. Hermes connects
the imaginary and sailing. Imagining a north-west passage might, in reality,
have ended in failure in the individual case, but it could also be said that to
imagine the passage – to produce a narrative of the journey whether real or
imaginary – is to be *in* the passage in a certain sense. Let us say in the spirit of
Serres that the journey cannot be reduced to a purely technical achievement
but includes a mythical and literary dimension, a dimension that is also
germane to success.

There could hardly be a genre of travel more susceptible of chance events
than sailing in the eighteenth century. A cursory reading of voyagers'
accounts soon reveals the way unforeseen circumstances – especially
meteorological – played a large part in the trajectory of the voyage. Ships plunged
into the unpredictable changes of wind and tide, not to mention the approximate
calculations of longitude – that is, sailing vessels, based in mechanics (not
steam) – were subjected to the play of disorder and order, a play, as we have seen,
that became particularly apparent in the age of steam. Nineteenth-century steam
power subsequently enabled a greater degree of control over disorder.

It is interesting to note that Turner's representations of snow, wind and rain
(i.e. of stochastics or chance events) often centred on sailing ships at sea (cf.
Snowstorm, 1842[18]), so that, once again, mechanical technology of order (of
pulleys, winches, levers, ropes and tackle) comes to illustrate the effects of
disorder and entropy, but without an awareness that this is what is being made
explicit.

---

18 See Tate Modern: https://www.tate.org.uk/art/artworks/turner-snow-storm-steam-boat-off-a-
harbours-mouth-n00530 (accessed 10 November 2022).

To perceive the interplay between order and disorder via historical eras is another instance of the work of Hermes, the medium. This is the essence of Serres's message to us, a message that is also the revelation of a passage, or of passages, a passage being the third party in the scene, a third party that is also the in-between.

*

What one is confronted with in the five Hermes volumes is the way that a certain Hermes – a Hermes of the sciences – becomes, like the angels, invisible in light of what he makes possible. This, to be sure, is Hermes as medium.

On the other hand, there is 'noise': noise in a channel; the 'noise' of the empirical mathematical model; the noise of excluded third; the noise, indeed, of entropy, of disorder. There is also the contention that with the in-between, philosophy not only creates concepts but, more pertinently for Serres's purposes, also creates personages (characters): compare with Hermes; the parasite; the Hermaphrodite; the instructed-third; the Harlequin. In this way, the excluded middle is included as an entity, if not as an object. Does not what we have said thus indicate that Serres is not at all happy with the idea of the medium as transparent – that he would be content to follow McLuhan rather than to counter him?

Here, there are two things that need to be taken into account: the first is that for our philosopher of Hermes, it is precisely the 'noise' dimension of science and culture that passed unnoticed, unaccounted for and uncommented upon. Who in the study of logic thought to focus on the excluded middle rather than on 'one' *or* the 'other'? Who would have thought that noise in a channel could result in greater creativity? It is as though what was originally 'invisible' was in fact very 'visible'.

The second thing to say is that despite highlighting the invisibility of what is very visible, it was, as we saw early in the chapter, that the imperfect empirical domain could lead to the ideal: thus, the imperfection of a circle, a triangle or a square drawn in the sand presupposes the ideal – is a passage to the ideal – rather than simply being a collection of distorted figures. Might not this be analogous with the fact that, while its material incarnation is an undoubted reality, only in its enactment does the medium come truly into its own? Serres does not explicitly include such a proposition, but his work also does not exclude it.

Finally, it is hardly as a series of obstacles or impossibilities that Serres embarks on a north-west passage. Rather, he is determined, that despite more than two centuries of struggle, the said passage will become transparent: that is, it will facilitate the movement between the exact and the human sciences, including myth and poetry. Truly, we will then have a medium in the fullest sense.

Object and medium: Technics in the
work of Bernard Stiegler

Bernard Stiegler's engagement with the *who* (Dasein) and the *what* (technics),
follows Heidegger but also the work of Gilbert Simondon, where 'the technical
dynamic *precedes* the social dynamic' (Stiegler 1998: 67; emphasis in original).[1]

For Simondon, technical objects are entwined in the process of
individuation. One would thus suppose that the relation between time and
its manifestation is an issue. But, as it turns out, this is only indirectly the
case. What is at issue in Simondon's book on the technical object is the nature
of this object and the human's relation to it. The reason for this is that, for
Simondon, culture is a 'defensive system against technics' (2012: 9). As our
author explains, 'so that the relation of the human to the machine becomes
stable and valid, it is necessary that the technical object be known in itself,
hence, the necessity for a technical culture' (102). We have arrived, then, at the
way Simondon privileges the *being* of the technical object over its function,
or over what it does. And, supplementary to this is the extent to which the
technical object does, or does not, assume the status of medium, even though
it is theorized as an object. In effect, we need to interpret the following
statement: 'through technical activity man creates mediations and these
mediations *are detachable* from the individual who produces and thinks them'
(332; emphasis added). This 'detachability' of mediations relates to Simondon's
concepts of 'ontogenesis' (the coming to be of objects) and 'transindividuality'
as the interhuman relations supported by technical objects. Or, as Simondon

---

1 This chapter on technics and the medium complements the chapter in (Lechte 2018: 59–188) on
 technics and the human, where Stiegler's philosophy is also the main focus.

says 'By the intermediary of the technical object an interhuman relation is created which is the model of *transindividuality*' (336).

Having raised the issue of the detachability of the technical object, we will now proceed to investigate Bernard Stiegler's notion of technics as constitutive of the human. Compared to Simondon, for whom culture is hostile to the technical object – to the 'machine' – Stiegler proposes that culture is the outcome of technicity; it is not prior to it, as is the case for Simondon. This, then, is a technicity based in time, which, for Stiegler, is strikingly exemplified by cinema.

Technics as medium

Bernard Stiegler argues that humans have 'forgotten' technics. But if technics is essentially a medium – a form of mediation – then it is in its nature to be 'forgotten', just as, for Heidegger, Being is forgotten, unless it is somehow objectified. If Mark Hansen is to be believed, we need to take note of 'Stiegler's attention to media specificity' (Hansen 2012: 45). The latter calls for evaluation in relation to Stiegler's epoch-making approach to technics. Stiegler brings to the fore the very issue addressed by this study, namely, how the medium can be thought (*pace* Hansen) other than as an opaque object – *other* than in terms of media specificity. In analogous fashion, it is a matter of how technics can be thought other than as object. Heidegger inveighed against thinking Being as a specific being – which means against Being as object. While technics must, however, be acknowledged to assume the status of an object, it is not as object (as opaque) that it is technics. Objectivity does not constitute its essential nature. Such a statement has the ring of paradox because in one sense, Stiegler refers constantly to an 'image-object'; but this is to be explained, as will become clear, by the fact that what the image-object (e.g. cinema, the phonograph) produces is the exact correlate of consciousness.

Before proceeding further, in an effort to eliminate ambiguity regarding Stiegler's approach to the medium, it is as well to clear the air and acknowledge criticisms of the theorist's approach even if these are not pertinent for demonstrating whether Stiegler focuses on medium specificity, rather than on medium transparency. For instance, it has been argued that because technics as Stiegler envisages it is effectively the supplement of a lack in the human, the temporal object and technics generally is privileged in the formation of the human. In other words, 'The concrete genesis of the technical temporal object from the I's inadequacy literally predetermines its scope: technics enters the scene *in order to supplement a lack on the part of the I*' (Hansen 2012: 59).

To this objection, one could briefly respond by pointing out that what the myth of Epimetheus, invoked by Stiegler in *Technics and Time I* (1998), signifies is that technics, for the human, presupposes an *essential* exteriorization – an exteriorization that makes the human human (more on this later). The point is that there is a clear difference between a supplementarity that is added to an essential human and an essential supplementarity that, as such, constitutes the human. In the latter case, technics ceases to be an object and instead becomes a medium integrated into the being of the human.

But Hansen goes further and claims that Stiegler privileges memory (and therefore tertiary retention) with regard to technics. And the philosopher of technics is criticized for being influenced by the early Husserl of time consciousness and the privileging of the *epochē* and *Erlebnis* (lived experience) over the phenomenologist's later writing on 'worldly appearing'. Moreover, it is claimed that Stiegler's focus on consciousness derives from a 'deep-seated Cartesianism' (60).

Added to the critical mix is Stiegler's later work on care, where, it is alleged, 'deep attention' is privileged over 'hyperattension'. Deep attention is attention focused on one task to its completion, while hyperattention means focusing on a number of tasks simultaneously ('multitasking') (see Hayles 2007). Stiegler's critique of 'hyperattention' in favour of 'deep attention' supposedly explains the theorist's hostility to the 'culture industries' and his recourse to the term 'adoption' in relation to the dissemination throughout the world of American 'Hollywood' culture. Such a relation is deemed to demonstrate that the symbiosis of consciousness and Hollywood film images inevitably comes to have deleterious results.

While Stiegler's theory of adoption is not the strongest part of his philosophy, the situation, as will be confirmed, is to do with the medium as film content, whether or not one agrees with the interpretation of this content.

But now, having interpreted Serres on science in the previous chapter, let us briefly compare this with Stiegler on science.

Stiegler and Serres on science

In his work on cinema, and film as a temporal object, Stiegler also speaks of science (2011: 187–224). But Unlike Michel Serres, for whom, as we saw, progress in science is not linear, Stiegler holds that science changes progressively, hence, the distinction between '*modern* science and *contemporary* science' (Stiegler 2011: 189), or between 'classical' and 'modern' science (204). When science 'is no longer classical', 'it *becomes* performative' (204). There is, at this point, no division between science and its application. Instead, we have 'technoscience', where science as theory and as application are totally integrated: 'it is science that becomes applied technology, and not technology as applied science' (189). Descriptions of reality are only one modality of technoscience. Indeed, rather than being charged with a description of reality, technoscience 'radically destabilises it'. 'It *creates* a new reality' (191). All facets of human action and endeavour are essentially technical – that is, are an exteriorization. Thus, with anticipation as an element of technics – a point initially signalled by Simondon – and the mind, we find that 'the possibility of anticipation, as I explore it throughout *Technics and Time, 1* and *2*, is itself conditioned and overdetermined through possibles of tertiary retentions – through the technical medium of the *mind*' (2011: 196). As Stiegler specifies, 'my claim is that *technics permits the construction of schema, including practical schema*; technics' connections to theory and its place in theory must therefore be disrupted' (197). This shows that technics exists in the unawareness of its presence. It suggests that it is completely transparent.

Certainly, as we shall see, Stiegler takes Derrida's notion of *différance* into account in his theory of technics. Does this mean, as Hansen has claimed, that technics is reduced to 'writing' – to text – in the narrow sense, as opposed to the 'robust *materiality* of technology'? (Hansen 2000: 4). As Hansen would have it, 'Derrida simply effaces the very category of radical exteriority and, along with it, all traces of materiality outside the space governed by textuality' (125). The point is that Derrida does not intend 'writing' or 'text' to be understood in the narrow, colloquial sense, but in the sense of 'programme' and 'organization', as order and as structure as opposed to disorder and entropy. Here is another echo of Serres and the play of entropy as disorder and structure as order. If materiality is also essentially a form of order (i.e. a mode of keeping entropy at bay) then Hansen – without recognizing it – is in keeping with Stiegler's and Derrida's take on technics rather than the opposite. But, in any case, why rule out discourse, language and textuality from materiality? The answer would be, because this is what the *doxa* decrees. If, however, entropy is taken as the main reference point with regard to materiality, a picture of materiality arises that is very different from that presented by Hansen.

Stiegler's technics

A key aspect of Stiegler's approach involves the emergence of new processes of retention, reproducibility and transmission (2011: 194). Types of memory referred to are: (1) genetic; (2) individual; (3) tertiary. 'But technics opens the possibility of transmitting individual experience beyond the individual's life: technics supports a *third* level of memory, the mechanisms of tertiary retentions' (206). It is the latter that is, as Hansen recognizes, crucial to Stiegler's project to rethink technics.

More broadly, Stiegler's work has become increasingly well known for having argued for the way the *who* (subject) confirms its being through the *what* (technics). In other words, the human is constituted through technics. This is the already mentioned 'fault of Epimetheus', where, in the myth, Epimetheus has to complete the human by adding artificial elements (technics). As we have seen, Stiegler proposes that the human, through processes of exteriorization – where tools (for example) come to 'make' the human – reveals itself to be in a symbiotic relation with technics. Even Donna Haraway's 'cyborg' is a combination of human (organism) and machine, rather than the human *as* machine. Similarly, the bionic being is one that has had 'artificial' organs replace 'natural' organs. The totally bionic being is, for much of the thinking on technics, still a foreigner, relative to the natural being of old.[2] Now, just as the human is in a transductive relation with technics (meaning that the one only exists in relation to the other), so the aforementioned technoscience

---

2 Compare with 'The prosthesis is not a mere extension of the human body; it is the constitution of the body *qua* "human"' (Stiegler 1998: 152–3).

is in a transductive relation with its application. There is no pure science on one side and applied technics on the other.

All this is relatively well known, and I have written on Stiegler's work in a number of places discussing his theory of the *who* and the *what* (Lechte 1999), his theory of the 'orthographic' (Lechte 2007), his approach to Kant and the schema in the context of a theory of the image (Lechte 2012: 80–2) and his writing on the nature of the human (Lechte 2018: 165–80). It is thus not necessary to repeat in detail the components of Stiegler's philosophy of technics and time. What I would like to return to, though, is the Kantian schema; for the latter reveals key issues with regard to the medium.

The schema

The aspect of the Kantian schema that is pertinent is its relation to the image. As is known, it is a product of the imagination and is invoked to enable thought to comprehend entities of the greatest generality, entities for which the part, represented by a particular image, cannot stand for the whole (as with synecdoche). Kant proposes that the schema is a 'universal procedure of imagination in providing an image for a concept' (Kant 1970b: 182). Given that, for example, 'no image could ever be adequate to the concept of a triangle in general' (182), a schema is necessary. In this regard, 'The schema of the triangle can exist nowhere but in thought' (182). Extrapolating from Kant's example, the following entities are such that no image could 'ever be adequate' to their generality: space, time, infinity, life, materiality, number, being (Heidegger), image, causality, reality. For Kant, 'the schema has to be distinguished from the image' (182) and the image of a particular number (Kant refers to the number '5') cannot stand for number in general. But in Stiegler's estimation, schema and image cannot be separated. As he explains,

> A number always in some way presupposes a capacity for tertiary retention – whether *via* children's fingers, a magician's body, an abacus, or an alphanumeric system of writing – which alone can facilitate numerization and objectification. This capacity has a history, during which at one point the concept of one thousand (1000) became possible. Properly understood, this conception is first and foremost a process. Until a certain point quite recent relative to the long history of humanity, the number 1000 was literally

inconceivable to a human consciousness without the tools for thinking it, when 1000 ('one thousand', or the figure/image above, or 1111101000) had not yet been elaborated. (2011: 51)

The schema, for its part, presupposes an image:

it remains the fact that there can be no manifestation of schema without image, whether mental or not. While Kant, giving an image to 'five' draws five dots in a row ([*sic*] thus inserting the *design* '... .' into a sentence, he unfortunately forgets that the *word* 'five' [*fünf,, cinq*] is *already* an image, and with a long history. (53) (Parenthesis not closed.)

Kant and much of the post-Enlightenment era have assumed that an image is a very specific object that does not embody the generality of a concept, whereas, for Stiegler, the image has the status (at least with regard to number) of a technical object. As such, it 'makes present' the thing itself. It is, therefore, transparent. Whether or not the technical object resembles what it makes present becomes irrelevant.

Technics: Its material support and exteriorization

As noted elsewhere (Lechte 2012: 95), the materiality of the technical support does not determine the nature of the imaged. Consequently, against Bergson, it can be said that a photograph can capture movement because an image is not reducible to its material support. Is the image representative of technics in general in this regard? Certainly, the fact that technics has historically been presented as an object makes it all the more difficult to grasp what is at issue here. From Ludwig Feuerbach to Guy Debord, it is assumed that one can chose reality *or* the image; for the image is deemed to be an object and as such, it is opaque, not transparent.

When Stiegler says that '*the image in general* does not exist' (2002: 147), what might be the implications of this statement? For Stiegler himself it is, in part, a matter of addressing the difference between a mental image and an image-object. But if a mental image is illusory in the sense that it depends for its viability on a certain exteriorization,[3] then we are looking at the primacy of

---

3 Even the unconscious – or, perhaps more correctly, particularly the unconscious – depends, not only on internal sources (drives), but also on external sources that are internalized (for example images, language, memories (primal scene)).

the medium itself where technics defines the human: to be without technics is not to be human. Does this mean that the medium (technics as media) is *in* the human and thus should not be thought of as an object outside the human? Or, as Stiegler, following the prehistorian Leroi-Gourhan puts it, with the evolution of language and tools the essence of the human becomes external to it. Or again, technics is equivalent to the human as exteriorization. What remains to be investigated is whether or not the exteriorization of the human is ontologically and epistemologically neutral. A McLuhan-inspired answer would be that they are not. Do Stiegler and Leroi-Gourhan – for that matter – follow McLuhan on this? What is the implication of Stiegler's notion of epiphylogenesis as the evolution and maintenance of life 'by means other than life' – that is, by technics? Is it that technics is a medium and as such 'disappears' into the human?

Crucial to understanding the significance of technics is the distinction between animality and humanity, especially as this is outlined in the work of Leroi-Gourham. If we forget for a moment, as I have previously indicated, that defining the human in relation to the animal entails a certain paradox (Lechte 2018: 140–1), Leroi-Gouhran's distinction between the 'zoological' and the 'anthropological' in the context of hominization is worth repeating the better to appreciate Stiegler's notion of technics.

Thus, rather than understating the human as a very sophisticated animal with, for example, a highly developed sense of communication, so that the human remains explicable within zoology, the prehistorian shows that the human emerges – to repeat – through processes of exteriorization – or through technics in the broadest sense. Or, again, as Derrida says, technics is the 'name' of the human.[4] Thus unlike the animal, the human does not have a nature.

The key stage of interest to Stiegler in the evolution of the human as specified by Leroi-Gourhan is the birth of graphism that is constitutive of uniquely human relations (Leroi-Gourhan 1964: 262 ff). What Stiegler, and before him, Derrida, deduce from this is the concept of the human as essentially processes of exteriorization. The latter enables a new relation to emerge between speech

---

4 Of course, questions remain as to whether the beings classed as animals are in fact entirely incapable of processes of exteriorization, such as a form of language. But this theme cannot be elaborated upon here. See, however, the reference to Merleau-Ponty's thinking on the animal and culture in Lechte (2018: 47–8).

and action. The conclusion to be drawn from this is that instead of a physical origin (let us say, biological) an entirely mediated origin is at play – or an origin *as* mediation is at play. The graphic revolution, which includes parietal art and the 'abstract' art of the Australian Aboriginal churinga, or sacred object (1964: 263), implies, as Derrida recognized, that no human culture – *qua* human – is outside the graphic process of exteriorization, with writing in the alphabetic, ideographic or pictographic sense being but three instances deriving from the 'birth of graphism'. The latter is the basis on which Leroi-Gourhan distinguishes the zoological from the ethnic or sociological status of the human. Not only is the human the being that exteriorizes, but the processes of exteriorization (from tools to every symbolic and artistic form) also constitute the human. This is what Derrida's notion of the 'grammē' implies. We are thus not just engaged in an encounter with language and writing in the narrow sense.[5] It goes without saying that the process in question is not simply the expression of an interiority, a point that the currently dominant form of psychological individualism is only too ready to embrace. Regarding expression, it is worth noting that Leroi-Gourhan attaches great importance to the fact that the first phase of the graphic revolution does not consist of a naïve realism, or figurative art, but is centred on the abstract, of which the Aboriginal churinga is an early and prime example (1964: 263). Such a form of exteriorization might facilitate participation in the sacred, but it is not an expression. Instead, it can be conceived as being a 'symbolic transposition' connected to language as writing (266).

'Graphism' – writing in the grammatological sense – also entails that the human (and maybe not just the human) is no longer defined biologically; or rather, to the extent that the human is also biological is the extent to which biology is now – as Derrida observes – 'writing and *pro-gram*' for the most elementary processes of information within the living cell' (2016: 9).

---

5 In an oft-quoted passage, Derrida states: 'the concept of writing [cf. *gráphein*, "to draw, to write"] exceeds and comprehends that of language' (2016: 9), and he continues: 'One now tends to say "writing" ... to designate not only physical gestures of literal, pictographic, or ideographic inscription, but also for the totality of what makes it possible; and further, beyond the signifying face, *the signified face itself*; and so for all that can make room for an inscription in general, whether it is literal or not and even if what it distributes in space is alien to the order of the voice: cinematography, choreography, of course, but also pictorial, musical, sculptural "writing" ' (9).

Michel Serres's interpretation of genetics also confirms Derrida's point, in that, as we saw in Chapter 5, genetics is fundamentally a 'pro-gramme'.

Stiegler's theory of technics comprehends the graphic revolution and grammatology as all forms of exteriorization, or inscription – as 'arche-writing' (Derrida) – and thereby demonstrates the 'invention of the human'. From this the conclusion can be drawn that the human *is* the medium. The human is that being whose distinguishing feature is that it is equivalent to the medium.

More precisely, though, how exactly does Stiegler approach Leroi-Gourhan's anthropology? Would the notion of the graphic ultimately result in the homogenizing of the human in the latter's separation from the animal? (1998: 136). The answer is that what Leroi-Gourhan's reflection shows is a version of the '*grammē*' as 'the pursuit of life by means other than life' (137). And Leroi-Gourhan does this in a way 'that does not take for granted the usual divide between animality and humanity' (137), even if this entails that 'the appearance of the human is the appearance of the technical' (141).

Dependence on technics – on exteriorizations – provides an opportunity for 'manipulation', the latter being exemplified for Stiegler – as we saw earlier – by the way Hollywood movies instil in consumers the 'American way of life', by the process of 'adoption'. Thus

> it nonetheless remains that the self is not simply *in itself* but originarily outside itself. The self is surrounded by [au milieu de] 'itself', by its objects and prostheses, a milieu that is therefore not only itself but its *other*.
>
> And this other precedes it, is already-there, as an unlived past that is only one's past on condition that it becomes one's future. (Stiegler 2011: 49)

Cinema as a case study

At the beginning of his engagement with cinema, Stiegler observes that there is a human desire for a narrative – for a story, that is 'the universal desire for fiction' (Stiegler 2011: 9).

From this it is deemed to follow that cinema, as a medium, is seductive. Humans are predisposed to take an interest in what it offers. World commerce plays on this desire for a narrative/story, so that cinema can be a vehicle for delivering its message – its world view.

Technically speaking, cinema is conceived as an extension of photography, But more than this the medium is a key instance of a temporal object. This raises the issue of entropy, as a temporal object is not eternal (2011: 36). In its symbiotic relation with the spectator, the film flux 'coincides' with the flux of consciousness. As a temporal object cinema, like melody, is modelled on Husserl's conception, which consists of a tripartite structure of memory as primary, secondary and tertiary. It is tertiary memory – memory as prosthetic – that most interests our theorist.

To connect the exterior image (image-object) to consciousness, and to demonstrate – as he says – the materiality of the image, Stiegler renders inoperative the distinction between the mental image and the image-object (2011: 36). Cinema as a temporal object becomes the vehicle for illustrating the way that consciousness is constituted through exteriorization, the latter being, as we have seen, the mark of the human. Now, the image-object is to be understood in terms of retentional finitude and thus in terms of the need for memory to be supplemented. Consequently, 'Tertiary retention is in the most general sense the prosthesis of consciousness without which there could be no mind, no recall, no memory of a past that one has not personally lived, no culture' (39). Tertiary retention is, then, a mode of exteriorization. Its promotion by Stiegler to a position of pre-eminence in grasping the essence of consciousness (which includes memory) contrasts with the conventional view of consciousness and mind as being interior and inaccessible to others. The inaccessibility of consciousness ('my' consciousness) to others breaks down as soon as it is a matter of self-consciousness. The latter, to be what it is, entails a certain objectification. As Stiegler explains, 'Consciousness can only become self-consciousness when it can be externalized, objectivized as traces through which at the same time it becomes accessible to other consciousnesses' (47). We could say, by way of elaboration, that every ego-self is aware of retentional finitude, hence the everyday efforts to counter it through the use of various memory aids. Indeed,

> no thought is possible without figurations that are themselves traces, gestures of thought as it must be subsumed into its inscriptions in space, inscriptions that within the intuition of an empirical given manifest a pure intuition of the formal conditions for this empirical intuition – and that, as has already been explored here, are the understanding's crutches, not just those of hope and of faith. (55)

Stiegler does not mention it specifically, but one could consider the phenomenon of the savant who is capable of recalling the past – as though it were yesterday. And that is it 'as though it were yesterday' – the point being that if the past were recalled as though it were *today*, meaning that nothing has been forgotten, that no selection has taken place, there would be no time (see 2011: 200) – there would be no entropy, no irreversibility.[6] So, although the savant might manifest a remarkable ability at recollection, it is still recollection that is at issue – yesterday is still imaginary, while today is still perceptual. Consciousness – always defined, in light of Husserl, as 'consciousness of' – is consciousness of an image, the image being tertiary memory. In short, both 'consciousness of' and retentional finitude give rise, in the context of the human, to the primacy of tertiary materialization and tertiary memory. Significantly, what is implied is that there is no consciousness in itself, just as there is no image in itself. Cinema and consciousness interact in the sense that 'I can also see "myself" as an other; I can film "myself", project "myself", graft "myself" onto myself, see "myself" as a tutor, as a support, a screen: writing, for example. That is, to "objectify", "exteriorize", express" myself: to "tertiarize" myself' (32). And this process/procedure, says our theorist, is already 'montage' (32).

Encountering the effects of cinema

The 'Kuleshov effect' is invoked by Stiegler to illustrate the aforementioned symbiosis of cinema and consciousness. It is a particular engagement by consciousness with the cinema image such that the interpretation or impact of a single image varies according to how it was juxtaposed with another image:

> the Kuleshov Effect consists of inserting the same image of the actor Mozzhukhin's face numerous times into a series of sequences constructed around the image, in which each time the actor's face appears it does so with three other quite different images. The image of Mozzhukhin's face, though it is always the same, is nonetheless perceived by viewers as three different images, each seeming to produce a different version of the same face. (2011: 15)

---

6 In fact irreversibility and the associated entropy are an important part of Stiegler's approach to time. Thus, 'the emergence of all protentions occurs through the irreversible nature of their unfolding. This irreversibility is precisely the protention containing all protentions' (Stiegler 2011: 30).

And Stiegler goes on to highlight the importance of this effect for understanding how time, the cinema image and consciousness are inextricably entwined: 'In fact, it is this cinematic effect that ceaselessly produces a particular consciousness, projecting onto its objects everything that has preceded them within the sequence into which they have been inserted and that only they produce. And in fact this is the very principle of cinema: to connect disparate elements together into a single temporal flux' (15).

Although Stiegler's main concern is to determine what gives cinema 'its specificity, its force, and its means of transforming life leading, for example, to the global adoption of "the American way of life"' (17), my concern is not what gives cinema as an institution 'its specificity', but to determine the status of the cinema image as a medium. In this regard, it is Stiegler's commentary on specific films that is of interest, namely: Fellini's *Intervista* (1987), Resnais's *Mon Oncle d'Amérique* (My American Uncle) (1980), Alia Kazan's *A Streetcar Named Desire* (1951), Selznick's *Gone with the Wind* (1939), Hitchcock's *Four O'Clock* (1957 – an episode of the series, 'Alfred Hitchcock Presents'), Woody Allen's *The Purple Rose of Cairo* (1985) and *The Eclipse* (1962) directed by Michelangelo Antonioni. Each of these films, or – as with Vivien Leigh in *Gone with the Wind* and *A Streetcar Named Desire* in which Leigh also stars – the relationship between films, Stiegler proposes, plays on the difference between the present, the past and the future, between fiction and reality, between life and death, between real time and the time of film (cf. *Four O'Clock*). All of these features are most strikingly apparent in *Intervista*, where

> We see an actress playing an actress watching an actress playing a 'real' character in a fictional film, but we know that she is 'playing' at watching herself having been, that what she is doing is no longer a simple portrayal, a pure performance any actor might be required to give (to play this or that character), but the absolutely tragic staging of her own existence, insofar as that existence is passing by irremediably and forever – forever, except for what concerns this silvery image she has left on a reel of film: an image in which she has been preserved. (22)

From this, there is no doubt that what the image delivers – beyond all media specificity – is the actors as real people. The spectator is not watching a film – or is not simply watching a film – but is watching the real Anita Ekberg, the real Marcello Mastroianni (the actors) and the real Federico Fellini (the actor), who are also characters in the Fellini films: *La Dolce Vita* (1960) and *Intervista*. Thus, 'we must mark as tertiary retentions all forms of "objective" memory: cinematogram, photogram, phonogram, writing, paintings, sculptures – but also monuments and objects in general, since they bear witness, for me, say, of a past that I enforcedly did not myself live' (28). To be noted here is the necessary priority of tertiary before primary and secondary memory, in the sense that tertiary memory is the basis of the history of the heritage that I have not lived, which is prior to what I have lived. As one observer astutely remarks, 'The tertiary retention is the sociocultural background or heritage that makes a temporal flux possible; it provides the foundation from which primary and secondary retentions can take place' (McGowan 2012: 395). Cinema is the conformation of this. Also, consciousness is 'built on archi-protentions: death, desire for reproduction and expenditure – whose core is the unconscious' (17). Tertiary retention, based on retentional finitude, together with archi-protentions, reinforce the notion that perception is not identical with itself. This is also a feature of the spectator's response to the films Stiegler selects for commentary.

I take *Intervista* to be the most significant film in demonstrating Stiegler's approach to the image, and so we shall return it. But first, let us briefly attend to Stiegler's commentary on the other films cited.

With Resnais's film, 'the great French actor, Jean Gabin' (famous for such pre-war classics as Renoir's *La grande illusion* (1936) *and La bête humaine* (1938)) appears in the memory of the character, René Ragueneau, played by Gerard Depardieu. The point is that Gabin is both actor and character. Fiction and reality intermingle to the point of becoming indistinguishable – indeed, to the point, the film shows where the actor/character can influence behaviour as much as a 'real' close friend or associate. One can become obsessed or 'haunted' by a character.

In another example, Vivien Leigh as Blanch Dubois in *A Street Car Named Desire* is 'haunted' (for the viewer) by Vivien Leigh as Scarlet O'Hara in *Gone with the Wind*. Just as actor and character here become confused, so, too, the spectator of these and other films is caught up in this same circle of enchantment.[7] Thus,

---

7 After the success of the James Bond movies, Sean Connery was supremely irritated by the fact that when off the set, people frequently greeted him as, 'Mr Bond'.

How not to shudder before such a psychotic, at the catastrophe that has unfolded when we see Blanche taken away forever from her 'sanctuary' with Stella and Stanley? How not to feel insane ourselves, carried along by this exemplar of the great, mad American destiny – that never fails at the same time to sell us, through making us laugh and cry in the face of our own fate, the American Way of Life? (26)

Now the working of the image as medium is revealed, even if Stiegler does not refer to it as such. It is the image that constitutes the condition of possibility of the confusion between actor and character, and between actor or character and spectator, as played out in Woody Allen's *The Purple Rose of Cairo*.[8] In the movie, the character, archaeologist, Tom, steps out of the film into the real world and engages with audience member, Cecilia. The actual audience member thus finds his or her position replicated by Cecilia in the film – or, indeed, via the image, the border between the audience in the film and the film spectators becomes porous. Such is the way that Allen's film calls attention to the transparency of the medium. Not only is disbelief suspended in relation to cinema's realism, but the image also becomes reality, that is, it disappears as image.

Commentary on Hitchcock's *Four O'Clock* (see 2011: 28–30) is intended to demonstrate the working of archi-protention, that is, the fact that the audience is already set up – programmed – to expect death. And so, the watchmaker, the key character in the film, is 'hoisted with his own petard' ('petard' means explosive device), when robbers in his house tie him up in the basement and thereby foil his plan to set a time bomb for his wife and her lover. The bomb was set to explode at precisely four o'clock in the afternoon, the alarm on an alarm clock being the detonator. As Stiegler observes, the last 32′ 33″ – the longest running sequence of the film – in fact represents two hours of the watchmaker's life, while the final minute before the anticipated explosion actually lasts 72 seconds. Through other examples of time contraction, Stiegler shows that the image of time (time as it unfolds in the film narrative) is quite distinct from real time and yet is no less convincing for the spectator for all

8 *The Purple Rose of Cairo* is referred to by Stiegler as having similar features to those observed in *Intervista*, but is not analysed in depth. Like *Intervista*, it had also been referred to briefly as an illustration of the narcissism of today's cinema in Stiegler's earlier volume, *Technics and Time 2* (2009: 24).

that. In short, the time image – the medium of time – works as real time even though it is not real time. This is why the tension remains even in light of multiple viewings for the film.

Stiegler's commentary on Antonioni's *The Eclipse* is also geared to demonstrate the autonomy of cinematic time. The film begins by showing the main character, Vittoria, visiting the Rome stock exchange, when suddenly one of the traders dies of a heart attack. There is, consequently, a minute's silence – that Stiegler times to be in fact 56 seconds – before the trading floor erupts into action again. Even though the image time almost replicates real time, there will always be a disjunction between real and cinematic time. Of course, given that we are talking here about consciousness as inexorably tied to the flow of cinema images, time for consciousness is also contraction, condensation, abbreviation – in short, 'the time of montage' (30). This is no doubt why the image for consciousness is always the 'presence of the thing in its absence'. For Husserl, by comparison, the image is always an object and thus not transparent.

The Secret of Intervista *and* Camera Lucida

Let us now return to Fellini's *Intervista*. We saw that in his initial engagement with this film, Stiegler remarks on the effect of character and actor coming together when, in the film, Anita Ekberg and Marcello Mastroianni meet at Anita Ekberg's home and view the famous Trevi Fountain scene from *La Dolce Vita*, a scene made some twenty-five years earlier. Ekberg and Mastroianni are actors who play themselves and who then become characters *as* real actors. The poignancy of the scene for the viewer derives precisely from the fact that it is the real actors (also characters) who view the Trevi Fountain scene. What is crucial, as Stiegler presents it and is thus crucial for our analysis in this study, is the reference to Roland Barthes's use, in *Camera Lucida* (2010), of the future anterior in referring to the image of a condemned Lewis Payne, subject of Barthes's paradox: 'He is dead and he is going to die' (95–6). Analogously, the actor viewing the Trevi Fountain scene is in the position of where he or she says '*I* am going to die' (2011: 23; emphasis added).

Stiegler thus deepens his analysis of *Intervista* by making the debt to Barthes's invocation of the future anterior quite explicit as is clear from the following famous passage from Barthes's *Camera Lucida* invoked to explain Anita's anguish:

> Watching herself performing thirty years earlier, Anita must feel the future anterior so striking to Roland Barthes as he looks at the photograph of Lewis Payne taken several hours before Payne's hanging:
>
> In 1865, young Lewis Payne tried to assassinate Secretary of State W. H. Seward. Alexander Gardner photographed him in his cell, where he was waiting to be hanged. The photograph is handsome, as is the boy: that is the *studium*. But the *punctum* is: *he is going to die*. I read at the same time: *This will be* and *this has been*; I observe with horror an anterior future of which death is the stake. By giving me the absolute past of the pose (aorist), the photograph tells me death in the future. What *pricks* me is the discovery of this equivalence. In front of the photograph of my mother as a child, I tell myself: she is going to die: I shudder, like Winnicott's psychotic patient, *over a catastrophe which has already occurred*. Whether or not the subject is already dead, every photograph is this catastrophe. (Barthes 2010: 96, cited by Stiegler 2011: 23)

From this extract, however, it seems clear that Barthes makes the photographic image the privileged bearer of time and thus the unique bearer of the future anterior as the evocation of death. Have commentators not, as a result, failed to notice that the significant thing about Barthes's position on photography is that it is a restatement of media specificity? Certainly, within photography and thus within cinema as derivative of photography, there is transparence: Anita Ekberg is thus genuinely faced with a premonition of death. The '*noema*' (the essential feature) of the photograph is the '*it-has-been*' ('*ça a été*'). This is the principle that applies to photography and not to any other medium – even if the '*noema*' of photography is also its essential transparence. Consequently, photography would have the feature of the medium as disappearing that this study attributes to all media *qua* media. By contrast, for Barthes, the photographic referent is the '*necessarily* real thing which has been placed before the lens, without which there would be no photograph' (2010: 76). As such it is distinct from all other media referents: 'Painting can feign reality without having seen it' (76), whereas, 'in Photography I can never deny that *the thing has been there*' (76).

Like Barthes, Siegfried Kracauer also defines photography by its rigorous presentation of the object before the lens: 'in photography the spatial appearance of an object is its meaning' (1995: 52). And, for Kracauer, this is what distinguishes a photograph from a painting. A painting is riven with symbolic traits, whereas a photograph is not. However, we can today observe experiments in blurring the border between painting and photography, as exemplified by super-realism, and in the work of artists such as Gehard Richter (b. 1932), who mixes painting and photographic images, and in the work of the American artist, Alexa Meade (b. 1986), who, in using amongst other things the human body as a surface, paints in imitation of photography.[9] In any case, the point is that the sheer variety of image content in the context of what is called 'painting' implies that generalizations about painting as a medium must remain problematic.

But be this as it may, once cinema and photography are conceived as temporal objects in the manner of *Intervista*, the *noema* of photography ceases to be important. Rather, how specific images are experienced takes precedence. This is no less true for Barthes in *Camera Lucida* than it is for other commentators on photography, such as Susan Sontag (2008).[10] For while the reader is shown that the *punctum* does ultimately come to coincide with the future anterior of the Lewis Payne photo – the '*ça a été*' – the notion of the *punctum* is only compelling when it becomes manifest in a range of photographs where the content is quite heterogeneous. Indeed, considered philosophically, the overriding principle of the future anterior would only require reference to a single photograph to be confirmed. The diversity (in terms of content) of photographs contained in *Camera Lucida* (and in photography generally) implies that it is photographs as specific images that hold sway overall, and not the single principle as adduced by Barthes. Thus, when considered in terms of

---

9 Certainly, I acknowledge that what has been said here regarding photography and painting raises more issues than can be dealt with in this chapter. For instance, one could ask what it is about photography that allows it to be imitated by painting – and, inversely: What is it about painting that enables it to be imitated by photography? What is implied here, too, is the question of the degree of fluidity of genres.

10 At one point, early in her text, Sontag – perhaps uncharacteristically – writes that 'photographs are as much an interpretation of the world as paintings and drawings are' (2008: 6–7). As the title of Sontag's book indicates, the topic is photography – not photographs: there are no images in *On Photography*.

what is imaged, rather than in terms of the materiality of the technical object, all media tend to converge. Such is the central thesis of this study.

Steigler's approach and adoption

By aligning consciousness, in the first instance, so closely to the unfolding of the film as temporal object, independently of content, is not Stiegler replicating Barthes's error when he reduces photography to the abstract principle of the future anterior? The answer would seem to be that in fact the same can be said of Stiegler as we said of Barthes. However, although he proposes a principle to apply to the relation between consciousness and films generally, it is the analysis of the varying images in a range of films that in fact characterizes Stiegler's approach. For, indeed, as soon as actual films (both fictional and non-fictional) are analysed, film content rather than film form is what is crucially in play. Thus – again like Barthes on photography – the principle of the coincidence of film with consciousness could be confirmed on the basis of a single example. There is no need to investigate a range of films. Once it is a range of different film content that becomes the centre of attention, the content of cinema similarly becomes the centre of attention.

What, however, are we to conclude regarding Stiegler's arguments that 'The very possibility of "culture", and thus of "spirit", relies on technics' (2011: 37), and that 'self-consciousness can only emerge through a process of exteriorisation' (47)? Do these propositions match up with the principle of the transparency of the medium? In response, let us consider Stiegler's concept of 'adoption'. The term is used to indicate, Stiegler claims, the way Hollywood came to dominate early cinema in such a way that the 'American way of life' was communicated to the rest of the world – or, should we say, that the rest of the world was – due to the parallel between consciousness and film – indoctrinated with American cultural forms and values. In Stiegler's words, 'In a war of images' America uses, and has used, cinema in order to ensure that 'the entire world would adopt '*the American way of life*' (Stiegler 2011: 116). This is obviously a big claim. At first glance it seems to be sustained by the very principle itself of the coincidence of consciousness and film flux. But when thought about more deeply, we are prompted to ask whether this is indeed the case. Surely, it is one thing to show how spectators are susceptible to being influenced by cinema; it is quite another to generalize about the nature of cinema content (the American way of life) and its impact on viewers, namely, the *adoption* of Hollywood ideology. This is not to deny that a case could be made about the content of Hollywood films prior to and after the Second World War, but it would require an engagement with the content – with the images – of these films and not just a philosophy of the relation between technics and consciousness. Would Hitchcock's most significant films (cf. *Vertigo* (1958); *Psycho* (1960)) made in America be included in the adoption thesis? It is unlikely, given that Stiegler chooses *Four O'Clock* for analysis.[11] The point to be reiterated is that it is the inherent variety of film content and the play of images that constitute the cinema as a true medium.

In the end, though, we should not forget that Stiegler begins his analysis of consciousness and cinema by positing the idea that, as humans, we have a desire for a story:

> The propensity to believe in stories and fables, the passion for fairy tales, just as satisfying in the old as in the very young, is perpetuated from generation to generation because it forges the link between the generations. Insatiable, they hold out the promise, to generations to come, of the writing of new episodes of future life, yet to be invented, to be fictionalized [*fabuler*]. (2011: 8)

And, as a consequence of the desire for a story, 'Global commerce now develops by mobilizing techniques of persuasion owing everything to the narrative arts. There is no event, no moment, independent of the desire for stories. Media networks and the programming industries exploit this fictionalizing tendency by systematizing the specific resources of audiovisual technics' (2011: 8).

My argument is that, given the unlimited range of the narrative arts, the focus once again must be on the film content – on the images – in order to appreciate cinema as medium.

In certain respects, then, one could designate as Stiegler's weakest argument the one concerning cinema and adoption, where he claims, especially with regard to Hollywood, that American cinema has been focused on the

---

11 On the other hand, Chaplin is not excluded from the process of adoption: 'When Chaplin, pursued by McCarthyism, filmed *A King in New York* and denounced America's duplicity, he nonetheless worked to celebrate American greatness, which had given him the means to become one of world's greatest artists, precisely in disseminating to the world the entire American adventure, through him' (2011: 117).

dissemination of the 'American way of life' throughout the world. To claim that *all* of American cinema is a purveyor of the way of life in question is, it has been argued, an overreach. Do the films of Hitchcock, Chaplin, Welles, Kazan – *A Streetcar Named Desire* analysed by Stiegler – and many others really purvey the American way of life? The thesis is hardly sustainable. Nevertheless, at issue above all is the interpretation of the *content* of films, just as the focus on films as the vehicles of stories is also to focus on film content. In other words, Stiegler's orientation is inexorably towards the essential transparency of the film image as medium. Thus, one can indeed challenge Stiegler's interpretation of film content, but one cannot deny that it is content that is at issue and not a supposedly cinematic view of the world.

Memory and archive

What, however, are we to make of the relation to transparency or opacity of memory and the archive – two themes also considered by Stiegler? If it is conceded that memory *qua* memory as medium is selective and that the archive as medium inevitably has a specific configuration (it is, after all, impossible to conserve all documents), does this not imply that recall is memory's recall and that it is the archive as such that speaks through documents? Do we not have here a version of medium specificity?

In response to this question, we know, since Freud (and Proust) that selection is an imprecise term where personal, individual memory is concerned. Certainly, what is recalled is finite, but it is only partially what is selected. Recollections, after all, frequently *arrive* in consciousness without being provoked – without, indeed, being wished for or sought after. Does this mean, then, that memory as such 'speaks'? Possibly, if one can accept that finitude is what memory reveals, but then, 'no', it is not memory that speaks once the focus is on the memory content. This is particularly important as regards Stiegler's emphasis on tertiary memory – a memory that flows over into the archive, a memory that I have not lived but which is part of my identity as a cultural and historical being.[12] Let it be accepted that one can concentrate

---

12 As Stiegler confirms, 'Tertiary retention is in the most general sense the prosthesis of consciousness without which there could be no mind, no recall, no memory of a past that one has not personally lived, no culture' (2011: 39).

on the finitude of memory (whether lived or tertiary) and the archive, but it is in delivering their content that both memory and archive are transparent and truly endowed with meaning even if the latter can, and indeed should be, on numerous occasions, contested. In other words, memory is the activation of memory and archive is the activation of the archive.

7

The medium and object-oriented ontology (OOO)

As was mentioned in the introduction to this work, object-oriented ontology (OOO) has become a significant movement in contemporary philosophy. It also offers an insight into the role of the medium in art. The question to be pursued is, does OOO's conception of the medium confirm or refute the notion of media specificity?

Prior to looking at OOO in relation to art, an examination of Graham Harman's reading of Heidegger on 'tool-being' is appropriate as it evokes the reality of the medium. As we saw in the introduction, in Heidegger's distinction between the tool as 'ready-to-hand' and 'present-to-hand', the tool in the former sense disappears in its use, while the tool in the latter sense appears as an object. The tool as ready-to-hand has been characterized as the tool as medium. The tool only appears to consciousness (as present-to-hand) when it breaks down, when it ceases to be used and becomes an object. This was also the case with Ernst's media archaeology. Harman's point in this regard is that tool-being (ready-to-hand) applies to all entities, not just to the examples of tools that Heidegger explicitly invokes. It remains to be seen, then, whether the medium as disappearance can encompass Harman's tool-being. Given that Harman explicitly says that 'there is no basis in tool analysis for any fruitful theory of modern technology' (Harman 2002: 4), the challenge is on.

Heidegger and technology as precursor to Harman's 'tool-being'

As we saw in the previous chapter, the tool constitutes, in Leroi-Gourhan's and subsequently in Stiegler's philosophy of technics, a mode of exteriorization. Technics in general would be a mode of exteriorization that distinguishes the human as human. Technics is not a mere addition (a prosthetic) that can be invoked or disregarded at will. For Heidegger, technics in the modern era is held to be an addition: a means to an end, a means used by humans. Thus is posed 'the instrumental and anthropological definition of technology' (Heidegger 1977: 5). The question, according to Heidegger, is, what is 'means'? And he famously relates the notion of means, historically, to causality, specifically to the four causes, and predominantly, the '*causa efficiens*'. When inquiring into the actual nature of cause, Heidegger breaks with the commonly accepted understanding and characterizes technology as enframing, which is 'a way of revealing' (12). As such, technology can thus be linked to the Greek word for truth as revealing: *alētheia*.

Although Heidegger links technology with revealing in his most well-known lecture on technology, 'The Question Concerning Technology' (given in 1953 and first published in 1954), he had, as Harman notes (2010: 17–18), already addressed the theme in detail in the earlier 'Bremen' lecture of 1949 (Heidegger 2012). There, the almost inscrutable character of technology derives, in part, from Heidegger's attempt to put very much to one side the notion of technology as means (the instrumental view), or technology as a human invention in favour of the key idea that 'the essence of technology is nothing technological' (2012: 33). We might designate this as the 'abstract' giving rise to the 'concrete' rather than the reverse, so that no individual instance (e.g. the machine) could be said to embody the whole of technology. Thus, 'Every construction of every machine already moves within the essential space of technology' (33). The instrument (machine) does not explain technology; rather, it is the essence of technology that explains the machine. All this is well and good. However, things become complicated when Heidegger endeavours to unravel the essence of technology through the concepts of positionality/enframing (*Ge-Stell*), standing reserve (*Bestand*), challenging forth and requisitioning/ordering (*Bestellen*). To recall, technology is neither a means, nor essentially something human; rather, the technological takes place autonomously as the unfolding of an epoch. The human, then, would also be part of the autonomous unfolding of the technological, from which nothing in the world is excluded: not nature, not machines, not human activity. Everything is now standing reserve – including nature – and thus available for exploitation or requisitioning. As challenging forth, the world is ordered in terms of specific goals: 'The earth's soil is forced into conscription' (26). Moreover, 'Through such requisitioning [*Bestellen*] the land becomes a coal reserve, the soil an ore depository. This requisitioning is already of a different sort from that whereby the peasant had previously tended his field. Peasant activity does not challenge the farmland; rather it leaves the crops to the discretion of the growing forces' (26).

Challenging forth can thus be understood to do with mechanization and in moulding standing reserve to serve planned ends. All of this occurs despite the human not because of the human: 'Requisitioning is no human deed' (29). Nevertheless, 'In the age of technological dominance, the human is placed into the essence of technology, into positionality, by his essence' (35). In other words, the human also becomes exploitable.

Interestingly, Heidegger cites radio and film as instances of the 'standing reserve of this requisitioning' (36), and he elaborates by referring to the fact that 'the public sphere as such is positioned, challenged forth and thereby first installed' (36). Radio, Heidegger finds, is illustrative of positioning and challenging forth – of the ordering of the public sphere. The impression given is that radio is 'imposed upon' individuals, not chosen by them: 'They are in their essence already imposed upon with the character of having to be a piece of standing reserve' (36). What is normally called a medium comes to have power in its own right with regard to the listener. While Heidegger does not refer explicitly to radio programmes, only to radio as an institution, the importance of programming, or radio content, is implied when, if one were to assume that radios were to disappear, Heidegger asks: 'who would be able to fathom the cluelessness, the boredom, the emptiness that would attack the human at a stroke and would completely dishevel their everyday affairs?' (37). It is as though the audience were addicted to radio *qua* content and would thus suffer withdrawal symptoms following its termination. However, as standing reserve and requisitioning, radio ceases to be conceived as a medium – that is, as transparent – in favour of it being part of the media industry that constitutes the 'coercive insistence of the public sphere' (36). No doubt, Heidegger is evoking part of what Adorno and Horkheimer will later designate as the 'culture industries'.

The urban public sphere and its media institutions, as part of standing reserve, are thus part of modern technology. But this generalization does not do justice to individual media events, specifically radio events and programmes in 1930s, Weimar Germany – one particularly notable event in terms of this study being Heidegger's 1933 radio broadcast, 'Why Do I Stay in the Provinces?' (Heidegger 1981). The broadcast is a talk given by the philosopher to explain why he did not accept an invitation to take up a chair at the University of Berlin and decided to remain in the provinces. Here, it is not, for our purposes, just a matter of understanding Heidegger's text as an insight into the true nature of his philosophical ideas,[1] but rather one of how the event might be interpreted in terms of Heidegger's own approach to technology, where radio is part of standing reserve. If, in terms of the latter, radio is essentially an institution that organizes the public sphere to the detriment of individuality, and if this means – to reiterate – that radio is not essentially its content, then how are we to understand Heidegger's talk? We have to understand it *against* Heidegger's approach to radio and no doubt to media in general. That is the short answer.

To follow Heidegger a certain way we can say that the essence of the medium is not any particular medium. Thus, taken individually, neither radio, nor film, nor television, nor painting or the other arts or other forms of technics constitute the essence of the medium. How, on this basis, does OOO and the work of Harman relate to the foregoing?

Tool-being

Although Harman's ambition in his book, *Tool-Being*, is to show that an analysis of Heidegger's study of the tool as 'readiness-to-hand' (*Zuhandenheit*)

---

1 Debate has centred on whether this talk is an 'apologia for a philosophy rooted in the countryside', as Wilding (2005: 110) has argued, thus conferring a potentially conservative, if not reactionary, take on Heidegger's philosophy. The latter, according to Wilding, was deeply affected by early sociology (Tönnies, Simmel), which could be interpreted as painting a negative picture of city life. For Heidegger scholar Jeff Malpas, the talk could be interpreted in a positive light as promoting the importance of the 'natural' environment and a necessarily solitary way of life conducive to thinking (see Malpas 2021: 40–1).

and as 'presence-to-hand' (*Vorhandenheit*) in *Being and Time* (1978) can illuminate the whole of Heidegger's philosophy,[2] our focus will be on the way Harman does, or does not raise the question of medium. Methodologically, Harman does not intend to reveal what Heidegger really meant but to develop a deeper understanding of tool-being that Heidegger was the first to bring to notice, but not the first to name. Rather, tool-being is the term Harman has coined to capture the gist of Heidegger's analysis of equipment.

What, then, is the significance of 'tool' in Harman's philosophy? In the first place, a tool, whether or not it is used in some way, is an object, and in the second place, 'it *is*' (Harman 2002: 20). Moreover, in a statement that foreshadows Harman's OOO, we read that 'the world is a geography of objects, whether these objects are made of the latest plastics or were born at the dawn of time' (21). And these objects are irreducible to any set of properties that might be 'tabulated by an observer' (21). In summary, objects are to be understood from a synthetic and not an analytic perspective.

Harman turns to the Heidegger-inspired invisibility of the tool or object as readiness-to-hand. And it transpires that the tool, in its working – in its readiness-to-hand – is essentially, and not just incidentally, invisible. It is not as though one could, if paying full and careful attention, observe the tool in its working. To some extent, readiness-to-hand presupposes this invisibility, but Haman wants to go further and claim that Heidegger places too much emphasis on the human use of tools rather than on tools as objects – objects that essentially include a dimension that is quite inaccessible to the human. In short, tools cannot be defined in terms of human use – or non-use – but rather in terms – as already mentioned – of their 'being'. Hence the notion of tool-being that will give rise to an 'object-oriented-philosophy' developed in Chapter 3 of *Tool-Being* (2002: 217–96).[3] If Heidegger's concept of present-to-hand, where the tool/object can be present to consciousness, does not capture what is essential, it is also the case that readiness-to-hand is defective with

---

2 Compare with 'the present book advocates a more extreme position: that the theory of equipment contains *the whole of the Hedeggerian philosophy*' (2002: 15).

3 It is notable that Harman's concept of the tool-being anticipates Quentin Meillassoux's rejection of a putative 'correlationism', where an object is always an object for a human subject (see Meillassoux 2011). In passing it can be observed that the subject–object relation specific to the concept of correlation as Meillassoux proposes it is an epistemological, rather than an ontological, notion. As such, it would seem to go without saying that the human cannot be excluded from knowing.

regard to bringing the essence of the object to presence. For an object is more than its use, more than any end to which it is oriented.

If, to grasp the full force of Harman's approach, we move from tool to objects in general it transpires that, in their being, objects are never fully present, which implies that an object is never reducible to a representation of it, unless the said representation is so constituted as to reveal an absence or gap at the heart of what is represented – the appearing of that which cannot appear, as it were.

In Harman's view, what he dubs the Heideggerian 'as-structure' must be fully appreciated before an assessment can be made of Heidegger's approach to tools and technology broadly understood. Thus the broken tool – the tool as *Vorhandenheit* – like technology as standing reserve, both fall into the as-structure – namely, the thing, object, being, *as* thing, object, being. Here, a qualification should be noted: 'the thing "as" thing is not the same as the thing itself, which can *never* be openly encountered' (69). Consequently, the 'as-structure marks an event of *simulation*' (69). Heidegger's 'as-structure' turns on the possibility of going beyond the presence-at-hand of the entity and accessing the thing itself – technology *as* technology; but, Harman contends, this is impossible as an aspect of the thing-entity always remains hidden, withdrawn. To focus again on Heidegger and technology, Harman argues that the notion of modern technology *as* 'standing reserve' or, for that matter, *as* enframing/positionality, falls down because it is analysed in terms of the as-structure and thus in terms of the appearing as such of the entity. Thus, an injudicious invocation of the as-structure 'undercuts Heidegger's technology writings, which culminate in the untenable claim that the technological world strips all reality down to its bare visibility or manipulability. Just as theory ultimately cannot be understood as the making present of thing "as" thing, technology cannot adequately be grasped if we regard it only as the univocal stripping away of secrets' (79).

To elaborate this point, Harman, in a short article that summarizes a number of the key points in *Tool-Being*, emphasizes the fact that technology for Heidegger is essentially *Vorhandenheit* – that is, technology as standing reserve is what appears. Therefore, '"standing reserve" is without distance, without true nearness, and is ontologically identical with what was earlier called presence-at-hand' (2010: 22). What Harman fails to notice here – or fails to comment upon – is that standing reserve cannot be understood to be an end in itself, but is clearly a means to an end. By way of illustration, we can refer to Heidegger's reference to the Rhine River and the hydroelectric plant: 'the river is dammed up into the power plant. What the river is now, namely, a water power supplier, derives from the essence of the power station' (Heidegger 1977: 16). Everything that is 'stockpiled' is '*on call*' (emphasis added): 'The sun's warmth is challenged forth for heat, which in turn is ordered to deliver steam whose pressure turns the wheels that keep the factory running' (15). Finally, 'Everywhere everything is ordered to stand by, to be *immediately* at hand, indeed to stand there just so that it may be on call for a further ordering' (17; emphasis added). In light of these statements, Heidegger can be clearly seen to revive the notion of 'means', even while denying that technology is a means to an end. Only if standing reserve is a means, does it make sense to say that 'standing reserve no longer stands over against us as object' (17). And the machine would be 'completely unautonomous, for it has its standing *only* from the ordering of the orderable' (17). Hence, if technology retains its status as means, it must be doubted that it can appear as such, whether or not this be in terms of Heidegger's *Vorhandendheit*. As a result, Harman's interpretation needs to be nuanced, if not entirely rejected.

Ultimately, for Harman, the writings of McLuhan and Latour 'put Heidegger's aloof reflections on hydroelectric dams to shame' (2002: 78). But it is McLuhan's notion of the medium as object that is also problematic. Given its putative impact in Heidegger's eyes on the formation of the public sphere, the example of radio would seem to confirm that, for the thinker of the question of technology, the 'medium is the message'. Might it be, then, that Harman employs his own version of the as-structure when it comes to considering the medium, whether as image or otherwise. And, in any case, if the as-structure in Heidegger's hands appears as a simulacrum, it remains to determine the exact status (opaque or transparent?) of the latter.[4] The hope is that a detailed engagement with Harman on art might throw light on this issue. To prepare for this, we need to understand what Harman means by 'object'.

---

4 By way of elaboration here, Harman states, in relation to Baudrillard – the famous theorist of the simulacrum – that: 'The works of Jean Baudrillard are also relevant on the theme of simulation, but these works are so non-Heideggerian in terminology and tone that excessive space would be required to demonstrate the strange but undeniable Heidegger–Baudrillard connection' (2002: 302, n76).

The object

Object now, according to Harman's conception – one that he claims distinguishes his approach from almost all others – is that no description, no itemization of qualities, no entire specification of relations – indeed no rendering of the object of whatever kind can do full justice to the *being* of the object. As an illustration, our author asks us to consider a bridge:

> No description of the bridge by a human being and no touching of the bridge by the sea or the hill that it adjoins, can adequately mimic the work of the bridge in its being. No perception of the bridge-thing however direct a perception might be, can accomplish the very actuality that brings the bridge about. The bridge is irreplaceable in an *absolute* sense. (224)

This is further testimony to Harman's engagement with objects as radically synthetic. Objects are *radically* synthetic because even indicating that the object never fully appears cannot be understood as a specific quality of that object. As mentioned earlier, Harman's general approach to the tool/object is nothing if not detached from the analytical. Of particular significance is the idea that a synthetic characterization applies to any object whatsoever. And Harman has become well known for his extended lists of objects that range from the most lauded and visible – artworks and buildings – to the most innocuous and inconspicuous – dust and bacteria. Specks of dust, like bacteria, are thus objects. In this light, the following question arises: are there, or are there not, entities that in their being are not objects – images, for example?

Object-oriented ontology, McLuhan and the medium made explicit

Harman's concept of the image is coloured by an explicit acceptance of McLuhan's theory of the medium, even if, in speaking about architecture, he also translates medium as 'form'. Thus, in an article on McLuhan and Heidegger, the philosopher observes that

> This is where McLuhan becomes relevant, since even more concretely than Heidegger it is he who relentlessly champions form. McLuhan's most famous

phrase, 'the medium is the message', also expresses his central idea: that the content of any medium is largely irrelevant compared with the structure of that medium itself … . To argue over good and bad printed books is to ignore the transformative effects of print itself. (2016a: 103)

We only need recall here the discussion, in the previous chapter, of Barthes and Kracauer on photography and the fact that photography in general can only become explicit in relation to the content of a range of *different* photographic images. There is no image that would capture photography as such. As far as Harman's example is concerned, print in general would only 'appear' via the content of specific books or newspapers. As a medium, print does not appear as such. Rather than follow up on the perception of media specificity and the essential nature of the medium, Harman, in the article cited, chooses to close with an explanation of why McLuhan is not a technological determinist. Part of the explanation lies in the 'retrieval' by artists and others of 'old' media so that the latter can take on a new life. This is evocative of Ernst's work discussed in Chapter 4 and, as we shall see, of the approach of Rosalind Krauss. But, in contra-distinction to what is evident in McLuhan's (and Harman's) thinking, the medium becomes transparent in Ernst's vision of revitalized vintage, media products.

Harman on art

To illuminate Harman's understanding of the image as medium, we turn now to the domain of aesthetics, which Harman regards as pivotal in the OOO understanding of the object.[5]

A quote on the medium from art critic Clement Greenberg can set the scene here, as Harman takes up Greenberg's position on the medium as the point of departure for his own thinking. Greenberg thus sets out his view on art as follows:

---

5 Harman defines aesthetics as 'the study of the surprisingly loose relationship between objects and their own qualities' (2019: xi–xii). See also in this light the notion of aesthetics as 'first philosophy' in Harman (2012).

Realistic, naturalistic art dissembled the medium, using art to conceal art; Modernism used art to call attention to art. The limitations that constitute the medium of painting – the flat surface, the shape of the support, the properties of the pigment – were treated by the Old Masters as negative factors that could be acknowledged only implicitly or indirectly. Under Modernism these same limitations came to be regarded as positive factors, and were acknowledged openly. Manet's became the first Modernist pictures by virtue of the frankness with which they declared the flat surfaces on which they were painted. The Impressionists, in Manet's wake, abjured underpainting and glazes, to leave the eye under no doubt as to the fact that the colors they used were made of paint that came from tubes or pots. Cézanne sacrificed verisimilitude, or correctness, in order to fit his drawing or design more explicitly to the rectangular shape of the canvas. (Greenberg 1995: 86–7)

This, then, is Greenberg's way of confirming the dictum that the 'medium is the message', a point that was taken up by Harman in a chapter appositely titled, 'The Canvas Is the Message' (2019: 83–109). Although, as we have seen, Greenberg acknowledges 'pigment', 'paint' and 'colour' as media, it is, for Greenberg, above all, as Harman recognizes, flatness (manifest in the canvas) that is the key 'medium' in modern art (Harman 2019: 85). Greenberg is thus opposed to 'nineteenth-century illusionism' based in perspective, since, on this reckoning, the content must give way to the primacy of the medium: the flat canvas, even if the latter does not appear as such and remains in the shadows, in a kind of twilight zone.

When referring to art more generally, Harman says that 'literalism' occurs when an object is made equivalent to its qualities (see Harman 2019: 26). Another way of putting it is to say that literalism means that an object is equivalent to a description of it. By contrast, aesthetically, an object cannot be reduced to its qualities. To reduce the message to the medium made explicit is a form of literalism, which is not necessarily Harman's position. In fact, to all appearances, Harman places art content on the side of literalism and the medium on the side of what is unique in art. Ultimately, literalism transcends the difference between content and medium, so that there can be a literalist interpretation of the medium as there can be a literalist interpretation of content. Here, much depends on what counts as 'content' and what as 'medium'. In this regard, the following points need to be taken into consideration, points that constitute elements of a discussion prompted by Harman's remarks in the work already cited, *Art and Objects*.

Then again, in opposition to Greenberg and Heidegger, Harman states that 'What OOO most rejects in Greenberg, as in Heidegger, is another aspect of their shared modernity. Namely, they not only oppose a deep medium to a superficial content, but further assume that this deep medium is One, making all multiplicity automatically shallow by contrast' (2019: 142). Consequently, 'OOO argues – against Greenberg and Heidegger – for a fragmented depth, so that the medium of the artwork is not found in the unified canvas, but in each and every element of the work, some of them left in suppressed literal form while others are freed up by way of the object–quality tension we call beauty' (142).

To reiterate, academic art for Greenberg is that which takes no account of its medium (Harman 2019: 99). But the problem is that medium is conceptualized as object rather than the 'disappearance of medium in its implementation' (Krämer 2015). If, for Heidegger, Being acts as medium (Harman 2019: 100–1), the question is: how is it possible to philosophize about Being? Even though Harman is critical of Heidegger on this point it is not because Heidegger objectifies Being. Rather, just as Greenberg and McLuhan have no time for content – Greenberg in art and McLuhan in relation to media – so Heidegger is deemed to have little time for the variety of particular beings – beings in their difference from one another. Just as Heidegger's project is to seek ways in which Being can be brought into the clearing of unconcealedness in the move of '*a-lethia*', so Greenberg and McLuhan seek ways to make the medium explicit. But, ultimately, rather than Being as such appearing, it is a matter of how Being enables beings to be in their differences. Because Greenberg and McLuhan are analogously fixated on the appearing of the medium (Harman confirms as much), they fail to grasp the nature of medium *as* medium. For the medium, as has been said throughout this study, is not reducible to a thing, object or specific entity. If something (the medium) does not appear as such, it can imply that it is in the shadows, in the darkness of the underworld and thus the harbinger of a threatening negativity and forgetfulness (cf. *lethia*). In this way, the medium can be linked to the mystical, which means that it is not available to normal sensory perception or to scientific verification. Harman does not go into this kind of detail, but it is clear that, in one way or another, the medium needs to be brought to light. So that if, for 'Heidegger,

Greenberg, and McLuhan ... medium refers to something hidden beneath the surface properties of the object', by contrast, the position of OOO is that the medium is 'located *above* beholder and work, which contains them like an unseen atmosphere' (2019: 173). As it turns out, what Harman means by this is that there is an essential relation between artwork and beholder. The beholder, in Harman's view, is part of a 'compound' that 'exceeds both parts individually and is not exhaustively knowable by the human beholder who forms part of it. Rembrandt's *Nightwatch* is not a painting if no one experiences it' (45). But, equally, the said painting is not reducible to an experience of it.

Where, then, is the medium? Specifying the medium in fact does not pose a problem. The medium can be equated with the physical being of the artwork/object. The medium of painting certainly includes, as Greenberg proposes, the flat canvas. As it turns out, the body is the medium of the beholder. Body is the condition of possibility of the beholder. But neither artwork nor beholder are reducible to the media of which they are composed. They are not medium specific – medium specificity being, as I have argued, the consequence of McLuhan's famous dictum.

The virtue of Harman's discussion of Greenberg, and the work of art historian Michael Fried, along with the work of various art theorists, such as Arthur Danto, is that the issue of the medium is addressed, even if one must also disagree with the philosopher's own conception of it as equivalent (in Heidegger and Greenberg, if not in McLuhan) to a homogenizing, deep structure behind the veil of reality. The problem with Harman's engagement with the medium – as with McLuhan and Greenberg – is that medium and content become separated from each other, so that there is the medium on one side and content on the other, whereas, in fact, I have argued, there is no medium without content: content is the 'presence' of the medium; the medium is the condition of possibility of content.

Harman and objects – including art objects

Effectively, in his evocation of *Night Watch* (1642), Harman does not treat the medium, for he does not comment on the content of *Night Watch*, whereas the following description is, I suggest, equivalent to the appearing of the medium:

Here a frisky dog barks; a drummer beats his big drum, readying to keep time with the marching guards; a boy is seen at the furthest edge to the left, looking back as he runs off carrying a gunpowder horn; a guard tinkers with the muzzle of his musket; behind the richly attired captain, another guard accidently fires his musket, its smoke mixing with the white plume on the lieutenant's tall hat (a comical near miss, and an actionable offence). Further to the right, a guard examines the barrel of his musket. Meanwhile, some figures, jostling behind the more prominent characters, are barely visible beyond a limb or, if you look very carefully, an eye and a partially glimpsed face. That eye to the upper left of Banning Cocq, belongs to the artist himself. Just as the Flemish artist Van Eyck loved to do, Rembrandt painted himself hidden within the scene.[6]

Thus, by way of the medium of oil paint, Rembrandt himself appears in *Night Watch*. But the appearing of Rembrandt does not relate, for Harman and others, to the medium as such. And it does not relate, despite his criticism of Greenberg and McLuhan, for neglecting content. As far as Harman's approach to the art object is concerned, we might ask whether the foregoing description of the content of *Night Watch* should be interpreted as 'undermining', that is, as reducing an (art) object to its qualities? Is a description of an artwork's content the same thing as reducing it to its qualities? Or is the point to accept that a description of an artwork is part of what it is, but it is not the whole story? The following statement by Harman seems to confirm the latter assumption: 'But with artworks the gap between the object and its qualities is far more pronounced, since no qualitative or quantitative analysis of Van Gogh's *Starry Night* or Wagner's *Tristan und Isolde* can possibly exhaust these works, just as no description of a person's traits can ever do justice to the person' (2013: 192).

On one level, this seems to be perfectly acceptable: a work of art or a person are more than any description can provide. On another level, however, a description – following Harman's (or is it Latour's?) quirky list – is *also* an object where the same divide is encountered between medium (language, signs) and content (the description). Does this imply that no interpretation of

---

6   BBC culture at: https://www.bbc.com/culture/article/20190214-does-rembrandts-the-night-watch-reveal-a-murder-plot (accessed 31 August 2022).

a description (or description of a description) can ever be exhaustive enough to do justice to the description? If this is true, it is also trivial, but still damaging enough to cause a problem for Harman's philosophy of the object. Perhaps, though, we have overstepped the mark and called description an object when Harman specifically rules this out. But no – here is a list that includes signs: 'wrenches and anvils and linguistic signs' and in fact, 'everything under the sun' (2002:10). So that 'moon-ray, wish, puppet, number' (2002: 43) are objects. How is a wish (my wish? – the other's wish?) communicated? Again, the divide between medium and content arises. Can a description of a wish ever be exhausted? With this example, we seem to have reached the *reductio ad absurdum* of OOO. As Lemke has pointed out, 'OOO does not offer any orientation on how differences between objects are enacted or established and how they become meaningful' (Lemke 2017: 134). To this we can add: if objects are truly diverse can they even answer to the term, 'object'? Can the '*punctum*', or subjective sting or point that Barthes invokes, be an object? Of course, one way to deal with this is employ the frequently used recourse to paradox and say that even a non-object is an object.

The *punctum* as object

The *punctum* disturbs the narrative aspect of a photograph (the *stadium*). Barthes says that it 'is also: sting, speck, cut, little hole – and also a cast of the dice. A photograph's *punctum* is that accident which pricks me (but also bruises me, is poignant to me)' (2010: 27). In Harman's framework, an artwork needs a beholder; in Barthes's framework, a photograph presupposes a viewer. Much has been made (and by Barthes himself) of the subjective status of the *punctum*: my *punctum* – the detail in the photo that attracts me – is, by definition, not your *punctum*. But while the *punctum* supposedly triggers something *in* me (hence, the possibility of the revelation of my singularity), in point of fact the detail is *in* the photograph or image.[7] Thus the *punctum* is not an object in any simple sense but is constitutive of a specific relation between image and viewer.

---

7 Why should the *punctum* not apply to any image, regardless of the medium?

Does it make any sense to say, in Harman's terms, that the *punctum* is an object and that, as such, it partly withdraws from view? In other words, in what sense is the *punctum* not fully present? A 'sting' or 'prick' that is not fully present is not a sting or a prick. Maybe, on the other hand, it is the detail constitutive of the *punctum* that withdraws – that is not wholly present. Yet, if this be the case, once again it would seem the very reality of the *punctum* is diminished.

Overall, though, whatever view one takes regarding the *punctum* as object, it is generated by an aspect of the content of the image, a content that is made possible by the medium. There are moments when Harman, too, seems to be heading in this direction – namely, when he refuses the idea of the medium as a 'One' and argues that the 'medium of the artwork is not found in the unified canvas, but in each and every element of the work' (Harman 2019: 142).

Harman on literalism in art

On the other hand, in a discussion of Dada and Surrealism – prompted by Arthur Danto's definition of art as meaning – Harman presents confusing messages about the medium and the notion of 'literalism' in art. Surrealism will turn to be less literalist – at least as exemplified by Salvador Dali – than Dada. How does our author arrive at this conclusion?

To begin with, he defines literalism, as we have seen earlier, as the reduction of an object to its qualities. How does this pertain to an artwork? Imagine if it became illegitimate in art criticism influenced by OOO to isolate for attention Mona Lisa's smile (a quality). Moreover, as has often occurred, the background of the Mona Lisa figure can be the focus of attention. The painting, *qua* art (as opposed to house painting), a critic might say, *is* its qualities. In Mark Rothko's *Untitled*, 1967,[8] we encounter two fields, each of different degrees of redness and the border in between (perhaps a horizon). The degrees, or intensities, of redness are not just the qualities *of* the work, but are the work *as* specific qualities. Let us say that a concern for the qualities of artwork does not automatically equate with literalism. After all, it is Mona

---

8 Oil on canvas, 81" × 76". Private collection. Reproduced in Waldman (1986: plate number 186).

Lisa's smile that is being referred to, not specific strokes of oil paint. Similarly, in Rothko's work it is redness as such, not the chemically constituted red paint that is encountered. In short, there is interpretation, not a mere listing of physical qualities, which would be true literalism. In what way, if at all, does Harman's position correspond to what we have said regarding the artwork and qualities? And what are the implications for an understanding of the medium?

Characteristic of Greenberg's modernism is the requirement that the painter/artist evoke the medium in the work, that is, the 'flat canvas'. Cubism fills the bill here because of its evocation of two-dimensionality (flatness), as opposed to the three-dimensional illusionism of nineteenth-century style art. The latter, for Greenberg, refuses the medium any visibility. Art critic and art historian Michael Fried also plumbs for the medium; it is just that, for him, the said medium is to be equated with 'shape' (see Harman 2019: 85). With Fried, the 'interplay between content and its ground' is at issue, a fact that links both Greenberg and Fried with Heidegger's Being and McLuhan's medium.

What is not acknowledged, however, is that it is the medium that enables the content of the artwork to appear – even 'to be'. To the extent that the flat canvas appears as content (in Mondrian's work, for example) it ceases to be a medium because it becomes content. The analogy that can be drawn here is the one already outlined in Chapter 1 with regard to Benveniste's theory of the *énonciation* (act of stating) and the *énoncé* (the statement made). The *énonciation*, it was said, is analogous to the medium as the condition of possibility of the *énoncé*. To experience the content of an artwork, for it to have an impact as immediately meaningful or significant in some way, is to experience it as equivalent to an *énonciation*, whereas, to address the content of an artwork as an example of a particular movement or genre or as typical of an artist's style is to encounter it as an *énoncé*. In short, the *énoncé* is an objectification, while the *énonciation*, *qua énonciation*, cannot be objectified. I am claiming, then, that the medium is equivalent to the *énonciation*. The denial of this distinction leads to 'medium specificity' or to what we could call the 'McLuhan factor'. Harman shows his commitment to this factor when he writes: 'To take one's medium for granted, *to focus thereby on content* rather than background, is another way to say one is a *literalist*' (Harman

2019: 145; emphasis added). What this statement forgets is that any focus on background – what I call the medium – begins to turn it into content. Would background include the paint (the medium) outside the frame, as we find in the image of Pollock's painting?[9] I would reply in the affirmative.

As soon as the medium's materiality is the focus of attention, it becomes 'content'. Put another – rather obvious – way, once the medium becomes the message it ceases to be medium.

Modal ontology as the 'presence' of the medium

Harman's claim that the medium that does not appear evokes the Heideggerian Being – a Being that, as 'Oneness', opens up new possibilities. For whether or not Heidegger's presentation of Being results in a Oneness, it is possible, in light of Giorgio Agamben's insight, to resort to a modal ontology.

As already outlined in Chapter 1, a modal ontology means that Being appears in a plurality of modes none of which (in keeping with the ontological difference) is equivalent to Being as Being. Even though it is not always possible to discern whether Heidegger intends that Being is never without beings,[10] Agamben points to the 'Postscript' appended to the 1949 edition of 'What Is Metaphysics', where we read that 'the truth of being never prevails in its essence without beings, that a being is never without being' (Heidegger 1998: 233). Agamben's translation concludes with '*beings* are never without Being' (Agamben 2015: 164; emphasis added).[11] And Agamben confirms that 'Being can never be separated from beings' (164). Whether or not the reading of Heidegger here is 'correct', the analogous argument to be made regarding the medium is that 'content' is never without the medium, and the 'presence' of the medium is content – whether this be of an artwork, a film, a photograph, a literary text or an architectural structure. With a modal ontology the middle voice also comes into play. For example, in Antonioni's 1966 film, *Blow-Up*,

---

9 See: https://artwizard.eu/jackson-pollock-ar-29 (accessed 27 October 2022). Also search art wizard.
10 For example, when Being is equated with nothingness in 'The Fundamental Question of Metaphysics' (Heidegger 2014: 1–56).
11 Elsewhere, Heidegger appears to confirm the relation between Being and beings, when he states that 'Being is thus dispersed into manifold beings' (2014: 112).

the photographic image reveals the body beneath the hedge. Again, artistic content shows the medium in action.[12]

Modal ontology is then invoked in order to emphasize the status of the medium as a mode because – in Agamben's words – 'the mode is at once identical and different – or rather, it entails the coincidence, which is to say the falling together, of the two terms' (164).

As it turns out, Harman also agrees in substance with a modal ontology in relation to Greenberg and to Heidegger as he refers to that fact that 'Tension between foreground and background is always needed for Greenberg, just as Heidegger requires that Being manifest itself in individual beings while also hiding behind them' (2019: 128). This more modal interpretation of Being and beings seems to be in opposition to Harman's claim that Being is 'this deep medium One making all multiplicity shallow by contrast' (142). For it is in the *diversity* beings that Being can be detected. Again, Harman nuances his position by acknowledging that the 'medium of the artwork is not found in the unified canvas, but in each and every element' (142). Harman's sensitivity to the medium in every element of the work and the fact that background (in collage) does not become present fails, as we have seen, to carry over to a consideration of the medium in general. And this failure is due to the anti-literalist stance Harman adopts, a stance he also attributes to the Kant of the Third Critique (141). This should be qualified: it is not literalism that reduces the object (whether art object or not) to a set of qualities, but the incorporation of art content into the definition of qualities.

Dada and Surrealism

In arguing that art is now related to meaning, Danto echoes Luhmann's claim that 'Art … establishes its own rules of inclusion, which are served by the difference of medium and form as medium' (Luhmann 1987: 105). Perhaps unlike Danto, Luhmann is sensitive to the role of the medium in art. Does

---

12 Thus, 'Modal ontology can be understood only as a medial ontology' (Agamben 2015: 165). Again, 'In a modal ontology, being uses-itself, that is to say, it constitutes, expresses, and loves itself in the affection that it receives from its own modifications' (165).

Luhmann then confirm Greenberg's stance? The answer is 'no', since for Luhrmann the form of art (the content?) renders the medium imperceptible, or, more generally, as absent, while Greenberg wants the medium to be entirely present. On the other hand, with statements such as the following, Luhmann's position is often ambiguous as when he views art 'as the development of ever new media-for-forms' (108). We are thus led to ask whether it is media as such that appear through forms or the reverse: that media enable the presence of forms.

To return to the Greenberg argument that Harman addresses in relation to Dada and Surrealism we find that the latter movements supposedly remain, in a crucial sense, academic in the execution of art; therefore, they 'take the medium for granted' and privilege content. For Harman, as we have seen, this is to take a *literalist* approach to art (2019: 145). On the face of it, illusionistic surrealist painting à la Dalí and Magritte seems to fill the bill. The flat canvas (medium) is ignored. On the other hand, Marcel Duchamp, 'author' of, amongst other things, ready-made objects and, subsequently, chief representative of Dada outrageousness, would supposedly privilege medium over content. To all appearances, then, Duchamp is not a literalist. And yet, Harman eventually concedes that Dada 'is an attempt to put a unified literal object in the usual place of an artwork, which … is necessarily non-literal' (155). Here, 'literalism' seems to mean an object *qua* object, while an artwork is more than this.

Harman could have made things clearer by making a distinction between content as physical qualities and the subject or theme of an artwork: what the work is 'about'. However, the response might be that a 'ready-made', for example, is not *about* anything: it just *is*. This is the point. But is this so? Even Duchamp's *Fountain* is placed – like any artwork – in a gallery setting. The ready-made is, in short, a de-contextualized object, as are the tools, weapons and artefacts of so-called primitive societies – items that have found their way into the Western gallery or museum system. As Denis Hollier writes, 'No art lover will ever ask what these objects [from other cultures] did before they cost so much money. No art lover will ever ask why they were never seen before they were put on exhibit' (1995: 137). The ready-made, then, becomes an art object once it no longer has a use-value – that is, once it is no longer a technical object (a means) and becomes vehicle of exchange-value (an end in itself). That is, the object becomes the *medium* through which art is experienced.

What better example could one find of an object that has absolutely ceased to have a use-value – that has been wrenched from its context – than Duchamp's *Fountain*? The latter thus becomes an end in itself.

Harman recognizes that a ready-made is something '*torn*' from its 'usual context' (2019: 156), but he does not concede that this alone can be sufficient for the said 'something' to became an artwork: 'the literal urinal is merely a bundle of qualities and by no means an object apart from its qualities' (157).[13] Through the objects in the paintings of Dalí, surrealism, according to Harman, subverts literalism in the same way that Heidegger's example of the 'broken hammer' puts us in touch with objects *qua* objects (162).

Artwork, medium and the surrealist object

In contrast to Harman, the question that this chapter has raised is, what is the status of the medium in the artwork? Clearly, two senses of 'medium' have arisen: the first is the one referring to the materials of which the artwork is composed – paint, canvas, photographic paper and so on. The second sense refers to the extent to which an object that has no use-value becomes the medium of what can be called art. If the paint, canvas and colour become invisible in light of the subject-matter of the picture, is it also true that, once in an art context (gallery), the object *qua* object also becomes, in a sense, invisible? In this regard, Duchamp's ready-mades might not be the best vehicle through which to answer this question.

We refer, now, to an aspect of surrealism that is entirely absent from Harman's account. This aspect concerns what are, initially, ethnographic items, items that, nevertheless, end up in Western museums and galleries – or in André Breton's Paris apartment.[14] Surrealism evokes Heidegger's 'broken hammer' in the sense that, as the quote from Hollier indicated, a Western

---

13 It is interesting that Harman frequently refers to Duchamp's object as a 'urinal' rather than as '*Fountain*', thereby diminishing its artwork status.
14 It is well known that Breton decked out his Paris apartment at 42, rue Fontaine, with Oceanic, North American, African and Australian Aboriginal art and artefacts. For a discussion plus images of Breton's apartment, and the implications of Breton's 'surrealist' appropriation of non-Western objects, see Conley (2015).

beholder becomes aware of an 'ethnic' artefact only after it ceases to have a use-value and enters the context of art, in other words, after it has been de-contextualized.

Surrealist object as ethnographic

James Clifford, in his highly regarded article, 'On Ethnographic Surrealism', presents an 'ethnography, which shares with surrealism an abandonment of the distinction between high and low culture' (1981: 549). What brings ethnography even more into the shadow of surrealism is its encounter with the sheer diversity of objects and ways of life: 'The surrealist moment in ethnography is that moment in which the possibility exists in unmediated tension with sheer incongruity' (563). Ethnography itself thus becomes a medium. As such, there is no limit as to what can come to have aesthetic value. While the ethnographer, as contemporary of surrealism, strove to render the strange object familiar, the surrealist approach was to render the familiar strange (542). For the surrealist – especially Breton – the very process of de-contextualization that the collection of non-Western cultural objects represented opened the way for such objects to assume an aesthetic value, that is, in fact, to become part of a collection, whether in a public gallery, or in a private collection – such as the one owned by Breton. While Breton aspired to demonstrate that non-Western objects were equally worthy of aesthetic appreciation, another tendency in surrealism argued that the origins (the 'use-value') of such an object should not be erased. In effect, against the commodification of the art object, the ethnographic object should be displayed so as to reveal its ritual significance – that is, its context.

Whatever position is taken regarding the object of indigenous cultures – whether as proto-artwork or as evocative of sacred or profane ritual – it would seem that, in either case, the object is a medium. This is to say, too, that in either context, the object is not reducible to an enumeration of its material qualities. In this, there is agreement with Harman. Where it is necessary to disagree is in the implication in Harman that the medium can appear as such. Counter to this is the idea that the medium does not appear as such because it is the condition of possibility of what does appear. Or, in the terms already invoked in this study, the non-appearing of the medium in what appears is 'evidence' of the medium. The medium appears in not appearing. As has already been acknowledged, this is not to deny that the medium requires a material element to be what it is; but it cannot be reduced to this – as is the case in McLuhan with whom Harman seems to be in agreement. Surrealism also becomes a medium to the extent that, like ethnography, it is implicit in a grand diversity of objects, but is not reducible to a single object. Through surrealism, objects and personages become fantastic, strange, extraordinary. But not only this; it is also the case that surrealism *valourizes* the aforementioned categories. It is thus due to surrealism that art and objects not necessarily produced by members of the movement, but also those hitherto unrecognized, become worthy of acclaim. Such is the case, for example, of the supposedly symbolist paintings of Gustave Moreau (1826–1898), along with the works of numerous poets and writers, including Lautréamont, Baudelaire, Mallarmé and Rimbaud.

*

I have suggested, then, that what is lacking in both Harman's and Greenberg's accounts of painting is a nuanced notion of content. For instance, while the viewer of a Cézanne painting might become aware of the pigments of which the picture is made, this is paint within the frame of the picture – it is paint *as* content, something that is very different from the paint outside the frame as was instanced in an image of Pollock painting. In sum, the medium as such – which is the medium in its implementation – cannot be depicted.

8

The probabilistic object as hyperobject and media specificity

Already, in considering Michel Serres's work in Chapter 5, the notions of entropy, negantropy, order and disorder came into view, especially with regard to information theory. The question that, for instance, Brillouin raised in relation to information theory as initially proposed by Claude Shannon is whether the transmission of information is unique within the field of physical entities and thwarts the tendency for order (i.e. any sort of pattern) to break down into disorder (no pattern is detectable). In the information context, 'negantropy' came to mean a counter-entropy and could be realized when 'noise in a channel' was – theoretically – reduced to zero in light of the flow of information. Like knowledge, information is a counter-entropic force. We saw that in his penchant to promote the productiveness and even the creativeness of noise (cf. the notion of parasite), Serres, at the same time, introduces the opacity of the medium. Creativity arises however in overcoming the noise in a channel or in whatever context it might arise.

The original formulation of the 'Clausius theorem' of entropy by Rudolf Clausius in 1855 still left open the question of human knowledge capacity in relation to the detection of disorder: might it be that entropy was really only an index of the limited capacity of the human mind – and thus of human knowledge – in discerning whether, in specific cases, disorder truly occurs? In this regard, it has been said by some contemporary observers that 'there remains at the present time a strongly entrenched view to the effect that entropy is a subjective concept precisely because it is taken as a measure of "missing information" – information which we *might* use but don't, due to thermodynamic systems being incompletely specified' (Denbigh and Denbigh 1985: 1). In effect, with perfect knowledge (cf. God's omniscience), there would be no disorder. The general consensus today, however, is that disorder and chance are true realities, while information, as has been indicated, is a counter to entropy – hence Brillouin's notion of 'negentropy'. But 'if', Brillouin says, 'we want to transmit information or store it in a memory device, we first select a physical medium, a cable, a radio link, a mercury line, a magnetic tape, etc., and we have to study the physical limitations of this medium' (2013: 28). In effect, if negantropy as the incarnation of pure information is to be realized, the necessary physical medium must become entirely transparent. Is the latter ever fully possible? Heisenberg's uncertainty principle and its appropriation in the notion of the 'hyperobject' reveal, as we shall see, another dimension of this issue.

The uncertainty principle

To gain an understanding of 'hyperobjects' – the main topic of this chapter – it is first necessary to return to the key aspects of Werner Heisenberg's 'uncertainty principle' – a principle that, in sum, brings the measuring instrument as such into full focus, as was shown with regard to Ernst's notion of 'chronopoetics' outlined in Chapter 4. In this light, we also return to the following question: does the instrument/medium always dominate what is measured in quantum physics? The answer to this question is in part provided in a biography of Heisenberg where we read that: 'the very procedures of laboratory observation and measurement [would this be equivalent to the medium? – JL], previously of only minor concern to the classical physicist, became a central concern of the quantum physicist' (Cassidy 1992: 227). The reason for this concern was Heisenberg's 1927 paper, 'On the Perceptual Content of Quantum Theoretical Kinematics and Mechanics'. As the biographer remarks, 'Previously one could always describe the motion of an electron by noting its position and velocity at any given moment. Now, Heisenberg argued in his essay, such concepts are meaningful only when they are referred to or defined by the actual experimental operations used to measure them' (227–8). The illumination of the electron under investigation requires 'very short wavelengths', which in turn means, says Cassidy, summarizing Heisenberg, that 'the greater [is] the energy of the light quantum … hitting the electron' (228). The upshot, as is now well known, is that the very action of measurement affects the position and velocity of the electron: ' "The more precisely we determine the position [of the electron], the more imprecise is the determination of velocity in this instant, and vice versa" ' (Heisenberg cited by Cassidy: 228). A further implication of the 'uncertainty principle' is that the outcomes of the study of electrons in quantum physics are, Heisenberg indicated, ' "of a statistical type" ' (Heisenberg cited by Cassidy: 229). In other words, the outcome is based on probability, not certainty. That the position of an electron cannot be specified with certainty entails that its future position cannot be accurately predicted. In this sense, the uncertainty principle undermines the Laplacian definition of causality, which states that if a current state can be accurately and fully described, or specified, a future state can be accurately predicted. The apparatus, or instrument, then, is a version of 'noise' that disturbs the observable X. On this basis, the instrument (e.g. 'very short wave lengths') is not a medium as it is not what could be called transparent. In a sense, 'the tool speaks'.

Another element of the tool or instrument is, according to Heisenberg in a text aimed at a non-specialist public, the fact that 'the influence of the interaction with the measuring device ... introduces a new element of uncertainty, since the measuring device is necessarily described in the terms of classical physics' (Heisenberg 1990: 41). And Heisenberg continues by stating that 'These uncertainties may be called objective in so far as they are simply a consequence of the description in terms of classical physics and do not depend on any observer' (41). So, should the 'terms of classical physics' be abandoned and a more rigorous medium employed? The physicist answers in the negative. For the 'concepts of classical physics are just a refinement of the concepts of daily life and are an essential language which forms the basis of all natural science' (44). Another way of putting it is to say that science inevitably has to use the language of everyday life to communicate its findings, which means that despite the perception of limitations, the transparency of the language in its use has to be assumed.

Hyperobjects and how they are known

As foreshadowed, a certain conception of Heisenberg's 'uncertainty principle' underpins key aspects of the notion of hyperobjects. It thus remains to be seen how this is the case.

According to Timothy Morton, the inventor of the term, 'hyperobject', 'Hyperobjects are entities that are massively distributed in time and space relative to humans. They are so massive that humans can think and compute them, but not perceive them directly' (2014: 489). Being essentially 'huge both spatially and temporally', means, for our study of the medium, that the most pertinent way to encounter and then to understand hyperobjects is in terms of the medium that gives access to them. This tunes into the issue that we have just been addressing in relation to both Brillouin and Heisenberg, namely, the effect – or non-effect – of the physical medium or of the detecting instrument on the object detected or searched for. In some ways, although Morton is not always this object's best advocate, the following passage is instructive in so far as it foregrounds the instruments (medium) necessary for the detection hyperobjects, such as weather systems, like El Niño and La Niña, the unconscious or capital:

> One is incapable of seeing them directly, but one can compute and map them. Yet they cause all kinds of weather that one can sense directly. Think about the Freudian unconscious, existent but inaccessible save obliquely through slips of the tongue and dreams. Think about capital: one can see its effects everywhere, but one cannot directly touch it. (Morton 2014: 492)

Similarly, global warming as a hyperobject can only be known by graphing the available data, a graphing that currently shows an upward trend in temperature over time.[1] But, as already intimated in the introduction, in Mark Hansen's estimation, this implies that 'measuring media literally produce time-critical phenomena' (2016: 388). And, even more pointedly he claims that 'When they [media] produce phenomena, these apparatuses are in fact performing ontological work' (396). In other words, media are the essence of the being of the world. The world and media are one. But this would imply that, like Being, media do not appear as such, whereas Hansen's emphasis on material apparatuses belies this fact.

As we have seen, a consideration of the medium in relation to fields like quantum objects opens the possibility not only that the medium is explicit but

---

1 As Morton would have it, global warming cannot be experienced as such; but it can be thought and understood via graphs and other visual data instruments, an example of which is the NASA graph of global warming (see Morton 2013: 3).

also that it is the medium as measurement that creates the object (this is Ernst's thesis). On this, Mark Hansen concurs with Ernst. In a discussion of media archaeology in relation to OOO and the notion of the hyperobject, Hansen develops an argument, the tenor of which is against OOO and Morton. He thus states that

> Just as there is no being of quantum objects independently of measurement, there is no being of the world in itself that would be separate from its manifestations.
>
> What this means, I suggest, is that the quantum phenomena produced through the technology of measurement are ontological: they are manifestations of the structure of the world as it is, and they are the only way in which the world is. (Hansen 2016: 396)

By, in effect, making quantum physics the measure of the world as such, the medium constitutes the world in as far as it is essentially implicated in the creation of appearances – of phenomena. Contra OOO and the positing of a noumenal realm withdrawn into itself and inaccessible to any medium, there would be nothing else but the phenomenal world. Again, let us refer to Hansen:

> I can thus agree with Morton that global warming is 'not a function of our measuring devices', but not for the reasons he offers: far from being radically disjunct from some real object called global warming, our measuring devices literally produce global warming as a phenomenon, indeed, as the originary phenomenon of climate. Outside of our perceptions and our data concerning climate, both of which offer access to climate, there simply is no such thing as global warming. (402)

Hence, the medium *produces* the object, as it were. Does this at the same time imply that the nature of the object is medium specific? That is, does this mean that phenomenality is medium specific? An affirmative response is difficult to avoid, so that, effectively, the medium would become the object. However, Hansen nuances his position: 'In stark contrast to object-oriented ontology, medium-oriented ontology insists on the reality of the phenomenal and insists that this constitutively partial and perspectival reality is consubstantial with reality as such, without having to ask what any given phenomenon really is' (403).

From this it can be argued that there is nothing other than what is made available by way of the medium; the medium is transparent.

For his part, Morton puts the opposite case: 'The very tools we were using to objectify things to cover the Earth's surface with shrink wrap become a blowtorch that burns away the glass screen separating humans from Earth, since every measurement is now known as an alteration, as quantum-scale measurements make clear' (2013: 37).

And so, when Morton sees the sun beating down on the solar panels of his house, he does not see global warming as such. 'Hyperobjects are *nonlocal*' (38). Quantum theory is true because it is not local – it is not constituted by perception or by human reason: 'Quantum theory is the only existing theory to establish firmly that things really do exist beyond our mind (or any mind). Quantum theory guarantees that real objects exist!' (39). Furthermore, 'Observation is as much part of the universe of objects as the observable, not some ontologically different state (say of a subject)' (40).

According to Morton, OOO is 'congruent' with quantum theory because the latter is 'object-oriented': 'OOO is deeply congruent with the most profound, accurate and testable theory of physical reality available. Actually, it would be better to say it the other way round: quantum theory works because it's object-oriented' (41). And Morton, invoking Niels Bohr, sides with the idea that quantum phenomena are identical with their measuring devices (2013: 41). According to Cassidy, though, Bohr speaks rather of the 'complementarity' of the wave and particle character of quanta, rather than of the merging quanta with the measuring device (Cassidy 1992: 243). One thing, let us note in passing, that a device of whatever kind cannot do is interpret the results of the interaction between device and entity. On this basis, 'uncertainty' is also an interpretation conveyed by a necessarily transparent medium, even if the key implication of uncertainty is the inseparability of the observing device (medium) and the object observed (the quantum particle/wave). In Cassidy's words, 'Together, uncertainty and complementarity [Bohr's thesis] represented the *interpretative* culmination of quantum mechanics' (1992: 243; emphasis added). And interpretation still applies when a probabilistic approach is taken with regard to the speed and location of electrons in Heisenberg's framework.

OOO and the true or false viability of quantum physics

Now, however, an examination of the way quantum physics is invoked by Morton is called for, while at the same time keeping medium specificity in view. We can note, first of all, that uncertainty in quantum mechanics is a principle of microphysics. Its focus is subatomic particles; it is thus analytically inclined. Indeed, the atom becomes significant *only* in light of its qualities. In terms of Harman's conception of OOO, such an approach to the atom would be a case of 'undermining'. And considering the atom only in terms of nuclear physics would be a case of 'overmining' – which entails a case of 'duomining'. Thus, the pursuit of the electron that results in the uncertainty principle – contra Morton – hardly fits an OOO conception of the object. In other words, the OOO approach would only be applicable to the atom as a whole, not to the parts of the atom.

Also at issue – as Hansen makes clear – is the a priori assumption by OOO of the object's withdrawal. In terms of this study the point to be made about the atom is that instruments (media), such as the electron microscope, provide true information about the components of the atom. If this were not so there would be no debate possible about the nature of uncertainty in detecting electrons. As we saw in relation to Ernst's media archaeological approach, it is one thing to valourize the historical, material version of a medium, it is another to conceive it as transparent, even in its historical version. In other words, it was argued that media *qua* media function independently of their materiality. The paradox of the uncertainty principle arises because under certain conditions, the light of the electron and the light of the observing instrument become one. This implies, as we have seen, that the observing instrument becomes equivalent to the entity observed.

I suggest that what has been described is analogous to the painting of paint, as for example in the work of Australian artist, Cj Hendry.[2]

Hendry's images of paint are not actually paint, but a *trompe-l'oeil* created using material other than paint, such as coloured pencils. As such they highlight the transparency of the medium.[3] Once the materials of painting

---

2 See: https://www.frankie.com.au/article/cj-hendrys-drawings-of-paint-544385 (accessed 11 November 2022).

3 In Australian artist, Ben Quilty's work, paint, colour and surface are all explicit, but this is because they are also part of the content of the paintings. See, for example, https://news.curtin.edu.au/stor ies/soldiers-internal-war-shown-ben-quilty/ (accessed 8 October 2022). Also see the paintings of

become integral to the content of the work, the medium still only appears in its transparency. This also applies to the works of Abstract Expressionism.

Hansen's notion of 'medium-oriented ontology' is instructive. However, this syntagma must be interpreted to mean that, due to its transparency, the medium delivers what is manifest in the form, we could say, of a modal ontology. That is, it is not a matter of the becoming-present of the medium. When this is extrapolated to the world in its entirety, it is still the world that appears, not the medium.

Again, when it comes to a computer simulation of climate, the issue is about the computer model 'creating' the reality. As Hansen says, 'computer simulations are concerned less with truth than with correctness. Emancipated from the need to decide on a true reality, simulations are able to embrace a "plurality of realities", each of which is possible and each of which has a distinct probability' (2016: 400). We can accept that this is so, but at the same time recognize that all pertinence lies in the information that the computer model conveys; it is not about the model as such. The following question nonetheless arises: in certain fields such as meteorology where the object is probabilistic, are we then getting a medium's-eye view of things? The hypothesis presented here is that, as with the quantum object, the medium 'disappears' into the 'plurality of realities', one of which is the weather system.

Although the OOO position of there being a deep reality of climate beyond the phenomenon of weather might be problematic, there can be no doubt that it does not privilege medium specificity, which is what the opposing view can lead to when it promotes a medium-specific view of reality.

The abject and the hyperobject

Timothy Morton's theory evokes the problem typical of OOO: namely, that of defining everything as an object.[4] If this were so, OOO would have to be defined

---

Nicolas de Staël (1914–1955): https://www.spellmangallery.com/artists/nicolas-de-stael (accessed 28 October 2022).

4 Notable in this regard is the sub-title – *A New Theory of Everything* – of Graham Harman's general outline of OOO (2018) and the title of Timothy Morton's article: 'Here Comes Everything: The Promise of Object-Oriented Ontology' (2011).

as an object that withdraws, even from itself. As this study (see Chapter 7) and other commentaries have noted (see Norris 2013: 27 and Lemke 2017: 137, 145), it is, precisely, the simple listing of a diversity of objects (a flat ontology) that becomes problematic in Harman's version of OOO. Moreover, contributing to the problematic nature of OOO's approach is the choice or the term 'object' – as opposed, perhaps, to entity, thing or phenomenon. How can 'object' not evoke the 'subject–object' relation? But even more pertinently for this study is the absence of any sense that reality might also be composed of non-objects, such as is highlighted by the 'abject' and 'abjection' – terms that have come into prominence through the theory of Julia Kristeva (1982). If objects are 'seductive' – and Harman, as a reader of Baudrillard, accepts this[5] – the abject is anything but seductive. Indeed, psychoanalytically, it is repulsive. As I have indicated elsewhere (see Lechte 2016: 19), just how the abject can appear in an artwork is an issue, given that, at some level, art objectifies. But following on from this is the question of how the abject appears at all. In a sense, the object is its appearance, whether this be partial (the object withdraws), as for Harman, or total, as for Hansen.

To make it more politically relevant, various writers[6] have continued to illustrate the abject by pointing to refuse, such as plastic, that pollutes the oceans of the world. While it might be possible to argue that the great majority find pollution undesirable and even repulsive, not all plastic is polluting and not all pollution is populated by plastic. An undesirable object is not necessarily abject. This is particularly the case with artworks, where a visceral encounter is more or less normal. How, then, does the medium figure in relation to the abject? If we take the meaning of 'non-object' seriously, a problem arises in any attempt to ascertain what the role of the medium might be. Certainly, objects can be made present via the medium, but it remains to be seen as to whether this is also the case with regard to the abject.

Previously, I have argued in relation to Philippe Grandrieux's film, *Sombre* – a work that focuses on a serial killer – that the abject is not to be found in the content of the film (objectional as the content might be), but in the film itself (Lechte 2016: 25). The abject permeates Grandrieux's art, much like style or

---

5 See Harman (2016b).
6 See, for example, Frantzen and Bjering (2020).

an overarching ambivalence. So, indeed, a medium is in play, and it is quite transparent, but it now operates at the level of the work as a whole and not just at the level of the content.

The point that I am making is even more clear-cut with regard to the photograph, Immersion (1987) (*Piss Christ*) by Andreas Serrano, where a crucifix is shown through the artist's yellow-coloured urine. In ethnology, urine as such is not abject unless it is out of place (cf. Mary Doulas). Clearly, the crucifix itself is not abject. However, the combination – that is, the totality – is potentially abject, an abjection that is more than the sum of the parts of the photograph. In this case, then, the artwork – if that is what it is – becomes the vehicle of the abject, but the latter does not appear as such.

Looked at independently of a psychoanalytic context, abjection envelopes like a fog. This is why, for the human, it is a threat that needs to be repulsed, if only one could be aware of its imminence. This is to say, further, that in not being an object, the abject is outside knowledge and being; it thus takes a very special medium to render it present.

One of the key markers of the abject is that it is neither one thing *nor* the other. In short, it defies a binary classification. In this sense, rather than confirming an object-oriented ontology, as Morton might have wished, quantum mechanics and the principle of uncertainty derived from the particle-wave notion of the electron evoke a non-object redolent of the abject. Moreover, in an article on ecology and waste, authors Frantzen and Bjering (2020) suggestively argue that, due to the incredible ubiquity of waste on the planet, the term 'hyperabject' is a term more appropriate for the times than 'hyperobject'. Even so, it is also true that the authors who have formulated the term 'hyperabject' tend, in their descriptions, to objectify waste, thus rendering it less abject.

Consequently, in the trajectory of this chapter, we have travelled from Heisenberg's uncertainty principle and its problematizing of the object in relation to the medium, through Morton's attempt to install 'hyperobject' as the key term of our time, to the notion of the hyperabject, where, again, the very being of the object is problematized. The upshot is that the gauntlet is thrown down to the theorist to come up with an even more nuanced conception of the medium than currently exists.

As a result, the goal of the conclusion to this study will be to reconsider and reflect on the state of play with regard to the medium, in part, through the presentation of possible counter-examples to the thesis of the medium as transparent or as disappearance.

Conclusion

On whether the medium is always transparent

This conclusion addresses further issues relating to the medium and provides pointers for future research. Also, in light of the foregoing investigation into the medium as transparent or opaque, a reflection is undertaken on the notion of soliloquy in order to determine whether Husserl's philosophy of 'indication' and 'expression' brings the transparency of the medium into question.

It has become clear that this study is oriented towards showing that the medium does not entail determinism: essentially, the medium *qua* medium does not determine an outcome. As a result, the medium is not viewed as a limitation but as a possibility. But does this mean that things have been pushed too far in favour of the transparency of medium in the preceding analyses? The following reflection includes a response to this question.

Indication, expression and soliloquy in Husserl

Ironically, in its everyday use, language is, for the most part, unproblematically treated as a transparent medium. Even the exact sciences, as we saw Heisenberg confirm, are reliant on the everyday use of language and thus on its transparency. This means that language as such does not appear but rather things indicated or expressed appear. If we use the terms 'indication' and 'expression' as Husserl defined them, indication refers to a concrete fact. In speaking this would include 'facial expressions and the various gestures which involuntarily accompany speech without communicative intent' (Husserl 1970: 275). Such features are excluded from the definition of 'expression'. As Derrida (1976: 38) notes, the external expression based in physiognomy is also the point at which the non-conscious, or the unconscious, or what is involuntary can appear and which may be revelatory of an interior state that is foreclosed from the one presenting the bodily gestures and so on. The body thus becomes the medium of both unconscious as well as conscious communication.

Expression, for its part, is both the conscious expression of a mental state and equivalent to a statement about something. Indication can 'indicate' the presence of thoughts or of the state of mind of the speaker, while 'expression' would refer to a statement made about something that has meaning independently of the mental state of the one making the utterance. A statement calls for interpretation. Even though the medium's transparency has been tirelessly argued for, the transparency of language in relation to 'indication' and 'expression' raises issues that could mean that the claim that the medium is absolutely transparent should be qualified.

But maybe what, first of all, needs to be questioned with regard to indication and expression is the incipient psychologism that serves as the basis of an unquestioned set of a priori assumptions concerning the nature of the communicative function. Indeed, Husserl, despite his constant disclaimers to the contrary (see *Ideas I* (1982)), would seem, according to the following passage from the *Logical Investigations* (1970), to run the risk of a certain psychologism. Thus, the philosopher argues that all expressions ultimately have an indicative function, since 'They serve the hearer as signs of the "thoughts" of the speaker, i.e. of his sense-giving inner experiences, as well as other inner experiences, which are part of his communicative intention' (277). And the phenomenologist goes on to designate the latter as the '*intimating function*' of 'verbal expressions' (277). Clearly, for Husserl – as for common sense – the intimate or interior being of the other as speaker – or, more generally as communicator[1] – is of immense interest, as the following passage confirms: 'The hearer perceives the speaker as manifesting certain inner experiences, and to that extent he also perceives these experiences themselves: he does not, however, himself experience them, he has not an "inner" but an "outer" percept of them' (278). The issue of whether language as such, or signifying as

---

1 The use of the term 'communicator' implies that not all linguistic or signing activity is of a verbal nature, however much Husserl largely assumes this to be the case.

such, is a factor in the constitution of interiority is absent from Husserl's frame of reference. As a result, we have an implicit characterization of the nature of the human, one that privileges a discontinuous and closed interiority to which no other person or thing has direct access. That is, it is not here a matter of a presentation of the ontological status of language and communication.

Of course, Husserl famously (as revealed by Derrida's commentary) holds that there is no indication in soliloquy: 'In a monologue', says Husserl, 'words can perform no function of indicating' (280); that is, the words – the medium – perform 'no function'. But what, we might ask, is it that is immediately experienced? If the imagination (medium) can bring centaurs into focus, might not thought itself be a medium – a medium of meaning with regard to 'communicative intention'? Does the centaur, or any imagined object, affect the possibility of self-presence in soliloquy? To the extent that we are dealing with an *imagined* object, the latter is absolutely present. Its 'being', in short, is absolutely transparent. A dream object – an object that brings with it an experience of strangeness – would seem by comparison (although Husserl never mentions dreams) to disrupt self-presence. A dream represents an encounter with the unfamiliar. As such, a dream also leads to an encounter with the enigma of the medium, since a dream is in fact an illusion of reality, given that it takes place entirely within the realm of the imaginary. But this can only be verified after the event of the dream in the waking state. What we cannot be sure of is whether a dream is the medium that bears within itself an uncanny content. In any case, the *issue* of the medium is here being brought to light. Indeed, it is the *issue* of the medium that Derrida's analysis of self-presence in Husserl – especially with regard to speech – brings to light.[2]

Whatever else Husserl might do in his study of the communicative process, he clearly raises the issue of the medium, since he draws attention to the possible effects of 'the sign *qua* sign, e.g. to the printed words as such' (282). For a successful act of communication the word must become transparent so that it is 'no longer ... the object of our "mental activity"'. Our interest, our

---

2 Compare with 'The operation of "hearing oneself speak" is an auto-affection of a type that is absolutely unique. Firstly, it works in the medium of universality; the signifieds that appear here must be idealities that must *idealise* [*idealiter*] to enable repetition or the transmission as the same indefinitely. Secondly, the subject must hear itself or speak to itself [*se parler*], allow itself to be affected by the signifier that it produces without any detour occasioned by something exterior, by the world, or by, in general, the non-self' (Derrida 1976: 88).

intention, our thought ... point exclusively to the thing meant in the sense-giving act' (283). Everything in an expression hinges on meaning, Husserl eventually concludes, 'A meaningless expression is ... properly speaking, no expression at all' (293). In short, the realization of meaning presupposes the transparency of language, even if the latter can also be approached in terms of its materiality, something that can become perceptible in 'senseless' statements, such as the 'square circle'.

Even if Husserl clings to a classical version of the self in soliloquy as self-present and self-identical, thus making indication and communication superfluous, it is difficult to say that the medium is equally superfluous, or, for that matter, that consciousness as medium (because it is always 'consciousness of') is superfluous. This is because, as a pure transparency, the medium is not present. Therefore, here, the issue of the presence or absence of the medium is without significance. On the other hand, 'medium' seems to have a real significance in the following passage from Derrida's analysis of the Husserlian 'ideality' of the self, where the latter 'must be constituted, repeated and expressed in a *medium* that does not breach the presence and the self-presence of the acts proper to it: a *medium* that preserves both the *presence of the object* before intuition and *self-presence* as the absolute proximity of these acts themselves' (1976: 85; emphasis added to 'medium'). Here, the 'medium' becomes crucial either to sustaining or constraining ideality.

The Husserlian 'self-presence' is problematized or 'deconstructed' by Derrida through reference to time or the process of temporalization (1976: 5). Colloquially, my self-presence cannot be fully sustained because I also remember the past: memory is constitutive of the self. I also anticipate in the future. This insight is of course contained in Husserl's conception of temporal object that we encountered in relation to the work of Bernard Stiegler in Chapter 6. However, in Derrida's approach, what further undermines self-presence is the very fact of the medium – and, specifically, language as medium. Indeed, language as medium comes to coalesce with consciousness as medium. Or, as Derrida says, language and consciousness become 'indiscernible' (15). Temporalization thus undermines the possibility of a 'present instant'. In short, 'the punctuality of the instant is a myth' (68).

Be this as it may, but for Derrida the medium has a presence. Because it has a presence (because it is not diaphanous or transparent), it can undermine presence in general. The clearest example of this is, to be sure, that of the medium of writing – 'archi-writing', or the trace, which is 'unthinkable in terms of the simplicity of a present [moment]' (95). Moreover, the distinction between fictional or imaginary language and external, factual, non-fictional language cannot be sustained (63). It is thus in the nature of language *qua* medium that one must conclude that 'there is no sure criterion for distinguishing between an external language and an internal language' (63).

Derrida, then, like a range of commentators, treats the medium as a kind of object – or at least as an entity that can have qualities and effects attributed to it. But what about the language that Derrida is himself using in order to communicate his ideas concerning language and signification – that is to say, language in its mode of *énonciation*? This is significant because Husserl in *Investigation I* discusses the role of pronouns, in particular, the 'I' and Derrida comments on this. We know – as has been mentioned in the introduction in relation to Benveniste – that pronouns only have meaning in relation to the context or the occasion in which they are enacted. Indeed, when addressing the issue of personal pronouns, and of deictic terms, Husserl anticipates Benveniste. Thus, with occasional utterances, 'Only by looking to the actual circumstances of utterance can one definite meaning … be constituted for the hearer' (1970: 315). And, concerning the personal pronoun, 'The word "I" names a different person from case to case' (315). With regard to deixis, ' "Here" ', for example, 'designates the speaker's vaguely bounded spatial environment' (315). As the full sense or significance of pronouns, demonstrative or deixis can only be grasped in the *énonciation* or act of uttering – the existential reality – no specific statement (*énoncé*) can do it justice.

It is notable that in his reading of Husserl's *Logical Investigations* Derrida's focus is on the level of the statement made (*énoncé*) rather than on the level of the *énonciation* (see 1976: 107). For it is the latter that tends to fit the notion of language as a process of idealities: thus, 'language' will be the same word no matter in what context it might appear. Moreover, the material form of the word supposedly has no bearing on its capacity to function in discourse regardless of context. Such an approach, as well as neglecting the role of the level of *énonciation* that Husserl endeavours to explicate, also neglects the aspect of connotation, something that Husserl does not neglect (see Husserl 1970: §16, 295–8).

Similarly, language for Husserl is always the medium of meaning and understanding, while for Derrida, words as such – independently of whether they are understood – can assume a certain opacity. That is, they can appear as such – as *énoncés* that call for interpretation. An *énoncé*, then, is never absolutely transparent. Indeed, the notions of 'interval', 'delay', 'spacing' and 'difference' would seem to render language – whether as text or speech – ever more present, that is, would render the medium ever more present as object.

Husserl on the materiality of language

Husserl's 'investigation', and Derrida's privileging of the *énoncé* can serve to prompt a reconsideration of the materiality of language and in particular the sense in which the medium might, or might not, appear. What, then, is the exact sense of the 'materiality' of language? In a modernist vein, poets such as Mallarmé and Apollinaire, to all appearances, engage with the materiality of words. And, of course, there is handwriting. Do we not have here in focus the materiality of the medium, the medium as opaque (in the sense of a perceptible object)? Is not the conclusion to be drawn that the medium as such is speaking? Here it is important to recognize both elements of the phrase – 'materiality' and 'language' – since it is possible that if language as medium is in play so too is a certain transparency.

As we saw in the introduction, Tzvetan Todorov's example of a text written in blood introduces a variant of connotation that needs to be acknowledged. Thus, connotation, amongst other things, can evoke the material in which a text, image or sign appears.[3] Nevertheless, to the extent that the material signifies (the blood, for example) – that is, to the extent that it ceases to be a pure materiality and constitutes another level of expression – the medium is transparent. Connotation, then, does not result in medium specificity.

J. S. Mill's theory of connotation, Mill claims, is illustrated by the chalk marks that the robber, in the story from the *Arabian Nights*, put on the wall of the house he intended to rob. This is not an example of connotation, says Husserl, but only one of 'a mere indication' (296). While Husserl does not

---

3 Connotation, as Husserl shows in referring to John Stuart Mill's theory, can be quite complex. For Mill, proper names and attributes '(e.g. "whiteness")' do not connote anything, whereas names in general do connote (Husserl 1970: 295).

elaborate on his own theory of connotation, it is clear that whether the chalk mark be defined as connotation or as indication, it cannot be reduced to a mode of materiality – that is, it signifies, and is therefore transparent.

The mirror as a challenge to the medium as transparent

We turn, now, to examples of phenomena that may well show a version of the medium that undeniably challenge the thesis of the disappearance of the medium.

To begin with, let us assume that we are dealing with a distorting mirror in which the reflected images appear to connote the mirror as such rather than the images as content in the mirror as medium. Here, it may prove instructive to recall aspects of the semiotic view of this phenomenon, specifically, as articulated by Umberto Eco (1984: 202–26).

What is interesting and possibly unique is that the image content of a mirror is undoubtedly the sign of the mirror as such. It does not make sense to say that the constitution of a mirror is independent of the image(s) in it, for it is indeed the reflected images in the mirror that confirm the presence of the mirror *qua* mirror. Viewed in this way, the mirror would seem to be a medium that appears as such – that, consequently, does not disappear.

On the other hand, while a child might believe that there is an image/person *in* the mirror, the latter entails that an image is a reflection, so that what might seem to be *in* the mirror is in fact external to it. A mirror has no interiority. In my everyday use of the mirror, I believe that what I see is 'me', but it is a me external to the reflection. With a photograph of myself, or with my painted portrait I am, by contrast, internal to the medium; the latter is thus transparent (disappears). To this, we can add Eco's remark that 'A mirror does not "translate"' (1984: 207); it reveals what truly exists. 'It tells the truth', says Eco, 'to an inhuman extent' (208). What we have with a mirror image is not a representation or a sign of what is reflected, but a double, meaning by this that the reflection and the reflected have the same qualities (see Eco 1979: 180–2). The experience of the mirror image as a double 'makes man's experience with mirrors an absolutely unique one' (Eco 1984: 210).

Another feature of the mirror relates to time. With the mirror, the reflection and the reflected exist in the same moment. Reflection and what is reflected are absolutely present to each other. The movement of the hand of the one reflected is immediately replicated in the reflection.

If, however, a mirror is, as Eco proposes, a 'prosthesis' (a technical device) and a channel or, material *medium* for the passage of information' (208), does it also appear as such? According to Eco, 'all prostheses are channels or *media*' (209). As prosthetic a mirror can be used, Eco adds, as 'the *symptom* of a presence' (209), the presence of the source of images. In such a situation, Eco claims, we learn about mirrors and not 'about mirror images' (209). This view is the opposite of the one stated earlier to the effect that, rather than being a special case, the presence of mirror images evokes the presence of the mirror. The fact that the reflection and the reflected are doubles and exist in the same moment serves to enhance this view.

Surely, more than anything, distorting mirrors must signal the presence of the mirror over the image, since it is clearly the distorted reflection that indicates the mirror's presence. This is the situation where the mirror image might be said to function exceptionally as a sign. Or, as Eco observes, 'we accept that the mirror, which usually tells the truth, is lying' (217). But what if the distortion goes undetected? Dire consequences are likely because the mirror habitually 'tells the truth'.

Perhaps, in the end, while the image/reflection makes the mirror present, the mirror also brings the reflected to presence – otherwise, rather than seeing myself in the mirror, I would only see a shiny surface.

Trompe-l'oeil, camouflage and the medium

Perhaps it is true that if the medium as such is to appear it may well be as a mirror. But we should also consider *trompe l'oeil* and camouflage as possible candidates for the appearance of the medium. With regard to the former, an illusion of three dimensions is created on a two-dimensional surface,[4]

---

4 Edward Collier, Trompe l'œil with a letter rack holding newspapers, letters, writing equipment and a comb, https://www.ngv.vic.gov.au/explore/collection/work/144815/ (accessed 4 May 2023).

whereas with the latter (camouflage) a three-dimensional surface (as with army camouflage uniform, or varieties of tree frog) gives the illusion of two dimensionality.

In Jacques Lacan's famous commentary, *trompe l'oeil* in painting amounts to 'the painting appearing to be other than it is' (1973: 102). How does this illusion occur? Let us note, first of all, that *trompe l'oeil* only works when the illusion is recognized. A *trompe l'oeil* that totally deceived the beholder would not, strictly speaking, be a *trompe l'oeil*. The beholder thus marvels at the illusion, as the content seems to be so real, while at the same time recognizing that it is only an illusion of realism. As Lacan explains, 'What is it that seduces and satisfies us in *trompe l'oeil*? When does it captivate us and give rise to our jubilation? At the moment where, by a simple movement of our gaze, we are able to notice that the representation does not move with it and that there is only a *trompe l'oeil*' (102–3). In fact, the thing we notice is the paint as such, independently of what is represented. At least this is possible in principle. Perhaps, though, there is here a similarity to the mirror effect, since the opacity of the paint is played off against the transparency of the painting content. Without taking account of the content of the work, there can be no illusion.

By contrast, in camouflage – for example, in an army jungle uniform – the aim is to make the illusion continuous. Once the medium (uniform) is detected there is no longer any camouflage. In short, the medium *must* remain transparent in camouflage.

The age of McLuhan again

This study has endeavoured to address what it has designated as the 'age of McLuhan' – the age in which media theory has embraced the now familiar claim that the 'medium is the message' – that, in other words, the medium signifies. This is what has also come to be known as 'medium specificity'. The 'age of McLuhan' is encapsulated by the concept of the mass media. Instead of being conceived as a transparent vehicle of information, 'the media' is understood as an institution that has its own view on things and represents the world according to its own interests, ideas and tastes. The media here is unproblematically thought of as the 'message' ('massage').

With the notable exception of Sybille Krämer, few media commentators and theorists have questioned the idea that the medium signifies. And, indeed, 'media specificity' accords perfectly with a theoretical – as opposed to an experiential – approach to the medium. However, the notion of medium specificity fails to capture the true character of the medium, since to the extent that there was such a thing as medium specificity, there would be no medium as such.

In its 'disappearance', the medium evokes Heidegger's notion of Being, in as far as the latter does not appear as such and only has presence through beings in what has been called a 'modal ontology'. Once the medium is conceived in terms of that which does not appear as such, a range of entities emerge that have the aspect of the medium.

The khora

For instance, *khora* can be interpreted as having the quality of the medium. Thus, Plato, significantly, calls the *khora* 'invisible' and 'formless', and says that it 'partakes of the intelligible and is most incomprehensible') (1980: 1178 (51b). It is an entity that is certainly not known through the senses and hardly even through the intellect. It is thus only knowable via a kind of 'bastard reasoning'. Debate has erupted during the past three decades or more as to the *khora's* exact status. The *khora*, the philosopher tells us, is like a container that in order to allow what is contained to appear does not itself appear. As Timaeus says in the Platonic dialogue, 'that which is to receive all forms should have no form' (50e) (Plato 1980: 1177).

Rather than remaining with the esoteric *khora*, a range of entities can, in light of the principle of a modal ontology, now be designated as having the quality of the medium. Time and space in general, for example, are not reducible to any specific instance, or instances and yet both time and space only appear via specific instances, just as Being appears through beings. Beauty, freedom and number, as such, find no incarnation in a particular instance and yet each of the foregoing only appears in a range of particular instances. For their part, specific numbers appear via the medium of number. To be sure, what has just been outlined requires further investigation. The idea of an incarnation of beauty as such in an entity has been an abiding myth and thus calls for investigation. No doubt, too, Christ as the incarnation of the word also calls for thinking and a response – if it is possible – to the question as to whether Christ is the incarnation of the medium.

The noumenon as medium

But now, at the risk of being overly speculative, if the Kantian domains of noumenon and phenomenon are not amenable to being interpreted in terms of medium as disappearing in relation to what appears, since this constitutes an epistemological orientation where human sensibility and intelligence mediate between noumenon and phenomenon,[5] it may be possible to move beyond human sensibility to the relation between the object-in-itself as reality and the phenomenon as appearance. For his part, Kant ever focused on the sensible as the key to the epistemological – any human access to the in-itself (or, what amounts to the same thing, to the transcendental object) would seem to be denied. Kant explains his position as follows:

> The sensibility (and its field, that of appearances) is itself limited by the understanding in such a fashion that it does not have to do with things in themselves but only with the mode in which, owing to our subjective constitution, they appear. The Transcendental Aesthetic, in all its teaching, has led to this conclusion; and the same conclusion also, of course, follows from the concept of an appearance in general; namely, that *something which is not in itself appearance must correspond to it. For appearance can be nothing by itself,* outside our mode of representation. Unless, therefore, we are to move constantly in a circle, the word appearance must be recognised as already indicating a relation to something, the immediate representation of which is, indeed, sensible, but which, even apart from the constitution of sensibility (upon which the form of our intuition is grounded), must be something in itself, that is, an object independent of sensibility. (Kant 1970A: 269–70; emphasis added)

---

5 OOO goes astray precisely here, for this movement that claims an affiliation with ontology in fact focuses on the noumenon–phenomenon relation, where it is all about human knowledge capacities and not about things-in-themselves. Harman writes, for example, 'The noumena, by contrast [to phenomena], are things-in-themselves' (2018: 68). Rather than escaping a humanist/epistemological framework, OOO simply offers another version of it.

This passage, from the first edition of Kant's *First Critique*, indicates that the object-in-itself, although unavailable to sensibility, nevertheless is presupposed by the very notion of appearance, albeit negatively. What is appearance if not the other of the object-in-itself – the other of reality? The whole tradition of Western philosophy from Plato to Kant confirms this. So, an opening for a modal ontology is hence detectable.

The realm of appearance is thus the realm of sensible objects. As another illuminating passage from the first edition explains,

> The object to which I relate appearance in general is the transcendental object, that is, the completely indeterminate thought of *something* in general. This cannot be entitled *noumenon*; for I know nothing of what it is in itself, and have no concept of it save as merely the object of a sensible intuition in general, and so as being one and the same for all appearances. I cannot think it through any category; for a category is valid [only] for empirical intuition, as bringing it under a concept of object in general. (1970A: 271; square brackets in the text)

The fact that sensible objects stand for 'appearance in general' implies that the transcendental object stands for reality in general. Again, therefore, an opening for a possible modal ontology emerges where appearance – that is, what is manifest – gives rise to that which appears in its non-appearing. That is, what is manifest is the mode of appearing of the transcendental object. For, without the latter, there would be no appearance – that is, there would be no sensible objects: 'the transcendental object lying at the basis of appearances (and with it the reason why our sensibility is subject to certain supreme conditions rather than others) is and remains for us inscrutable. The thing itself is indeed given, but we can have no insight into its nature' (Kant 1970B: 514).

Moreover, Kant says that it is not possible to 'know' the 'non-sensible cause' of sensibly perceived objects (1970b: 441). To say that the thing-in-itself is unknowable does not just mean that human faculties are incapable of knowing it, but, rather, that it is not the object of any knowing whatsoever. This is what makes it 'in-itself' and 'transcendental'. Thus, even God does not 'know' what is in-itself and transcendental.

How, then, can the 'in-itself' become present in the sensuous world? Only by its non-appearing, while at the same time being the basis of appearance. If the in-itself, transcendental realm creates a problem for knowledge, what is to be made of the realm of appearance? How is it possible to be certain about appearance *as* appearance? Indeed, if appearance is the result of the 'in-itself', appearance is not simply appearance, but becomes a complex totality of appearance *and* reality. In short, it is necessary to be far less certain than Kant about the actual parameters and nature of the human and sensuous knowledge.

What this implies is that not only does the medium have a far broader and deeper significance than has hitherto been understood, but also that there is only *one* reality, a reality that is already contained in the notion of appearance.

Moreover, there is, for Kant, knowledge that is a priori rather than deriving from sensuous experience. Here, the Kantian schema should be recalled – where the empirical opens the way to the ideal.[6] And we should also recall the fact that the schema is supplemented in philosophy by '*knowledge gained by reason from concepts*' (Kant 1970b: 577). In addition, 'mathematical knowledge is the knowledge gained by reason from the *construction* of concepts' (577). Philosophically, we can thus speak of the *concept* of beauty, of freedom, of virtue, of time and space, of mathematical figures, such as a triangle and so on. It could thus be proposed that the concept here corresponds to the medium – that concepts point towards the 'in itself'.

Consequently, even though it might well be thought by some commentators that Kant's dualist philosophy is hardly germane to a philosophy of the medium, one can appropriately respond by pointing to the critical significance of Kant because the medium is in fact far more than what a McLuhanesque media philosophy claims for it. Kant, indeed, opens the way to the insight that the medium appears in its non-appearing or in its 'disappearance', while for the age of McLuhan, it is precisely the medium that appears and thus gives rise to medium specificity. This means, too, that the medium is ontological and *essential* rather than epistemological. In short, the medium cannot simply be the object of an empirically based science, but is nevertheless presupposed by such a science, as is illuminated by Michel Serres's and Wolfgang Ernst's work.

Regarding the latter, it has been shown that, for Ernst, the measuring instrument is implicated in what is measured. Ernst's model, ultimately, is the

---

6 Compare with 'The single figure which we draw is empirical, and yet its serves to express the concept, without impairing its universality' (Kant 1970B: 577). Also, 'the object of the concept, to which the single object corresponds merely as its schema, must likewise be thought as universally determined' (577).

quantum object that is time critical. What is clear from this is not that the medium (measuring instrument) appears as such, but that the appearing of the measuring instrument is the appearing of the object.

To engage with Kant on the noumenon, then, is to find further confirmation of Jan Patočka's key idea that – as we saw cited by Hansen – there is no 'being of the world in itself that would be separate from its manifestations' (Hansen 2016: 396). From this it follows that the medium as such does not manifest itself separately from what it mediates. In short, manifestation and medium are become indistinguishable.

But despite Hansen and others (see Plotnitsky 2016: 158) viewing the 'reality' exhibited by the quantum object as having ontological ramifications, it is still a matter of knowing – or not knowing[7] – the object in question. The status of the conclusions drawn is still epistemological rather than ontological. The reason for the epistemological slant is that quantum mechanics has raised the possibility of a knowledge of the ultimate basis of reality. By comparison, the status of the medium is fundamentally ontological. We should not now seek to *know* the medium, for it is the latter that, in good measure, is the precondition of knowledge. Such, at least, is what this study has striven to show during its entire trajectory.

Epilogue

It has now become clear to me that a division – one that has become increasingly evident – has emerged. This division has to do with the fact that the media referred to throughout the study tend to fall into one of two categories: that of concrete, material media, and that of the medium as immaterial. In the first category we have the commonly recognized examples of media, such as art work (Harman, Greenberg, Krauss), books, canvas (Greenberg), channel (Shannon, Serres), chronometer, clock (Heidegger), codex, doors (Siegert), film (Stiegler), gramophone, typewriter, computer (Kittler), manuscripts,

---

7 Compare with 'the mathematics of quantum mechanics enables us to make such estimates without our being able to *know* anything about quantum objects themselves, or even being able to conceive of what they are and how they behave' (Plotnitsky 2016: 104; emphasis added).

maps (Krämer), newspapers, paint, radio (Ernst, Heidegger), railway carriages (Kittler), telephone, television and so on.

In the second category, the one that gives a modal ontology its *raison d'être*, we have: archaeology, archive (Foucault, Ernst), art, beauty, Being (Heidegger), consciousness (Husserl), *énonciation* (Benveniste), ethnography, *khora*, language, middle voice, noumenon (Kant), number, space, surrealism, technics (Stiegler), time (Heidegger, Ernst, Stiegler), Turing machine and so on.

It goes without saying that the content of the two categories is far from exhausted. But it does offer an idea of the permanent division in the nature of media. It also goes without saying that the contents of the first category are more easily appropriated as objects in themselves, while those of the second category more readily facilitate an understanding of the medium as transparent – indeed, as that which only appears in its disappearing.

A future study could well aim to render more profound our understanding and knowledge of the difference between the vehicle of the medium as material and concrete, as compared to the medium that would only 'appear' by way of a modal ontology. Such a study might also lead to understanding certain media as unclassifiable – as both material and immaterial. An example could well be that of Jeremy Bentham's Panopticon, a structure that has a definite visual form and yet – if we accept Foucault's analysis – was only ever actualized as a principle underlying the introduction in the modern era of numerous processes of discipline. The Panopticon appears on paper but disappears in its actualization, just as Krämer shows is also the case for maps.

Another theme that awaits elaboration is that of abstraction in mathematics, art and philosophy. Might not abstraction be equivalent to the medium in its disappearance in being actualized, or, maybe we could say after Simondon, that the medium's disappearance is in being concretized. In this context, we return to the Kantian schema and to Serres's notion that the material, graphic form (a symbol, let us say) is still understood as a repetition of the same ideal principle, despite every empirical or concrete repetition being different. The same is true of a signature, as Derrida recognized, and of the letters of a handwritten text, as Saussure demonstrated. The aim, then, would be to show that the appearing of the medium in its disappearance along with a modal ontology open up a rich terrain for a new philosophy of the medium.

References

Agamben, Giorgio (1998) *Homo Sacer*, trans. Daniel Heller-Roazen, Stanford, CA: Stanford University Press.

Agamben, Giorgio (2002) *Remnants of Auschwitz: The Witness and the Archive*, trans. Daniel Heller-Roazen, New York: Zone Books.

Agamben, Giorgio (2005) *State of Exception*, trans. Kevin Attell, Chicago: University of Chicago Press.

Agamben, Giorgio (2015) *The Use of Bodies*, trans. Adam Kotsko, Stanford, CA: Stanford University Press.

Aristotle (1984) 'On the Soul' (*de Anima*) in Jonathan Barnes (ed.), *The Complete Works of Aristotle: The Revised Oxford Translation*, Volume One, Princeton, NJ: Princeton University Press.

Bakhtin, Mikhail (1984) *Rablais and His World*, trans. Hélène Iswolsky, Bloomington: Indiana University Press.

Barker, Timothy (2021) 'Michel Serres' Messengers', *Media Theory*, 5 (1), 163–84.

Barthes, Roland (2010) *Camera Lucida*, trans. Richard Howard, New York: Hill and Wang.

Baudrillard, Jean (1989) 'Simulacra and Simulations', in Mark Poster (ed.), *Jean Baudrillard: Selected Writings*, 166–84, Cambridge: Polity Press in association with Blackwell.

Baudrillard, Jean (1993) *Symbolic Exchange and Death*, trans. Iain Hamilton Grant, London: Thousand Oaks.

Benjamin, Walter (1986) 'Critique of Violence', in *Reflections: Essays, Aphorisms, Autobiographical Writings*, trans. Edmund Jephcott, 277–300, New York: Shocken Books.

Benveniste, Émile (1966) *Problèmes de linguistique générale, 1*, Paris: Gallimard 'TEL'.

Benveniste, Émile (1971) 'Active and Middle Voice in the Verb', in *Problems in General Linguistics*, 148–9, Coral Gables, FL: University of Miami Press.

Benveniste, Émile (1974) *Problèmes de linguistique générale, 2*, Paris: Gallimard 'TEL'.

Bianchi, Pietro (2017) *Jacques Lacan and Cinema: Imaginary, Gaze, Formalisation*, London: Routledge.

Bourdieu, Pierre (1965) 'La définition sociale de la photographie', in Pierre Bourdieu, L. Boltanski, R. Castel and J.-C. Chamboredon (eds), *Essai sur les usages sociaux de la photographie*, second edition, 107–38, Paris: Minuit.

Brillouin, Léon (2013) *Science and Information Theory*, second edition, Garden City, NY: Dover.

Cacciari, Massimo, and Vedova, Emilio (1989) *Vedovas Angeli*, Klagenfurt: Ritter.

Carroll, Noël (1985) 'The Specificity of Media in the Arts', *Journal of Aesthetic Education*, 19 (4), 5–20.

Cassidy, David C. (1992) *Uncertainty: The Life and Science of Werner Heisenberg*, New York: W. H. Freeman.

Clausewitz, Carl von ([1832] 1985) *On War* [Abridged], trans. J. J. Graham, Harmondsworth: Penguin Books.

Clifford James (1981) 'On Ethnographic Surrealism', *Comparative Studies in Society and History*, 23 (4), 539–64.

Conley, Katharine (2015) 'Value and Hidden Cost in André Breton's Surrealist Collection', *South Central Review*, 32 (1), Special Issue: Dada, Surrealism, and Colonialism, 8–22.

Dastur, Françoise (2014) 'Time, Event and Presence in the Late Heidegger', *Continental Philosophy Review*, 47, 399–421.

Davis, Colin (2005) '*État Présent* Hauntology, Spectres and Phantoms', *French Studies*, 59 (3), 373–9.

Debray, Régis (2000) *Transmitting Culture*, trans. Eric Rauth, New York: Columbia University Press.

Denbigh, K. G., and Denbigh, J. S. (1985) *Entropy in Relation to Incomplete Knowledge*, Cambridge: Cambridge University Press.

Derrida, Jacques (1972) *Marges de la philosophie*, Paris: Minuit.

Derrida, Jacques ([1967] 1976) *La voix et le phénomène*, Paris: Presses Universitaires de France.

Derrida, Jacques (1993) *Spectres de Marx: L'État de la dette, le travail du deuil et la nouvelle Internationale*, Paris: Galilé.

Derrida, Jacques (1999) 'Word Processing: An Interview with Jacques Derrida', in 'Technologies of the Sign', special issue, *Oxford Literary Review*, 21, 3–17.

Derrida, Jacques (2016) *Of Grammatology*, trans. Gayatri Chakravorty Spivak, Baltimore, MD: Johns Hopkins University Press.

Doane, Mary-Ann (2007) 'The Indexical and the Concept of Medium Specificity', *Differences*, 18 (1), 128–52.

Eberhard, Philippe (2006) 'The Medial Age or the Present in the Middle Voice', *International Journal of Humanities*, 3 (8), 125–34.

Eco, Umberto (1979) *A Theory of Semiotics*, Bloomington: Indiana University Press.

Eco, Umberto (1984) *Semiotics and the Philosophy of Language*, London: Macmillan.

Ernst, Wolfgang (2005) 'Let There Be Irony: Cultural History and Media Archaeology in Parallel Lines', *Art History*, 28 (5), 582–603.

Ernst, Wolfgang (2011) 'Media Archaeology: Method and Machine versus History and Narrative of Media', in E. Huhtamo and J. Parikka (eds), *Media Archaeology: Approaches, Applications and Implications*, Berkeley: University of California Press.

Ernst, Wolfgang (2013) 'From Media History to *Zeitkritik*', *Theory, Culture & Society*, 30 (6), 132–46.

Ernst, Wolfgang (2016) *Chronopoetics*, trans. Anthony Enns, London: Rowman and Littlefield.

Faurisson, Robert (1980) *Mémoire en défense: Contre ceux qui m'accusent de falsifier l'histoire*, Paris: La Vielle Taupe.

Fenves, Peter (1998) '"Order of the Number": Benjamin and Irigaray towards a Politics of Pure Means', *Diacritics*, 28 (1), 43–58.

Foucault, Michel (1974) *The Archaeology of Knowledge*, trans. A. M. Sheridan Smith, London: Tavistock Publications.

Foucault, Michel (1982) *The Order of Things*, translated from French, London: Tavistock.

Frantzen, Mikkel Krause, and Jens Bjering (2020) 'Ecology, Capitalism and Waste: From Hyperobject to Hyperabject', *Theory, Culture and Society*, 37 (6), 87–109.

Freud, Sigmund (2001) *An Outline of Psychoanalysis*, trans. James Strachey in *The Standard Edition of the Complete Psychological Works of Sigmund Freud*, Volume XXlll (1937–1939), 141–207, New York: Vintage.

Genette, Gérard (1980) *Narrative Discourse: An Essay in Method*, trans. Jane E. Lewin, Ithaca, NY: Cornell University Press.

Goody, Jack (2000) *The Power of the Written Tradition*, Washington, DC: Smithsonian Institution Press.

Greenberg, Clement (1995) *The Collected Essays and Criticism, Volume Four: Modernism with a Vengeance, 1957–1969*, Chicago: University of Chicago Press, Paperback edition.

Grimm, Jacob, and Grimm, Wilhelm (1954) in M. Heyne (ed.), *Deutsches Wörterbuch*, 16 vols. rpt. Leipzig: Hirzel.

Hansen, Mark (2000) *Embodying Technesis: Technology Beyond Writing*, Ann Arbor: University of Michigan Press.

Hansen, Mark B. N. (2002) 'Cinema Beyond Cybernetics, or How to Frame the Digital Image', *Configurations*, 10 (1), 51–90.

Hansen, Mark B. N. (2003) 'Affect as Medium, or the "Digital-Facial-Image"', *Journal of Visual Culture*, 2 (2), 205–28.

Hansen, Mark B. N. (2006) 'Media Theory', *Theory, Culture and Society*, 23 (2–3), 297–306.

Hansen, Mark B. N. (2009) 'Living (with) Technical Time from Media Surrogacy to Distributed Cognition', *Theory, Culture and Society*, 26 (2–3), 294–315.

Hansen, Mark B. N. (2012) 'Technics beyond the Temporal Object', *New Formations*, 77 (77), 44–62.

Hansen, Mark B. N. (2016) 'Medium-Oriented Ontology', *ELH*, 83 (2), 383–505.

Harman, Graham (2002) *Tool-Being: Heidegger and the Metaphysics of Objects*, Chicago: Open Court.

Harman, Graham (2010) 'Technology, Objects and Things in Heidegger', *Cambridge Journal of Economics*, 34, 17–25.

Harman, Graham (2012) 'Aesthetics as First Philosophy: Levinas and the Non-human', *Naked Punch* 9, Summer/Fall, 21–30.

Harman, Graham (2013) 'An Outline of Object-Oriented Philosophy', *Science Progress (1933–)*, 96 (2), 187–99.

Harman, Graham (2016a) 'Heidegger, McLuhan and Schumacher on Form and Its Aliens', *Theory, Culture and Society*, 33 (6), 99–105.

Harman, Graham (2016b) 'Object-Oriented Seduction: Baudrillard Reconsidered', in Lars Spuybroak and Sjoerd van Tuinen (eds), *The War of Appearances: Transparency, Opacity, Radiance*, 128–43, Rotterdam: V_2 Publishing.

Harman, Graham (2018) *Object-Oriented Ontology: A New Theory of Everything*, London: Pelican.

Harman, Graham (2019) *Art and Objects*, Cambridge, MA: Polity Press.

Havelock, Eric A. (1986) *The Muse Learns to Write: Reflections on Orality and Literacy from Antiquity to the Present*, New Haven, CT: Yale University Press.

Hawkins, Paula (2015) *Girl on the Train*, New York: Riverhead Books.

Hayles, N. Katherine (1988) 'Two Voices, One Channel: Equivocation in Michel Serres', *SubStance*, 17 (3), 3–12.

Hayles, N. Katherine (1991) 'Introduction: Complex Dynamics in Literature and Science', in N. Katherine Hayles (ed.), *Chaos and Order*, 1–36, Chicago: University of Chicago Press.

Hayles, N. Katherine (2007) 'Hyper and Deep Attention: The Generational Divide in Cognitive Modes', *Profession*, 2007, 187–99.

Heidegger, Martin (1977) *The Question of Technology and Other Essays*, trans. William Lovitt, New York: Harper Torchbooks.

Heidegger, Martin (1978) *Being and Time*, trans. John Macquarie and Edward Robinson, Oxford: Basil Blackwell.

Heidegger, Martin (1981) 'Why Do I Stay in the Provinces?', in Thomas Sheehan (ed.), *Heidegger: The Man and the Thinker*, 27–30, Chicago: Precedent.

Heidegger, Martin (1992) *Parmenides*, trans. A. Schuwer and R. Rojcewicz, Bloomington: Indiana University Press.

Heidegger, Martin (1998) *Pathmarks* (translated). Cambridge: Cambridge University Press.

Heidegger, Martin (2012) '"Insight into that Which Is": Bremen Lectures 1949', in *Bremen and Freiburg Lectures*, trans. Andrew Mitchell, Bloomington: Indiana University Press.

Heidegger, Martin (2014) *Introduction to Metaphysics*, trans. Gregory Fried and Richard Polt, New Haven, CT: Yale University Press, Second Edition.

Heider, Fritz (1925) 'Ding und Medium', *Symposium*, I, 109–158.

Heisenberg, Werner (1990) *Physics and Philosophy: The Revolution in Modern Science*, London: Penguin Books.

Hepp, Andreas (2012) 'Mediatization and the "Molding Force" of the Media', *Communications*, 17 (1), 1–28.

Hollier, Denis (1995) 'The Use-Value of the Impossible', in Carolyn Bailey Gill (ed.), *Bataille: Writing the Sacred*, 133–53, London: Routledge.

Holmsten, Brian, and Lubertozzi, Alex , eds (2001), *The Complete* War of the Worlds: *Mars' Invasion of Earth from H. G. Wells to Orsen Welles*, Naperville, IL: Sourcebooks.

Hubert, Henri, and Mauss, Marcel ([1898] 1981) *Sacrifice: Its Nature and Function*, trans. W. D. Halls, Chicago: University of Chicago Press, Midway Reprint.

Husserl, Edmund (1970) *Logical Investigations, Volume One*, trans. J. N. Findlay, London: RKP.

Husserl Edmund (1982) *Ideas Pertaining to a Pure Phenomenology and to Phenomenological Philosophy, First Book*, trans. F. Kersten, Dordrecht: Kluwer Academic Publishers.

Ihde, Don (2010) 'Heidegger on Technology: One Size Fits All', *Philosophy Today*, 54, Issue Supplement, 101–5.

Jacob, Christian (1996) 'Towards a Cultural History of Cartography', *Imago Mundi*, 48, 191–8.

Jacob, François (1970) *La logique du vivant: Une histoire de l'hérédité*,
   Paris: Gallimard. In English as: *The Logic of Life: A History of Heredity* (1993),
   trans. Betty E. Spillmann, Princeton, NJ: Princeton University Press.

Jagoda, Patrick (2018) 'Media Specificity, Comparison, Convergence: Legacies of the
   Chicago School of Literary Criticism', *Modern Philology*, 115 (4), 500–11.

Jones, Barry (1982) *Sleepers Wake! Technology and the Future of Work*,
   Melbourne: Oxford University Press.

Joyce, James ([1939] 1975) *Finnegans Wake*, London: Faber and Faber.

Kant, Immanuel (1900) *Kant's Cosmogony*, trans. W. Hastie, Glasgow: James
   Maclehose and Sons.

Kant, Immanuel (1970A) *Immanuel Kant's Critique of Pure Reason*, trans. Norman
   Kemp Smith, London: Macmillan. First edition as cited in Kant (1970b).

Kant, Immanuel (1970B) *Immanuel Kant's Critique of Pure Reason*, trans. Norman
   Kemp Smith, London: Macmillan. Second Edition. Reprinted.

Kim, Ji-hoon (2009) 'The Post-Medium Condition and the Explosion of Cinema',
   Screen, 50 (1), 114–23.

Kisiel, Theodor (1995) *The Genesis of Heidegger's* Being and Time,
   Berkeley: University of California Press.

Kittler, Friedrich (1990) *Discourse Networks, 1800/1900*. Stanford, CA: Stanford
   University Press.

Kittler, Friedrich (1996) 'The City Is a Medium', *New Literary History*, 27 (4), 717–29.

Kittler, Friedrich ([1986] 1999) *Gramophone, Film, Typewriter*, trans. Geoffrey
   Winthrop-Young and Michael Wutz, Stanford: Stanford University Press.

Kittler, Friedrich (2006) 'Number and Numeral', *Theory, Culture & Society*, 23 (7–8),
   51–61.

Klee, Paul ([1956] 1973) *Paul Klee Notebooks, Volume 1: The Thinking Eye*, trans.
   Ralph Manheim, London: Lund Humphries. Reprinted.

Kracauer, Siegfried (1995) 'Photography', in *The Mass Ornament: Weimar Essays*,
   47–64, trans. Thomas Y Levin. Cambridge, MA: Harvard University Press.

Kracauer, Siegfried ([1947] 2019) 'Caligari', in *From Caligari to Hitler: A Psychological
   History of the German Film*, 61–76, Princeton, NJ: Princeton University Press.

Krämer, Sybille (2006) 'The Cultural Techniques of Time Axis Manipulation on
   Friedrich Kittler's Conception of Media', *Theory, Culture and Society*, 23 (7–8),
   93–109.

Krämer, Sybille (2015) *Medium, Messenger, Transmission: An Approach to Media
   Philosophy*, trans. Anthony Enns, Amsterdam: Amsterdam University Press.

Krauss, Rosalind (1997) ' "… And Then Turn Away?" An Essay on James Coleman',
   October, 81, 5–33.

Krauss, Rosalind (1999a) 'Reinventing the Medium', *Critical Inquiry*, 25 (2), 289–305.

Krauss, Rosalind (1999b) *'A Voyage on the North Sea': Art in the Age of the Post-Medium Condition*, New York: Thames and Hudson.

Kristeva, Julia (1982) 'Word, Dialogue, and Novel', in *Desire in Language: A Semiotic Approach to Literature and Art*, 64–91, trans. Thomas Gora, Alice Jardine and Leon S. Roudiez, Oxford: Basil Blackwell.

Kristeva, Julia (1998) 'Towards a Semiology of Paragrams', in Patrick F. French (ed.), *The Tel Quel Reader*, 25–49, trans. Roland-François Lack, London: Routledge.

Kristeva, Julia (2020) 'Reply to Edward S. Casey, Alina N. Feld, Michal Ben-Naftall, and Keren Mock', in Sara G. Beardsworth (ed.), *The Philosophy of Julia Kristeva*, 491–512, Chicago: Open Court.

Lacan, Jacques (1973) *Le Séminaire, Livre XI: Les quatre concepts fondamentaux de la psychoanalyse, 1964*, Paris: Seuil.

Lacan, Jacques (2006) *Écrits: The First Complete Edition in English*, trans. Bruce Fink in collaboration with Héloïse Fink and Russell Grigg, New York: W. W. Norton.

Laplanche, J., and Pontalis, J. B. (1988) *The Language of Psychoanalysis*, trans. Donald Nicholson-Smith, London: Karnac Books and the Institute of Psycho-Analysis.

Large, Duncan (1997) 'Hermes Contra Dionysus (Serres and Nietzsche)', *Horizons Philosophiques*, 8 (1), 23–39.

Large, Duncan (1999) 'Hermes Contra Dionysus: Michel Serres's Critique of Nietzsche', in B. Babich (ed.), *Nietzsche, Epistemology, and Philosophy of Science: Nietzsche and the Sciences II*, 151–9, Dordrecht: Kluwer Academic Publishers.

Large, Duncan (2016) 'Nietzsche's Conceptual Chemistry', in Gregory Moore and Thomas Brobjer (eds), *Nietzsche and Science*, 189–96, Abingdon: Routledge.

Lechte, John (1999) 'The *Who* and *What* of Writing in the Electronic Age', *Oxford Literary Review*, 21, 135–60.

Lechte, John (2007) 'Technics, Time and Stiegler's "Orthographic Moment"', *Parallax*, 45, 64–77.

Lechte, John (2012) *Genealogy and Ontology of the Western Image and Its Digital Future*, New York: Routledge.

Lechte, John (2016) 'Abjection, Art and Bare Life', in Rina Arya and Nicholas Chare (eds), *Abject Visions: Powers of Horror in Art and Visual Culture*, 14–29, Manchester: Manchester University Press.

Lechte, John (2018) *The Human: Bare Life and Ways of Life*, London: Bloomsbury.

Lemke, Thomas (2017) 'Materialism Without Matter: The Recurrence of Subjectivism in Object-Oriented Ontology', *Distinktion: Journal of Social Theory*, 18 (2), 133–52.

Leroi-Gourhan, André (1964) *Le geste et la parole II: La mémoire et les rythmes*, Paris: Albin Michel.

Lettvin, J. Y., Maturana, H. R., Mcculloch, W. S., and Pitts, H. R. (1959) 'What the Frog's Eye Tells the Frog's Brain', *Proceedings of the IRE*, 47 (11), 1940–51.

Loeb, Paul (2013) ' "Eternal Recurrence" in The Oxford Handbook of Nietzsche', in Ken Gemes and John Richardson (eds), *The Oxford Handbook of Nietzsche*, 645–71, Oxford: Oxford University Press.

Luhmann, Niklas (1987) 'The Medium of Art', trans. David Roberts, *Thesis Eleven*, 18/19, 101–13.

Malpas, Jeff (2021) *Rethinking Dwelling: Heidegger, Place, Architecture*, London: Bloomsbury.

Maras, Stephen, and Sutton, David (2000) 'Media Specificity Re-visited', *Convergence*, 6 (2), 98–113.

McGowan, Todd (2012) '*Technics and Time, 3: Cinematic Time and the Question of Malaise* (review), *symploke*, 20 (1–2), 395–7.

McLuhan, Marshall (1954) 'Joyce, Mallarmé, and the Press', *The Sewanee Review*, 62 (1), 38–55.

McLuhan, Marshall ([1962] 1967) *Gutenberg Galaxy: The Making of Typographic Man*, Toronto: University of Toronto Press.

McLuhan, Marshall (1975) 'McLuhan's Laws of the Media', *Technology and Culture*, 16 (1), 74–8.

McLuhan, Marshall (1992) *Understanding Media: The Extensions of Man*, Cambridge: MIT Press.

McLuhan, Marshall ([1964] 2008) *Understanding Media. The Extensions of Man*, London: Routledge.

Meillassoux, Quentin (2011) *After Finitude. Essay on the Necessity of Contingency*, trans. Ray Brassier, London: Continuum.

Mondzain, Marie-José (1996) *Image, icône, économie: Les sources byzantine de l'imaginaire contemporain*, Paris: Seuil.

Monod, Jacques (1972) *Chance and Necessity: An Essay on the Natural Philosophy of Modern Biology*, trans. Austryn Wainhouse, New York: Vintage Books.

Morton, Timothy (2011) 'Here Comes Everything: The Promise of Object-Oriented Ontology', *Qui Parle*, 19 (2), 163–90.

Morton, Timothy (2013) *Hyperobjects: Philosophy and Ecology after the End of the World*, Minneapolis: University of Minnesota Press.

Morton, Timothy (2014) 'Victorian Hyperobjects', *Nineteenth-Century Contexts*, 36 (5), 489–500.

Musil, Robert (1982) *The Man Without Qualities, Volume One*, trans. Eithne Wilkins, and Ernst Kaiser, London: Picador Pan Books. Third printing.

Nietzsche, Friedrich (1974a) *The Anti-Christ* in *The Twilight of the Idols and The Anti-Christ*, trans. R. J. Hollingdale, Harmondsworth: Penguin Books.

Nietzsche, Friedrich (1974b) *Beyond Good and Evil: Prelude to a Philosophy of the Future*, trans. R. J. Hollingdale, Harmondsworth: Penguin Books.

Nietzsche, Friedrich (1989) *Human, All Too Human*, trans. R. J. Hollingdale, Cambridge: Cambridge University Press.

Norris, Christopher (2013) *Philosophy Outside-In: A Critique of Academic Reason*, Edinburgh: Edinburgh University Press.

Ong, Walter J. ([1982] 1997) *Orality and Literacy: The Technologizing of the Word*, London: Routledge.

Parikka, Jussi (2011) 'Operative Media Archaeology: Wolfgang Ernst's Materialist Media Diagrammatics', *Theory, Culture and Society*, 28 (5), 52–74.

Parikka, Jussi (2012) *What Is Media Archaeology?* Cambridge: Polity Press.

Pecora, Vincent P. (1991) 'Ethics, Politics, and the Middle Voice', *Yale French Studies*, 79, 203–30.

Peters, John Durham (2015) *The Marvelous Clouds: Toward a Philosophy of the Elemental*, Chicago: University of Chicago Press.

Plato (1980), *Timaeus*, in *Plato: The Collected Dialogues*, ed. Edith Hamilton and Huntington Cairns, trans. Benjamin Jowett, Bollingen Series LXXI, Princeton, NJ: Princeton University Press. Tenth printing.

Plotnitsky, Arkady (2016) *The Principles of Quantum Theory, from Planck's Quanta to the Higgs Boson. The Nature of Quantum Reality and the Spirit of Copenhagen*, Switzerland: Springer.

Sartre, Jean-Paul (2004) *The Imaginary: A Phenomenological Psychology of the Imagination*, trans. Jonathan Weber, London: Routledge.

Schmidgen, Henning (2019) 'Successful Paranoia: Friedrich Kittler, Lacanian Psychoanalysis, and the History of Science', *Theory, Culture and Society*, 36 (1), 107–31.

Schmitt, Carl (1918) 'Die Buribunken: Ein geschichtsphilosophischer Versuch', *Summa*, 1 (4), 89–106.

Schmitt, Carl (2019) 'The Buribunks. An Essay on the Philosophy of History', trans. Gert Reifarth and Laura Petersen, *Griffith Law Review*, 28 (2), 99–112.

Scott, Charles (1988) 'The Middle Voice in *Being and Time*', in John C. Sallis, Giuseppina Moneta and Jacques Taminaux (eds), *The Collegium Phaenomenologicum, The First Ten Years*, 159–73, Dordrecht: Kluwer Academic Publishers.

Scott, Charles (1989) 'The Middle Voice of Metaphysics', *The Review of Metaphysics*, 42 (4), 743–64.

Serres, Michel (1968) *Hermès I. La Communication*, Paris: Minuit.

Serres, Michel (1972) *Hermès II. L'interférence*, Paris: Minuit.

Serres, Michel (1974) *Hermès III. La traduction*, Paris: Minuit.

Serres, Michel (1977) *Hermès IV. La distribution*, Paris: Minuit.

Serres, Michel (1980) *Hermès V. Le passage du nord-ouest*, Paris: Minuit.

Serres, Michel (1982a) 'Turner Translates Carnot', trans. Marilyn Sides in *Hermes: Literature, Science, Philosophy*, 54–62, ed. Josué V. Harari and David F. Bell, Baltimore: Johns Hopkins University Press.

Serres, Michel (1982b) 'Turner Translates Carnot', trans. Mike Shortland, *Block* 6, 46–55.

Serres, Michel ([1980] 1983) *The Parasite*, trans. Lawrence R. Schehr, Baltimore, MD: Johns Hopkins University Press.

Serres, Michel (1991) *Le Tiers-Instruit*, Paris: François Bourn.

Serres, Michel (1995) *Angels: A Modern Myth*, trans. Francis Cowper, Paris: Flammarion.

Serres, Michel (1997) 'Science and the Humanities: The Case of Turner', trans. Catherine Brown and William Paulson, *Substance*, 26 (2), Issue 3, 6–21.

Serres, Michel (1998) (with Bruno Latour) *Conversations on Science, Culture and Time*, trans. Roxanne Lapidus, Ann Arbor: University of Michigan Press.

Serres, Michel (2002) *Genesis*, trans. Geneviève James and James Nielson, Ann Arbor: University of Michigan Press. Reprinted.

Shannon, Claude E., and Weaver, Warren ([1949] 1998), *The Mathematical Theory of Communication*, Urbana: University of Illinois Press.

Siegert, Bernhard (2013) 'Cultural Techniques: Or the End of the Intellectual Postwar Era in German Media Theory', *Theory, Culture and Society*, 30 (6), 48–65.

Simmel, Georg (2004) *The Philosophy of Money*, trans. Tom Bottomore and David Frizby, London: Routledge.

Simondon, Gilbert (2012) Du mode d'existence des objets techniques. Nouvelle édition revue et corrigée, Paris: Aubier.

Sontag, Susan ([1971] 2008) *On Photography*, London: Penguin Classic Books.

Stiegler, Bernard (1998) *Technics and Time, 1: The Fault of Epimetheseus*, trans. Richard Beardsworth and George Collins, Stanford: Stanford University Press.

Stiegler, Bernard (2002) 'The Discrete Image', in Jacques Derrida and Bernard Stiegler (eds), *Echographies of Television: Filmed Interviews*, 145–63, trans. Jennifer Bajorek, Cambridge: Polity.

Stiegler, Bernard (2009) *Technics and Time 2. Disorientation*, trans. Stephen Barker, Stanford, CA: Stanford University Press.

Stiegler, Bernard (2011) *Technics and Time, 3: Cinematic Time and the Question of Malaise*, trans. Stephen Barker, Stanford, CA: Stanford University Press.

Sutherland, Thomas (2021) 'Communicating the Incommunicable: Formalism and Noise in Michel Serres', in Timothy Barker and Maria Korolkova (eds), *Miscommunications: Errors, Mistakes, Media (Thinking Media)*, Chapter 7, London: Bloomsbury, Online resource.

Todorov, Tzvetan (1967) *Littérature et signification*, Paris: Larousse.

Uricchio, William (2014) 'Film, Cinema, Television ... Media?', *New Review of Film and Television*, 12 (3), 266–79.

Vidal-Naquet, Pierre (1981) 'De Faurisson et de Chomsky', *Esprit, Nouvelle série*, 49 (1), 205–8.

Waldman, Diane ([1978] 1986) *Mark Rothko, 1903–1970: A Retrospective*, New York: Harry N. Abrams in collaboration with The Solomon R. Guggenheim Foundation.

White, Hayden (1978) *Tropics of Discourse: Essays in Cultural Criticism*, London: Johns Hopkins University Press.

Wiener, Norbert (1961) *Cybernetics or Control and Communication in the Animal and the Machine*, second edition, Cambridge: MIT Press.

Wilding, Adrian (2005) 'Why We Don't Remain in the Provinces', *Philosophy and Social Criticism*, 31 (1), 109–29.

Williams, Glyn (2003) *Voyages of Delusion: The Question for the Northwest Passage*, New Haven, CT: Yale University Press.

Williams, Raymond (1985) *Keywords*, London: Oxford University Press.

Wolf, Herta (2007) 'The Tears of Photography', *Grey Room*, 29 (Fall), 66–89.

Yates, Frances (2001) *The Art of Memory*, Chicago: University of Chicago Press. Reprint edition.

Index

www.ingramcontent.com/pod-product-compliance
Lightning Source LLC
Chambersburg PA
CBHW070240290326

41929CB00046B/2270